cross world

cross world

One Man's Journey into America's Crossword Obsession

MARC ROMANO

BROADWAY BOOKS

New York

PUBLISHED BY BROADWAY BOOKS

A hardcover edition of this book was originally published in
2005 by Broadway Books.

Published in the United States by Broadway Books, an imprint
of The Doubleday Broadway Publishing Group, a division of
Random House, Inc., New York.
www.broadwaybooks.com

BROADWAY BOOKS and its logo, a letter B bisected on the
diagonal, are trademarks of Random House, Inc.

The author and publisher gratefully acknowledge the following
for the right to reprint material in this book:
Tournament crosswords copyright © 2004 American
Crossworld Puzzle Tournament. Used with permission.
www.crosswordtournament.com

Book design by Donna Sinisgalli

Library of Congress Cataloging-in-Publication Data
Romano, Marc.
Crossworld : one man's journey into America's crossword
obsession.— 1st ed.
p. cm.
1. Crossword puzzles. I. Title.
GV1507.C7R574 2005
793.73'2—dc22
2004063434

ISBN-13: 978-0-7679-1758-2
ISBN-10: 0-7679-1758-8

PRINTED IN THE UNITED STATES OF AMERICA

10 9 8 7 6 5 4 3 2 1

First Paperback Edition

To Alan D. Williams,

in very fond memory of

a punster, a polymath,

and, best of all, a gentleman

contents

This is a book about my yearlong journey into the world of competitive crossword solving—although saying that is a little like saying "Lucy in the Sky with Diamonds" is a song about a girl or *The Scream* is a painting of a guy standing on a bridge. The real topic of any book about crosswords is all the information in the world; more to the point, it's about the type of person who has enough of that information at his (or her, of course) disposal to walk into a tournament and know with a degree of confidence that he will be able to accurately finish in a few minutes a puzzle it would take most ordinary civilians several hours or more to complete.

Specifically, *Crossworld*'s subject is the American-style crossword as exemplified by the *New York Times* puzzle, whose defining characteristics are a symmetrical grid, a ban on the use of words fewer than three letters long, the absolute avoidance of stand-alone letters, a proportion of white squares to black that never falls below 70 percent, and the injunction that a clue and its answer must be substitutable for each other if used in a sentence. The use of rebuses (symbols that stand in for a word or phrase), multiple letters within the same square, and numerals (Arabic or Roman) have all, over the last two decades, become increasingly popular and acceptable elements within American puzzles.

Like all specialized fields in the realm of human endeavor, over the years crosswords have engendered a specific vocabulary that constructors and editors use to describe the technical aspects of what they do; the average solver can live a perfectly normal life without needing to know these terms, but in a book about crosswords they will inevitably make frequent appearances, so it would be best to explain what they are at the outset. (Should you forget what they are, no worry—they are explained again in the text.)

A crossword puzzle is made up of three parts: the grid, the fill, and the cluing. The grid is the arrangement of black-and-white squares you see when you open up your newspaper and turn to the puzzle page; the fill is the set of correct answers that, when you're done, will populate the puzzle; the cluing is the list of prompts and hints, numbered sequentially across and down, that when interpreted correctly will yield the fill. The only other term you'll need to know is "keying"—the placement of letters so that they form a word, phrase, or abbreviation. A stand-alone letter would be completely unkeyed; a letter in a corner, where it becomes part of the 1-Across and 1-Down word, would be double-keyed. In crosswords, a "word" is defined as any single answer across or down; quite commonly, a "word" in the puzzle sense is in fact made up of several real words.

Not all people like solving crossword puzzles, and not many of those who do spend a whole lot of time talking about them, so there won't be many occasions, unless one day you attend the American Crossword Puzzle Tournament (held annually every spring in Stamford, Connecticut), when you'll be called upon to know the activity's specialized vocabulary.

But this knowledge still could be useful to you. Imagine you're at a cocktail party and fall into conversation with a knot of particularly wonky guests who are talking about that day's *New York Times* puzzle. Even if you don't know anything about that puzzle except the name of its constructor (a piece of information made available by only a small number of crossword venues, including the *Times*), you can pretend that you do by saying something like: "Ah, yes— elegant grid, fresh and creative fill, great cluing. Classic Cathy Millhauser." The mavens might think you're a puzzle expert and, with luck, start talking about another and more congenial subject. Congenial to you, that is.

Chapter 1

MY PUZZLING
PROBLEM

I am hopelessly addicted to the *New York Times* crossword puzzle.

Like many addicts, it's taken me time to admit I have a problem. The hints I was heading for trouble came, at first, only occasionally. The moments of panic when I realized that for whatever reason I might not be able to get my fix on a given day. The toll on relationships. The strained friendships. The lost hours I could have used to do something much more productive.

It gets worse, too. The high no longer lasts as long as it once did; what initially could occupy me for a whole afternoon now takes me twenty minutes or less to get through. I have become increasingly alarmed that the supply of the thing I need is limited. The *Times* publishes only one puzzle per day, and when that's done I find myself rooting about for substitutes—the *Wall Street Journal*, *Philadelphia Inquirer*, and *New York Sun* puzzles, to name just a few—that are somehow less satisfying. Sure, there are a couple of thousand puzzles in the *Times*'s electronic archive. But a puzzle you've already done being something of a dead letter, falling back to that recourse is something like accepting an herbal cigarette when you're a smoker plumb out of Camels. There is no substitute for the genuine article, and a sort of panic sets in once it's no longer available. To badly paraphrase the British novelist C. S. Forester, it is prospect and not possession that affords the greatest pleasure, and the delicious agony of the twenty-four hours between completing one puzzle and starting another makes up the circadian rhythm by which my life has been regulated for nigh on two decades now.

If you've ever been to or listened in on a meeting of any of the twelve-step groups—Alcoholics Anonymous, Narcotics Anonymous, Overeaters Anonymous—you may have noticed the pattern that emerges from the narratives of the people who get up to publicly confess their addictions. These men and women all seem to be describing, in their own ways, how they were caught blindside by their particular object of desire. At an AA meeting, it may be the woman whose parents owned a tavern; all those surreptitious sips of liquids from colorful bottles as a little girl transmuted, for her, into a spiral of inebriation and promiscuity that ended only six months before in this very room. At an NA meeting, it may be the regional salesman whose toots of cocaine on the road, originally just to help clear his head, paved the way for divorce, petty theft, and finally grand larceny and imprisonment.

What these stories say, in essence, is that all addicts go through a lapsarian event of some sort or another, which may be why so many twelve-step meetings take place in churches: It's comforting to explain one's own fall from grace in an environment where the concept of grace itself is dwelt upon so constantly. Addicts seem to fetishize the fact of their own fall, even though the process of falling is, in the end, rather the same whether you happen to be the reformed floozy, the now reemployed and sober salesman, or Adam and Eve. Only the substance changes: alcohol, cocaine, knowledge of good and evil. Or crosswords.

My own fall was right down the pipe, in addiction-narrative terms. Along with a few friends from my hometown at the northernmost end of Boston's North Shore (white-clapboard public buildings, preppies, gulls wheeling in the deep, snug, boat-filled harbor), I was invited down to New Canaan, Connecticut, for a house party hosted by a friend of ours whose parents had, the year before, moved from the Bay State to the Nutmeg State. This was late summer 1985; I was between my sophomore and junior years in college. The six of us drove down in two cars at far too great a speed, with me at the helm of a Ford F250 pickup whose nervous owner sat beside me, constantly doling out advice about the way I was handling his beloved truck.

Apart from the nagging, which occurred both on the way down and the way back up (and which I resented from someone who not only regularly treated his friends to hundred-mile-an-hour dirt-road horror shows, but who also needed me to do the piloting because the Commonwealth of Massachusetts had suspended his license for drunken driving a month before), it was really a perfect weekend. New Canaan was in its late-summer torpor, the hired band was unexpectedly decent, the cold beer flowed, and our friend's new Connecticut crew was so much like we six in thought, dress, and background that everyone seemed to have known one another for ages. We had, in short, a ball.

I went to bed late but woke up, as I generally did then and still do now, early. No one else in the house was stirring except the mother of the family. When I appeared in the kitchen, seeking coffee after a dip in the pool, she said the newspaper hadn't appeared and wondered if I'd be good enough to pick one up at a store in town (or village, really, at the time).

"Or two," she added. "With so many of you kids in the house, someone else is bound to want another magazine."

I drove into town and bought, as specified, two copies of the *New York Times*. When I returned, coffee was ready, no one as yet had emerged from the bedrooms upstairs, and my friend's mother was dropping a celery stalk into a Bloody Mary. With a grunt of thanks, she took one of the papers, extracted from it the *New York Times Magazine*, and flipped it open to the puzzle page.

Then she sipped her drink, examined the black-and-white grid, and set to work. The house was silent but for her sipping (Bloody Mary), my sipping (coffee), and the rapid-fire scratching of her pencil. I didn't know yet that it's perfectly acceptable in *Times*-buying households to say nothing to a houseguest, even if the guest is your daughter's and not your own, until you've finished at least half the puzzle and a Bloody Mary.

Feeling vaguely offended, I reached for the spare magazine out of sheer retributive spite. The next moment, I became a puzzler.

This is not to say that I'd never done a crossword before. I had, in spades: the *Boston Globe* puzzle, most of the time, or the puzzle in *TV Guide*, or any other puzzle one picks up at moments when one needs distraction. The one common denominator is that they were easy, pastimes rather than challenges, so at the time I preferred reading to puzzling. I still do, except for when a fresh *Times* puzzle is to be had.

Ten minutes later, my friend's mother mixed herself another Bloody Mary and returned to the kitchen table. After maybe another twenty minutes, she sighed contentedly. Then she mixed herself a third Bloody Mary and rummaged through the other sections of the paper. My coffee was cold and barely touched and I'd completed less than a third of my puzzle when the daughter of the house appeared, with the other houseguests more or less in tow, if two hours later counts as "in tow." My friend said good morning to her mother and then drifted over to ask me how I was doing with the crossword. I grunted by way of answer. I had begun, you see, to understand.

I couldn't believe that a New Canaan matron with two stiff pre-breakfast drinks under her belt had managed to complete the same puzzle I was working on a full three hours before I did. I was at least thirty years younger than she and the lazy salutatorian of my high school graduating class—and a second-year student at Yale, for God's sake, even if an unmotivated one. My performance was shameful.

When I finally did finish, barely minutes before we were all due to drive home again, and after having spent several hours skulking around the house, avoiding the presence of people who wanted to "help" with the puzzle, I glanced at the top of the page to see who was responsible for it. The only hint that it had not been constructed by Satan himself—that there was a human agency behind the puzzle—was the single line, "Edited by Eugene T. Maleska."

Maleska Versus Shortz

That name "Maleska" imprinted itself upon my brain at once and forever. It was an odd-sounding collection of syllables: odd-sounding in the sense that it echoed any number of East European names whose possessors had bedeviled me up to then with their machinations physical (Erno Rubik), literary (Ernst Kantorowicz, Mikhail Bakhtin), and scientific (Dmitry Mendeleyev, cursed be all chemistry).

"Fine," I thought to myself as we piled into our cars. "Fine, Eugene T. Maleska, from this day onward, you'll publish no puzzle but that I'll complete. Eugene T. Maleska, you probably Slovakian evil genius, from this day on your ass is mine."

In truth, from that day on, the ass-ownership situation was the other way around completely. Eugene T. Maleska had possession of my puzzler's soul from that day in August 1985 until he died in 1993; I mourned his passing the way someone else might mourn the closing of a favorite corner restaurant—with a sense of grief partly admixed with an anticipatory dread of what new institution might come to take the departed one's place.

Many others, over the ensuing years, were also to mourn Eugene T. Maleska. A former teacher of Latin and then administrator in the New York City school system, he was an iconoclast and, some had it, a world-class curmudgeon, famous for developing instantaneous and permanent grudges against crossword constructors who violated any of the myriad iron (but never actually spelled out) rules he seemed to believe governed the world of puzzles. Yet he had built up an ardent following of people who agreed with him that puzzles should mainly concern themselves with high culture and disdain words or phrases that had originated since roughly 1960. If you knew the names of opera stars, the titles of popular songs from the 1930s and '40s, and which horses had won the Kentucky Derby in the first half of this century, you stood a fair chance of completing any crossword the *Times* published under Maleska's tenure, which began in 1977. If, like me, you didn't have this body of knowledge to hand—or if you were unfamiliar with Maleska's favorite filler words, such as "adit," "oryx," "ani," and "esne," among a dozen or so others—you were forced to rapidly develop a working understanding of both the references and the vocabulary. If you were of a certain age or a cultural snob or raised in or around New York City (or, ideally, all three), he was your hero: You knew what to expect from the crossword that would appear on your doorstep the following morning, and you could be reasonably certain you'd eventually finish it. In a sense, consistently solving Maleska's puzzles made you an honorary New Yorker, back when New York was Ed Koch and not Rudy Giuliani or Michael Bloomberg.

All that changed when Maleska went up, in 1993, to that big crossword grid in the sky. The puzzle's new editor, a person named Will Shortz, had a very different understanding of what a crossword should be, and, for the effect he would have on me as well as on literally millions of other puzzlers, he turned out to be a far, far more baneful figure than his predecessor. Largely this is due to the fact that Shortz is a much cleverer puzzle editor than Maleska or his predecessors, Margaret Petherbridge Farrar and Will Weng (my deep apologies, Eugene T.; you were fun while you were around, and I do still miss you). Shortz is also a more technical, more engaged, and more democratic puzzle editor than any of his forebears.

What the words "clever," "technical," "engaged," and "democratic" mean when applied to crosswords is an indication of the changes Shortz was to bring about in the august institution of the *Times* puzzle (which began running every Sunday as of 1942 and daily as of 1950). For now, the words "fiendish," "difficult," "evangelic," and "irksome" can stand in for them. But the point, again, is that the old *Times* puzzle used to demand of its solvers little more than a general body of knowledge acquired over a lifetime spent in the United States from about 1935 to about 1985. This is not to say that Maleska's puzzles weren't difficult enough. Under Will Shortz's direction, however, the puzzle began to demand much more extensive knowledge of contemporary culture, plus the ability on the would-be solver's part to come to terms with a number of other puzzle dimensions: themes that bear on how one interprets clues correctly, rebuses, squares containing more than one letter or figure, graded levels of difficulty, and so on.

Perhaps the most significant change instituted by Shortz was radically reenforcing the policy of scaling puzzles by difficulty, with the week's easiest appearing on Monday and its hardest on Friday or Saturday. (Although larger than the weekday crossword, Sunday's is usually, in terms of difficulty, at about the Thursday level.) For many, including me, this meant it soon became almost pointless to pick up a copy of the *New York Times* on Monday or Tuesday, since the puzzles appearing in them were constructed with the beginning or inexperienced solver in mind and, in a noncompetitive context, simply weren't worth doing. For many other people, this time not including me, it also soon became pointless to pick up Friday or Saturday's, either, since their difficulty upped the frustration factor manyfold, causing legions of faithful crossworders to abandon a particular puzzle for perhaps the first time in their lives. And, needless to say, to curse this interloper who had ruined the classical crossword experience so carefully nurtured by Maleska.

Even Shortz's name seemed an ill omen, since all his predecessors had sounded, or at least on the printed page looked, more imbued with gravitas than he. Margaret Farrar (née, and for a while editing puzzles as, Margaret Petherbridge, which sounds like a character out of Wodehouse) had echoes of Farrar, Straus and Giroux and serious books; the unusual moniker of the *Times*'s second puzzle editor, Will Weng, didn't bring any specific image to mind, but that odd combination of Western-sounding first name and Asian-sounding last certainly caught the eye. "Eugene T. Maleska" is of course a showstopper, evoking images of scholars poring over massive tomes in the lugubrious silence of the Slavic Reading Room at the New York Public Library. By contrast, "Will Shortz" sounds like someone you'd meet in the cattle-feed section of a farm-supply store in Indiana.

Shortz was in fact born in Indiana, and when you meet him in person he's every bit as warm, open, enthusiastic, and friendly as you'd expect someone from the Hoosier State to be, but that's about where the whole expectations-met game comes to a shuddering halt, Shortz-wise. Sometime around 1960, when he was less than ten years old, he fell in love with puzzles. After a couple years of practice, he sold his first one for publication when he was fourteen. He entered Indiana University as an economics major, but soon realized the school had an independent-study program that allowed a limited number of students to design their own major. He applied and, as every press piece on Shortz since has reported, he convinced the docents to grant him an undergraduate degree—the only such degree granted by any university anywhere, ever—in the field of enigmatology, or the study of puzzles and games and their relationship to the cultural environment in which they are created and solved. After college he went to law school, and for a while it seemed that, his unusual undergraduate concentration aside, Shortz was headed for a career that would raise no eyebrows in his Indiana hometown.

While contemplating a life of torts and contracts, he continued to pursue his passion, constructing and publishing puzzles for, among others, *Games* magazine. When the editorship at that periodical opened up in 1978, the publishers offered him the position. Of course he accepted, and so became one of that very rare breed of persons whose consuming passion corresponds precisely to his career arc. Before he even joined *Games*, Shortz founded the American Crossword Puzzle Tournament, held annually in Stamford, Connecticut (the next town over from New Canaan, for what that's worth), and now in its twenty-ninth year. Shortz also created the World Championship Puzzle Competition, which features four-person teams from various nations vying with one another to solve a series of language-neutral math and visual problems. When Eugene T. Maleska sloughed his mortal coil in late 1993, the list the

New York Times Corporation's headhunters came up with as potential replacements probably numbered only one.

Once he was hired, Shortz's decision to begin instituting more carefully calibrated levels of difficulty in the *Times* puzzle may have shocked and horrified many longtime and faithful solvers, but it did have the effect of radically broadening the base of people who at least try to do the crossword on a regular basis. The *Times* has apparently never audited itself to find out how many copies the puzzle was responsible for selling under Farrar, Weng, and Maleska. But under Shortz, and with the advent of the World Wide Web, some pretty astounding numbers have begun to come in. The *Times* puzzle Web site has forty thousand subscribers (or more—the nonpublic Times Corporation holds this number pretty close to its chest) each paying $34.95 a year; *Times* puzzle books, all published by St. Martin's Press, regularly sell in the tens of thousands. And five hundred or so highly motivated solvers actually go to Stamford every year. By any measure, it looks like Shortz's decision to make the puzzle at once much easier on some days, much harder on Fridays and Saturdays, and more contemporary every day has paid off handsomely for the *Times*—which, incidentally, only in 2003 raised the remuneration for a given freelance-constructed weekday puzzle to $100 and for the Sunday puzzle to a dizzying $350. My on-the-napkin calculations indicate that the *Times* puzzle as edited by Will Shortz probably adds a hundred thousand newsstand sales of the newspaper per day and maybe two hundred thousand every Sunday, and this at $1 and $3.50 per issue, respectively. Whatever the real numbers may be, they're definitely large.

Yet Shortz's policies have also alienated some—for example, Michael D. Coe, professor of anthropology emeritus at Yale University and author of, among others, *Breaking the Maya Code, The*

Maya, and (with his wife, Sophie) *The True History of Chocolate*. A lifelong *Times* puzzle solver, Michael is the person you'd want on the phone if you ever needed a lifeline on *Who Wants to Be a Millionaire*. Soon after Shortz was named puzzle editor, an annoyed Coe vowed never to try the crossword again, since it had, in his view, become filled with impenetrable clues involving rap artists and the like, not to mention what, in his view, amounted to product placements (all those anathema-to-Eugene brand names). He in fact canceled his *Times* subscription because of Shortz, or rather because the puzzle under Shortz no longer made up for the fact that, to Coe, the *Times* seemed an insular, self-congratulatory newspaper not really worth the cover price it kept jacking up. He bought a computer and went online a few years later, however, rediscovered the *Times* puzzle in its electronic version, and now scans the occasional *People* magazine in an effort to absorb the contemporary cultural information he needs to solve it, at least Sunday through Thursday—Fridays and Saturdays remain impenetrable to him.

More than anything, though, Shortz has, via personal magnetism (he hosts the popular "Puzzler" section of National Public Radio's Sunday broadcast every week) and sheer hard work (he provides about half the clues, on average, for any given puzzle the *Times* publishes 365 days a year, while at the same time maintaining a busy speaking schedule and organizing a dozen or more cruciverbalist gatherings per year), built around crosswords a thriving, very active, and very social community of solvers and constructors. Their annual gathering in Stamford is an energetic geekfest the likes of which you haven't seen unless you've been to the annual high school Math Olympiad or, to use a cognate from the animal world (and to mix a metaphor), seen the swallows flocking at San Juan Capistrano. It's hard to imagine how the grumpy and reclusive Eugene T.

Maleska could ever have broadcast the love of crosswords as widely as has Will Shortz in the space of just over a decade—and as Shortz looks to continue doing for decades to come.

Perhaps only marginally less important than the grades of difficulty that Shortz has imposed on the *Times* puzzle is the technical virtuosity he has built into it, or caused to be built into it by the sort of constructor whose work he chooses to publish. Simply put, the crosswords are marvelously engineered now in a way they never have been before—including the way they are today in, for instance, British newspapers, whose cryptic puzzles have baffled and delighted countless millions for almost eighty years. (And that, for the record, have also completely mystified billions of others who aren't acculturated Englishmen and Englishwomen and haven't the slightest idea how those jokes, free associations, and puns could ever cohere into the specific answers that show up in the newspaper's next-day edition.)

Word-Cross

Given the millions upon millions of people who do them every day all over the world, it would seem that crossword puzzles must have an ancient history, but they don't. The first one appeared in December 1913, in the "Fun" section of the *New York World* newspaper, and was constructed by the section's editor, Arthur Wynne. The concept of the crossword, which at first Wynne styled "word-cross" until a salubrious typographical error reversed the order of the words a month after the first one appeared, found nearly instant mass appeal. By the early 1920s, several dozen American newspapers carried their own, usually weekly, version of the puzzle. Internationally, crosswords caught on almost equally as quickly, with British,

French, German, and Russian examples coming into print a few years after the conclusion of World War I. (In his autobiography, *Speak, Memory*, Vladimir Nabokov claims that his father, the jurist and politician Vladimir Dmitrievich Nabokov, coined "*krest-noslovo*," the Russian equivalent of "crossword"; the Russian word used for "crossword" today is in fact *krosVERD.*)

In the early 1920s, the youthful founders of the publishing house Simon & Schuster took a gamble on their first book, a collection of commissioned crosswords, but hedged their bets by making sure their company's name appeared nowhere on or within it. After the first four-thousand-odd-copy run sold out in a few weeks, the next run that came to market bore their imprint; it sold about a quarter-million copies in its first year, launching not only one of the two new major American publishing companies to set up shop that decade (the other being Random House), but also bearing witness to the fact that the crossword had within eleven years graduated from transitory fad into a full-fledged—and, for the people who published it, either in newspapers or in collected forms in books, an extremely profitable—national institution. From the beginning, publishers found that crossword constructors would work for either very low pay or for free, while crossword solvers would shell out lots of good hard dollars for both the newspapers in which the puzzles originally appeared and the volumes into which they could eventually be collected. The same dynamic still operates today; now, though, a star system is beginning to emerge in which constructors can make money on the book end of the crossword-publishing spectrum by demanding standard author's royalties for volumes made up entirely of their work. At the American Crossword Puzzle Tournament, the only place where high-profile constructors reliably appear en masse, they're even mobbed by autograph seekers.

Since such books commonly sell in the tens of thousands of

copies apiece, a good year's work for one of these constructors (about 1.2 puzzles a week) could, today, conceivably translate into a solid upper-middle-class income. On the other hand, constructing a crossword publishable in the *Times* takes a huge amount of time and energy, even given the development and brisk sales, over the last decade, of crossword-building computer software. To make a living off his or her work, the busy constructor has to wonder whether he or she can keep up the pace. This is why there are three hundred–odd people in the current roster of *Times* puzzle writers and why the crossword editor in America is so much better-known than the average constructor—because he or she is the person whose name most frequently and most prominently appears on the masthead. Millions of people will spend anywhere from three minutes to several hours focused intently on the puzzles editors coproduce and publish day in and day out. A crossword constructor doesn't necessarily have to worry about being crucified by millions over a minor mistake; crossword editors do.

Throughout the 1920s in America, crosswords were both a phenomenally successful fad and, again, a burgeoning national institution. Hit songs and stage shows were based on them; women and men sported crossword-themed clothing (as some of them do still at the American Crossword Puzzle Tournament). But while other fads from that ditzy age, such as bobbed hair or flagpole sitting or goldfish-swallowing, came and went, crosswords remained, if anything growing more entrenched as time went on. In 1942 the *New York Times* was then (as now) the highest-profile American newspaper, and its undoubtedly much-cogitated decision to begin publishing crosswords on a regular basis—and to keep publishing them from that date to now—was and is a singular vote in favor of the puzzles' powerful cultural status and likely staying power. And yet like rock and roll and chewing gum, they're one of those homegrown American cultural inventions that were somehow destined not only to thrive in North America but also to find resonance among peoples as fundamentally different as, say, the Russians and the Japanese.

What is it about crosswords that made them an instant public sensation, and keeps them a sensation today, pretty much all over the globe? One reason might be that they act as a sort of barometer of one's own acculturation; if you can do the crossword in your nation's newspaper of record, it means you're smart and mentally agile and hip enough to say "I belong here"—a pretty persuasive reason to do big-city-newspaper puzzles, especially if you're a second-generation immigrant or (as I was when I ran across that first *Times* puzzle in New Canaan) a provincial kid aiming to make it in the big city someday. Another reason, which a lot of people I've raised the question with bring up, is that crosswords are the ultimate way of dealing with immediate worries, or at least burying them for a determinate amount of time: Trying to figure out what seven-letter word begins with "p" and ends with "a" and has a "k" or a "g" in the sixth position is an almost magical way of forgetting, for instance, that your live-in girlfriend is coming home in twenty minutes and that you just happen to have spent the night with a different girl entirely, but neglected to explain beforehand that you were going to do so. When your girlfriend does come home, slamming the door on her way in, there'll be hell to pay, but in the meantime you think to yourself, "Way to go, pal: The answer is probably PAPRIKA!" And you get that amount of time off from the otherwise relentless dread hanging over you, which while it's happening is a very good thing indeed. Except for writing or (so I'm told) engaging in close combat, nothing removes imminent social contingency from one's life better than solving crosswords.

Overlord

The odd thing about crosswords, though, is that they work as a psychic balm for you only if you've developed the knack for solving them, and that's not as easy as it might seem. Learning to solve one crossword doesn't necessarily give you the tools to solve all others. The person who has spent a decade decoding the way Will Shortz thinks a *New York Times* crossword should be built may be good at solving Shortz-edited puzzles, but will likely be helpless when confronted with a *Times of London* puzzle. Let's say the scenario with the cuckolded lover above involves a British girlfriend, that you've already done that day's *New York Times* crossword, and that all there is in the house as you're waiting for the sword to fall when your loved one appears in twenty minutes is the cryptic puzzle in her *Times of London*. (You have, naturally, already done the American-style "Quick" puzzle you've found in the same paper.) The puzzle that remains would be a cryptic crossword, and the references it makes use of are, broadly speaking, utterly impenetrable to you. You don't know what on earth the constructor may be driving at with a clue such as "Goes back on a tractor with Stalin to spare." You think it might have something to do with Russia under Soviet collectivism, or perhaps with an older Stalin growing fatter around the middle, and hence maybe with Russia in the early 1950s, but you know the answer is likely to be something reconditely British, such as BOVRIL or BEDLAM (assuming you've figured out the first letter of the answer is "b," in which case all I'll say is "Good for you"). You know your English girlfriend isn't going to be of a mood to help out with nation-specific insights once she does get home. Under these circumstances, crosswords will help you out not one jot, and you'd better hope the other girl has a spare room in her apartment, because, without the familiar *New York Times* puzzle to calm your nerves, you'll be jittery and incoherent and will plead for hopeless mercy as soon as your girlfriend tosses her bag on the table beside you.

One particularly interesting example that may shed light on the cultural specificity of crossword puzzles comes from the late stages of World War II. Building on work already accomplished by the French and Polish intelligence services before their two nations were overrun by the Germans, the British had done wonders breaking the enemy Enigma code (or, actually, reverse-engineering the encipher-ing machinery that made Enigma possible) and by May 1944 were pretty much—though not entirely—on top of all nontelephonic communications the Germans maintained worldwide. A great part of the Enigma code-breaking effort was housed at a facility outside London called Bletchley Park; included among the linguists and mathematicians and WRENs hired to staff it were crossword-puzzle experts, who presumably had some talent in the field of deciphering hidden clues and messages. Some or all of these experts must have been doing the *Daily Telegraph* cryptics over May and June 1944, since someone noticed that five of its answers over the period looked suspiciously like code names for various components of the Allied assault on occupied France scheduled for early the following month: OVERLORD (the code for the whole Allied assault opera-tion), MULBERRY (the artificial British harbors meant to supply the invasion forces until French ports could be secured), NEPTUNE (the Allied supporting naval forces), UTAH, and OMAHA (the two Normandy beaches assigned to American landing forces).

British counterespionage agents promptly visited the *Daily Telegraph*'s puzzle editor and no doubt put him through the third degree, though they quickly exonerated him after it became clear he hadn't the slightest inkling about anything in the real world except puzzles. But the assumption that he might have been passing on vital military information to potential German spymasters through the *Daily Telegraph* puzzle is wonderful, though perhaps as reflective of the paranoia reigning at the time as of anything else. The clue that resulted in the answer OVERLORD, for instance, turned out to be "But some big-wig like this has stolen some of it at times." Even after two decades of close analysis, I haven't the slightest notion how to go about squaring the answer with the clue. (Though, to be fair to British counterespionage, the other four clues are more solvable; the clue for UTAH, for instance, was "One of the U.S.," and with a four-square blank to fill in you couldn't go very wrong, given a brain or at least an atlas.) The point is, the OVERLORD answer was apparently obvious to the couple hundred Englishmen who solved the *Telegraph* puzzle daily, but crosswords have fine margins that are not exportable. Americans have a tough enough time solving American crossword puzzles dating from before about 1970; that temporal gap, though, is infinitely easier to overcome than the cultural gap between British and American puzzles, and infinitely more so than the cultural gap between English and American puzzles and, say, German puzzles (and, of course, vice versa).

So let's call the solving divide insurmountable and set the odds against the Germans gleaning information from British cryptic clues in any reasonable amount of time at close to infinite. Granted, the correct answers would appear the day following the publication of a given puzzle; yet the most critical of the five clues, OVERLORD, appeared on June 4, meaning the answer appeared on June 5, the day originally scheduled for the Normandy invasion. By that time, five thousand Allied ships would have been off the French coast anyway, and five thousand ships were likely to tip off the Germans to the fact that something big was up. The British intelligence community's response to the *Daily Telegraph* crosswords in June 1944 was perhaps wise, given the scope and risk of what the Allies were then undertaking; but definitely paranoid and ultimately groundless, had anyone had the leisure to think the matter out in relative peace.

The Puzzler's Paradise

Relative peace, indeed, is what a puzzler needs while going about solving a crossword. At the American Crossword Puzzle Tournament, where hundreds of people sit elbow-to-elbow at scores of long banquet tables, sensory deprivation is ensured by the positioning of barriers between each contestant and his or her neighbor. (When I asked Will Shortz if these are there partly to prevent peeking, he tersely answered, "No one here cheats.") At the 2003 tournament, these barriers were makeshift manila-paper contraptions because the Stamford Marriott had lost the sturdier usual ones. These occasionally fell over, since the hotel's cavernous Grand Ballroom, where the event is held, is prone to drafts, which means that, during each of the eight heats, the termitelike sound of hundreds of no. 2 pencils scratching on paper is regularly punctuated by the swish of falling partitions—a distinct combination of sounds you'd be unlikely to hear anywhere else on earth.

A measure of how important this temporary separation from the world is for crossword puzzlers comes from a comment made by Jon Delfin, a New York–based pianist who has won the tournament seven times in the last ten years. By way of practice, Delfin sometimes solves puzzles with his right hand (he's a leftie) while listening to the radio or talking on the telephone. Doing crosswords while deliberately distracting oneself is, it seems, a great way to hone solving skills that will eventually be called on in the much quieter ambience of the competitive environment. Or at least the tactic seems to have paid off handsomely for Delfin, whose apartment must look, by now, like a museum for first-place crossword-tournament trophies.

While I'm nowhere near Delfin in terms of solving skills (he can do the Sunday *Times* puzzles in less than ten minutes with something approaching 100 percent accuracy, while it takes me an average of twenty-three or so minutes to do the same), I did, over the years, lower my time on the Sunday puzzle from three hours to less than half an hour by adopting certain techniques, at first unconsciously, then very consciously. Until about 1996, my puzzling was purely recreational and was likely to stay that way until I heard about the American Crossword Puzzle Tournament and decided that, one day, when I was ready, I'd compete in it.

I had moved from Boston to New York City in 1991 and have remained there pretty much ever since. As it turns out, life in the city is ideal for the dedicated puzzler, simply because it offers so many opportunities for downtime increments of twenty minutes or less in which to complete a crossword—the level of speed one needs before even contemplating doing reasonably well in a puzzle competition. Since most New Yorkers use buses, trains, and cabs instead of cars to get around, arrival times at mutually agreed meeting spots can vary dramatically; a crossword (or two) reliably takes the edge off waiting a half-hour for someone to show up. A ride in a cab through rush-hour traffic is excruciating, but not to someone equipped with a pen and that day's *Times*, especially if it happens to be later in the week.

For most non–New Yorkers, one's downtime between, say, work and home is spent either driving or being driven or bicycling or walking to and fro, none of which is safely or conveniently conducive to doing crosswords. Unless you enjoy walking into street signs, cycling into ditches, driving into other cars, or falling victim to motion sickness, you're not going to be motivated to solve puzzles while commuting; your time with a crossword will happen at breakfast, at lunch, or after dinner, none of which offer automatically structured time limits. In a city with a large and relatively undercrowded subway system, though, the chances are high that you'll spend a limited but temporally predictable (usually) stretch every day either sitting in or leaning against the door of a train car.

One of the virtues—one of the few, some would say—of the New York City subway system is that it forces its users, at least when they're traveling in Manhattan or in the immediately outlying districts of the other boroughs (trains go elevated in each after several stops), to do something other than stare out the window (there's nothing to see but dark tunnel walls most of the time) or at other passengers (which can be dangerous in many respects). New York subway riders tend to read, write, or doze. A good proportion of them put the enforced downtime to an arguably better use, and instead do puzzles.

Many a first date, I suspect, has been arranged after Party A on the subway asked Party B what his or her take was on the answer to 22-Down, because to some people crosswords are only slightly less sexy in and of themselves than are the people who do them. (In one 1998 puzzle that has become famous among the solving community, one hopeful suitor even managed to convince Will Shortz to encode a message asking the woman of the young man's dreams—an avid daily puzzler—to marry him. Shortz agreed, as did the girl.)

Once, one Saturday, as I was taking the ferry out to the island beach house I was sharing that summer with a dozen or so friends, I thought that I, too, was on the verge of stepping into the place where sex and crossword puzzles meet. The ferry ride was twenty minutes long, perfect for doing a Saturday-level puzzle, but in this case I was only about a third of the way through when the ferry reached the midpoint of its passage, and I was beginning to feel nervous. Someone interrupted me, and, waving the person off, I forced myself to concentrate on the puzzle in my lap. As the ferry was wheeling its stern around to greet the tail end of the dock, I finished. When I looked up, a young woman was smiling at me.

As a general rule, it's impossible to tell from just looking at someone if he or she is a crossword person; in terms of personal appearances, we're kind of unexceptional. But when it's summer, you're on your way to a beach house, and a pretty woman is smiling at you, it's one and the same if she wants to hit on you or talk about the puzzle, since both will be pleasant experiences. I smiled back and said, "Hi. Sorry about being rude, but I was doing the crossword."

"I know," she said. "I was watching. You were doing it in pen. Can I—" I didn't know what she was going to say, but my male ego was preening itself for something nice, so it was something of a letdown when she said, "Can I have your paper if you're done with it?"

I rarely actually read the *New York Times*, so giving it away was okay by me, but something about her made me feel it was the puzzle she was really interested in. Some crossword fanatics like to put their completed oeuvres into dated scrapbooks, but I've always been the sort who looks at a finished puzzle as a done thing, and it's of no more interest to me than a spent shell would be to your average marksman. I could no more imagine someone would want an already-completed crossword than I could imagine someone wanting, say, an item pulled out at random from my kitchen trash can.

"Of course. But the puzzle's done."

"Thanks. I just want it to show my friends."

I don't think I would have been more taken aback if the young woman had announced she was Mother Teresa's secret love child. She obviously wasn't going to show the puzzle to her friends and say some guy had done it on the ferry trip over; she was going to toss it on the kitchen table and let them think *she* had done it. Maybe I have a suspicious mind—but for what other reason on earth could she want an already-completed crossword? Granted, she may have already done the puzzle herself and simply wanted to check her answers against someone else's, or maybe she liked the look of the thing and wanted to frame it and hang it on her wall. If you believe the first reason, you're no cruciverbalist; if you believe the second, I really, really hope to meet that young woman again, because I could sell her enough completed puzzles to wallpaper the den, too.

I suppose it was this incident with the young woman on the ferry that finally made it clear to me that there are puzzlers and non-puzzlers, and that we—that is, puzzlers—are somehow more honest, in the main, than our nonpuzzling fellow humans. That's maybe an extravagant claim to make on the basis of an action committed by one single person in one specific place at one particular time, an action whose guiding logic, granted, I was then and am now unable to understand. At the time, however, that's how it felt. Now that I've twice been to the largest single gathering of crossword aficionados in the history of humankind and have seen and talked to the people who were there, I can't help but believe the world would be a much better place if everyone in it did puzzles, and took pride in doing them, and didn't go around asking other people for theirs (not that this is a very common activity, at beach resort towns or elsewhere, but in this case I'm speaking metaphorically). Will Shortz often argues that doing crosswords makes for better people: Those who solve puzzles need to know a lot about the world around them and have to think in a very closely directed way, and this combination,

Shortz believes, is a positive good. After talking to so many cross-word solvers and constructors, I'm increasingly beginning to think he's on to something.

Crossworld

Will Shortz is right—no one who takes part in the annual American Crossword Puzzle Tournament ever cheats. I'll go even further and say that no one *ever* will cheat there. To a puzzler, cheating is more than just a poisoned chalice—it's almost an impossibility, since the things you're vying against when you do a puzzle are, in this order, the puzzle maker, your control over the workings of your own brain, and, if you're in a competitive situation, the clock. Almost by definition, none of those things can be hoodwinked. If you look over your shoulder at the grid being filled in by the puzzler compet-ing beside you (which, if you're a true puzzler, you won't have time to do), you're in effect admitting that that person has better control over his or her brain than you do over yours (since neither of you has any control over the two other variables facing you: the puzzle maker's deviousness and the ticking of the clock), and that would be an intolerable thought. If you're desperate to become at any cost the best solver of the *New York Times* crossword in history, in other words, you won't get there using underhanded tricks.

At the American Crossword Puzzle Tournament, there are a lot of clear contenders for the title of best solver, though among them is certainly Jon Delfin. I was lucky enough (or guileful enough) to attend the 2003 competition as a reporter and had the chance to witness Crossworld in operation firsthand. I had convinced my ed-itor at the *Boston Globe* that it would make for a diverting human interest story, which it did, though I felt vaguely guilty throughout, like a chocolate fiend who's wangled a reporter's badge at the annual conference of the National Confectioners Association. The feats of solving to be seen there are astounding—Friday- and Saturday-level puzzles finished in six minutes or less, Sunday-size puzzles in ten; the top placers, though, usually take longer than that to get through a heat, since correctly finishing a puzzle is worth more points than doing it in so many minutes under the time limit. Competitors leave the Grand Ballroom at the Stamford Marriott (which I described in the *Globe* as "the size of a Zeppelin hangar," though that is perhaps an understatement) as soon as they've completed a puzzle and a referee has picked it up. After about three minutes, they begin flooding out to gather in the hotel's hallways and breathlessly compare notes, which means that about eight minutes into a given heat the place is filled with a conversational hum equivalent to a jet engine at full throttle. The hotel employees, after about the first two hours of this, walk around glazed-eyed and not saying much, knowing they still have another two days of it to endure.

Before heading up to the tournament with a photographer in tow, I'd called an acquaintance at St. Martin's Press and asked for the name of a puzzle constructor I could get in touch with once there. The name I was given was that of Brendan Emmett Quigley, which sounds like a character in a Raymond Chandler story. This impression was only reinforced when I asked him to describe himself so I could pick him out of the crowd: He said he was tall, very thin, red-haired, with red muttonchops, a combination Chandler would have been ecstatic about. The Grand Ballroom was packed with puzzlers, who sometimes tend to have eccentric sartorial styles, and I was having a hard time trying to spot Quigley; the *Globe* photographer, whose stock-in-trade is separating signals out of visual noise (and with the crossword-themed clothing and excited toing-and-froing, there was a lot of the latter), pegged him immediately.

Puzzle constructors are the crème de la crème of the crossword world, but as a group they don't tend to do that exceptionally well in a competitive environment; like National League pitchers, other practitioners of their rarefied trade can often stump them. Jon Delfin, who has published puzzles in the *Times* a couple of times to date, is one exception, as are Trip Payne, Tyler Hinman, and a handful of others. For constructors, whose work is exceptionally difficult (and, again, very much underpaid, for the most part), attending the competition is really more about collecting a year's worth of kudos and having a lot of shop talk than actually vying for the top prize— and there's a lot of kudos and a lot of shop talk.

For three days the amount of ambient energy at the Stamford Marriott is almost alarming, since it's the only time every twelve months when puzzlers, who one would imagine are introspective and solitary creatures, can get seriously social about their obsession. Perhaps the swallows at San Juan Capistrano aren't the best analogy from the animal world. The American Crossword Puzzle Tournament is more like those few nights in May or June when, all along the East Coast of the United States, horseshoe crabs, those 350-million-year-old arachnoid relics of the Paleozoic, clamber up onto beaches from Florida to Maine for their annual mating festival. Horseshoes spend the rest of the year solitarily hoovering the ocean floor for food (sort of like puzzlers hoovering for puzzles, though horseshoe crabs don't have Internet chat rooms). On their one group get-together each year, they make for a spectacle one really has to witness to understand, which is sort of what it's like being at the Stamford Marriott on the March or April weekend devoted to the tournament.

It's an eclectic group that comes to Stamford, insofar as any solidly middle-class group can be eclectic. The crossword-themed clothing makes them seem like a modern throwback to the early 1920s, when the fad initiated by the first Simon & Schuster puzzle book had millions of people wearing crossword earrings or crossword ties or smoking crossword-branded cigars. It's also, in the main, white, although Will Shortz strives mightily to broaden the demographic appeal of crossword puzzles and consequently of the tournament itself. There are two reasons why the participants look, at first glance, so—well, homogeneous. As the difference between British cryptics and American crosswords goes to show, puzzling—or at least puzzling that involves words as opposed to images or symbols, including mathematical ones—is intensely associated with one's degree of acculturation in a given society; immigrants don't do well at them, and immigrants are disproportionately poor and usually nonwhite. There's also the socioeconomic factor: To attend the tournament, you need to be able to afford the entrance fees (a couple of hundred dollars) and travel expenses, plus two or three nights at a relatively pricey hotel. On the whole, the tournament—like the National Spelling Bee—is, barring sponsorship arrangements, biased toward the middle class, and the East Coast middle class at that.

It also helps a lot to be a mathematician or a musician. Eric Wepsic, a usually strong finisher who didn't attend the 2003 event because he was getting married (which shows that being a word geek doesn't necessarily preclude having a functional love life), was a winner of the high school Math Olympiad, a managing director of my old hedge fund in New York at the age of twenty-nine, and generally the sort of individual you wouldn't want to meet late at night in a dark algorithm. Jon Delfin is, of course, a professional pianist. Will Shortz himself was, again, very nearly an economics major at Indiana University. Doing crosswords well involves having what I call a "garbage mind" (a strong associative memory, coupled with a magpielike obsession with collecting trivia) as well as an unusual ability to pick up on patterns and symbols. In practice, this means that the people who do best at crossword tournaments are the more quantitative types, which is counterintuitive—you'd think writers, editors, and translators would trounce pianists, systems analysts, and physicists at puzzles, but the opposite is the case. The line of demarcation between the okay crossword solver and the brilliant one isn't gender or age or degree of education. It is, purely and simply, how quickly one can crack a puzzle's specific, individual code, and it happens that a very small percentage of us can do that extremely well.

This book, then, is the story of my quest, born in that one almost revelatory moment watching a room filled with hundreds of the most accomplished crossworders in the nation at work, to place at least near the top half of the single largest such competition in the nation. It's also the story of crosswords themselves, and of word puzzles, and of the people who make them, solve them, and occasionally become consumed by them.

A fascination with crosswords being very personal, this book is also, for better and worse, a participatory rather than reportorial undertaking; like a book about alcoholism or sex addiction, a book about the crossword obsession has to be either first-person and funny or objective and not funny. I'm aiming for funny. So if the author occupies rather more of the center stage than other authors do in other books about quirky competitive endeavors (Scrabble or spelling bees, for example), it's because of the nature of the crossword itself: There's little competitive drama in any crossword tournament, but there's a lot of it in the small, quasi-solipsistic mental battle that breaks out in your head the moment you're presented with a new puzzle and reach for a pen or pencil to solve it.

Enter the
crossword

Arthur Wynne was born in Liverpool, England, in 1862, and as a young man emigrated to the United States, where he hoped to make his fortune in the newspaper business. As it turned out, he was no Adolph Ochs, Joseph Pulitzer, or William Randolph Hearst; his contribution to American journalism was, in the conventional sense, utterly negligible. But among his baggage on the packet boat that brought him across the Atlantic Ocean in the 1880s were the metaphorical seeds of what, in December 1913, would become the most singularly popular word game in history and an absolute financial windfall for publishers in every nation in the world. Unfortunately for Wynne, he never patented the idea.

The ancestors that begat the crossword puzzle have a long, long history. When, many millennia ago, one human uttered to another a word with a definite and specific meaning, some wag in the clan likely used it the following in day some unexpected manner that had all his caveman friends scratching their heads and wondering at the perverse nature of this new means of communication. That a word has a fixed relationship to a thing or concept that everybody can agree on is a great net advantage: Yelling "Tiger!" is a much more effective way of alerting your friends that a saber-tooth is prowling just beyond the flickering light of the campfire than a series of gibbering shrieks that could mean anything from "Rocks are falling down from the cliff" to "I think a scorpion just crept into your loincloth." But "tiger" can also be used metaphorically. There are those in our times, for instance, who'd characterize their bedmate as a tiger, and everyone would understand what they meant when they said it; I can imagine some well-rattled cavewoman fifty thousand years ago postcoitally whispering the same thing to her swain, only to have the poor fellow leap off the straw and reach, panic in his eyes, for the nearest sharp stick.

What I'm trying to say, I guess, is that words are good things, very useful, sometimes pretty and evocative in their own right, and always fun to play with. From the day they were developed, though, they've been used to confound, befuddle, and amuse their hearers, or at least a high enough proportion of them: In the same way that some people don't have a head for mathematics or an ear for music, there are others who lack an affinity for, or ability to do, wordplay— such as the troglodyte mentioned above, who probably spent the rest of the night at watch against a large imaginary cat, when a more word-disposed individual might have enjoyed a second go at his witty and logophiliac bedmate. (One psychotherapist, Evangeline Kane, argues—convincingly, in my opinion—that particularly violent criminals such as rapists display an inability to understand the multivalent value of words. They don't *get* concepts such as irony and rhetorical overstatement; all they know is that other people are constantly trying to pull verbal tricks on them, which may be one of the reasons for their huge reservoir of pent-up anger. Someone should probably look into this question from a statistical angle, although I'm not sure what could be done about the problem of violence even if an inability to handle words correctly were proved to be associated with it. What I do feel confident saying is that violent felons rarely attend crossword-puzzle tournaments.)

The fact is, enough people have enjoyed wordplay for so long that there exist examples of it dating to the birth of recorded writing itself—which, to be true, isn't that long, if you exclude hieroglyphs and ideograms found in the Egyptian and Chinese systems and concentrate solely on alphabetic writing, which postdates Homer by at least three centuries. I've yet to find a clear instance of hieroglyphic wordplay in the modern sense of the word. Chinese and Japanese writing are eminently suited to punning, I'm informed—Will Shortz once told me that there exists a great Japanese book on the subject, but, speaking no Asian languages, I'll take him on his word for it.

Primitive word squares—stacked words that read the same if looked at vertically, horizontally, or crosswise—appear on Greek stelae dating from the early part of the first millennium BCE. The Hebrew Bible is rife with acrostics—a game in which the first or second or whichever letters of lines in a passage themselves add up to a new sentence. A particularly fine example of anagramming—in which the letters in a word or sentence are rearranged to form an entirely new word or sentence—involves the apocryphal exchange between Jesus Christ and Pontius Pilate in which Pilate asks Jesus about the nature of truth. Supposedly, Pilate asked, "*Quid est veritas?*" Jesus answered, "*Est vir qui adest*"—"It [truth] is the man who stands before you." The reply uses precisely the same letters as those that appear in the question: A neat conceit, and it would be lovely were the anecdote true, but the whole exchange, famous as it is, ignores the fact that Jesus and Pilate would have been conversing in Aramaic or Greek, not Latin, and so is obviously the invention of some brilliant if anonymous medieval cleric, who probably bored the daylights out of the local gentry by repeating the squib at every possible opportunity.

Although they liberally make use of anagrams, puns, and other forms of wordplay, crosswords are by definition architectural creatures. Apart from Greek stelae squares, the earliest example of a diagrammed and structured word puzzle is a mysterious thing called the Phaistos Disk, which was discovered on the island of Crete, in the eastern Mediterranean, in 1908. (You can check it out in person at Greece's Iraklion Museum, in the island's capital city of Heraklion.) The object—a clay disk measuring about six and a half inches across, with some forty-five glyphs making up perhaps 241 distinct words that spiral around both the obverse and reverse sides—must have had some sort of religious or political import to whomever its makers were. It was found in what appears to be either a reliquary or counting room in the great palace at Knossos. (The interpretations you find in scholarly books and on the World Wide Web are as divergent as can be—some think the disk is a representation of a complex mathematical calculation, others say it's a prayer wheel, still others think it might be a property record of landholdings in a Mycenean mountain town. Like people who speculate about the location of Atlantis or the oracular meaning of the Mayan calendar, though, you can be pretty sure that anyone expressing a definitive view about the disk is both deeply passionate and supremely clueless, and so hardly a scientist.) It's always problematic to ascertain the age of a fired clay object, but this thing has to have been made somewhere around 1600 BCE, if you accept the rough archaeological consensus.

Whoever made the Phaistos Disk used forty-five manufactured dies, pressed into wet clay, with the divisions between "words"—in effect, clusters of die imprints—apparently predetermined, given their regularity. In reality, the disk cannot be translated—whatever language the dies represent is impossible to determine, given that they're the only extant example of their own peculiar letterforms, and the sample is too small to draw any conclusion from. In English, an equivalent problem would be to assume you have an eight-letter word with one "c" in it; based only on one thin shred of information—that the letter "c" is in there somewhere—you could argue it has to be "concrete" or "accruals" or any of a thousand other similar words, but in no instance could you bring to the table any proof one way or the other weightier than the extent of your own personal convictions. Plenty of people apparently want to knock their brains on the subject of the Phaistos Disk, to no avail. I suppose it's preferable to, say, applying that same intellectual energy to the invention of stock-market prediction scenarios that get people to invest Junior's college funds in a pyramid scheme, but still you wonder why so many people seem to have so much free time on their hands.

The point, though, is that someone, more than three millennia ago, had both the desire to make the letterforms and the foresight to ensure their aggregate impressions would fit perfectly on a pre-formed disk of set proportions—it would have been an embarrassing disaster to everyone involved in the project had a crucial word been abbreviated or dropped entirely, given that the consequences of such a thing happening would have been great. Gods don't like half-assed measures on the part of their followers; nor do deed holders on the part of their registrars.

The fact remains that someone in the age of Homer knew a letterform of a given size would produce marks of a certain size that would fit into a template of a given size and produce an artifact of record important enough to preserve in the inner sanctum of the great palace of Knossos on the island of Crete. The one thing everybody who writes books or posts Internet messages about the Phaistos Disk can agree on is that it's the first instance ever of the use of movable type, whatever that series of imprinted words or syllables actually means. We'll never know what the maker of the Phaistos Disk was trying to do with his piece of wet clay, but we certainly know that as he constructed it, he experienced an anxiety that has bedeviled crossword builders since the crossword was first invented: how to fit words into a delimited space.

And the crossword constructor has ancient cognates, at least in terms of the anxiety imposed upon him by his profession. Think of the nervous soul who had to make sure that a phrase—let's say "*Senatus Populusque Romanum*," SPQR, "The Senate and People of Rome"—would fit onto the pediment of a building erected in the City of Seven Hills a millennium and a half later. He's being asked to provide what a crossword constructor would call a "fill," or in other words the letters that fit perfectly into the spaces left for the answers; the only real difference is that he'll lose his livelihood—and perhaps his life—if he doesn't do it correctly. I suspect the maker of the Phaistos Disk, like the person who had to chisel "*Senatus Populusque Romanum*" onto a Roman temple face, was someone who sweated a lot until the task was satisfactorily completed. (As long as I'm pulling theories about the disk out of thin air, I might as well add that it looks a lot like those spiral puzzles that occasionally appear in the *New York Times Sunday Magazine*: the ones where numbered clues heading inward are overlapped by numbered clues heading outward from the center. Those puzzles give me hope that the Phaistos Disk isn't a prayer wheel or a record of landholdings on some stepped Thessalian mountainside, but simply the work of a puzzle maker of genius whose task it was to divert good King Minos—a sort of proto–Will Shortz in a Cretan tunic now lost to the mists of time.)

The Crossword's English Cousins

Also among Arthur Wynne's baggage were a number of cross-wordish precursors that may have served, at least partially, as inspiration for that magical creation of December 1913. First among these, I conjecture, were Yuletide ecclesiastical banners. Consider the heritage of the Celtic script so beloved of High Church Anglicans and various Catholic denominations today; attend a Christmas mass at Canterbury Cathedral or a Californian mission, and you'll see what I mean. Strung along the central aisle will be a series of banners, all in Latin, expressing some traditional epithet of the Lord Savior. For "O, King of the Gentiles," you'll see something like this:

O

R

GENTILUM

X

Depending on your linguistic capabilities and familiarity with the ins and outs of Celtic typography, it may take some time before you decipher each—depending also on your level of tolerance for liturgical ritual, the task of decipherment itself might represent the difference between a tolerable night out at church or a bottomless pit of excruciating boredom. You'll discover a darn interesting phenomenon in that vertical-and-horizontal arrangement of letters, with the "e" in "REX" and the "e" in "GENTILUM" intersecting so intriguingly. You will if you're into crosswords today; you certainly would have were it the late fall of 1913, you were Arthur Wynne, and the prospect of having to come up with an entirely new form of puzzle entertainment in time for the Christmas season lay before you like the pitiless chasm of Hell itself.

Fun, Victorian-Style

Let's say you're the fifty-one-year-old Arthur Wynne, tired, expatriated, whose dreams of a vigorous newspaper career in America have turned into the reality of being the "Fun" pages editor of a middling daily in New York City. You go to church, as all good Welshmen do in your time, and on this first Advent day you note, at Sunday mass, that words can cross. You reach into your mind in the hopes of looking for a way for words to cross in a fun way—because you've accepted that fun, not reportage, is your lot in the afternoon of your existence. As you look back to the British morning of your life, two distantly related word games would come to mind as possible sources of help. First you think of the acrostic puzzle. Second, you think of the word square.

An acrostic is a puzzle in which the first letter of each word in a stacked series of answers to specific clues combine to form a word of their own, a word usually relating thematically or otherwise explaining each other element in the puzzle. A simple one might involve each answer to a clue yielding the names of nonhuman, oxygen-breathing, red-blooded creatures, the names of which stack up to form the theme word ANIMAL, like so:

Aardvark

Narwhal

Iguana

Manatee

Antelope

Llama

Queen Victoria herself was a dab hand at creating acrostic puzzles, which may have been one of the reasons there was such a craze for them in England during the later part of her sixty-year reign—as was the case with many of her other pet concerns, including Christmas trees, temperance, sexual prudery, all things Indian, and Scottish ghillies. In his quite excellent *Oxford Guide to Word Games*, Tony Augarde cites a *double* acrostic the queen conceived for the entertainment and consternation of the royal brood. In this game, not only the first but also the last letters of the correct answers to the clue questions yielded related theme words, in this case NEWCASTLE and COALMINES. The fill words—NAPLES, ELBE, WASHINGTON, CINCINNATI, AMSTERDAM, STAMBOUL, TORNEA, LEPANTO, and ECLIPTIC—had nothing to do with either coals or Newcastle, and so technically the acrostic didn't quite work, but you have to give the old girl credit anyway: She was, at the time of its making, distracted by the administration of approximately one-sixth of the world's population.

The other Victorian-era puzzle craze was the word square, which involves the creation of a grid in which an initial word is written out both vertically and horizontally, as is the terminal word as determined by the last letter of the initial one. It sounds complicated—and it is, if you want to try creating one—but appears eminently elegant once you take a glance at the thing on the page. The example I use is also taken from the *Oxford Guide to Word Games*:

CREST
REACH
EAGER
SCENE
THREE

In every case, each word appears precisely twice in the square, in the mirror inverse of its original position. It may seem like child's play to construct such a thing, which, granted, it is—if you limit yourself to squares made up of three- or four-letter words. A square made up of five-letter words should take the averagely talented smith about an hour or so to construct; a six-letter-word square would take, if you're lucky, a rainy afternoon. To go beyond that, you'd need to be an idiot savant with an infinity of time on your hands, although I'm told that quite normal (*sic*) people like Lewis Carroll would think nothing of spending a week on creating eight-letter doozies with which to amaze their friends and impress little girls. Word-squaring is a constructor's activity, mainly, since the possibility exists—faintly, of course—that the seed word (CREST, in the example above) could yield more than one fill, which means that squares aren't reliably a one-possible-answer-only sort of puzzle you'd want to print in a newspaper without risking a torrent of angry mail. Apparently, only some nine hundred nine-letter squares are possible, according to Augarde (and you'd have to use unabridged dictionaries in a hundred languages to manage even one of those), and no ten-letter ones are at all.

But I like to think that Wynne's prime inspiration for the crossword was the city of New York itself. One day in 1913 the harried editor of the *World*'s "Fun" pages is late for an appointment and thinking about puzzles. He catches a hansom cab on Seventh and gives the driver an address—maybe 228 Fourteenth Street. "Take Thirty-eighth across town," he says, "then Second Avenue down." As the blocks fly by, he fantasizes that each could represent a letter in a word. And suddenly he knows that next week's puzzle will feature words that cross one another, just like the numbered streets and avenues of his adoptive hometown.

Crosswords Come of Age

Arthur Wynne died in 1945 and, being by all reports a reserved and rather retiring individual, did not leave behind memoirs or notes or much of a hint about how he came up with the concept of the crossword puzzle. Yet his invention caught the fancy of the *New York World*'s readership instantly and remained a popular weekly feature until the newspaper's demise in 1931. (Wynne himself retired in 1918.) Initially the puzzle was not subject to the rules that govern its appearance today: In terms of size, shape, ratio of black to white squares, symmetry, use of words less than three letters long, and content, it was a rather free-form affair, and prone to erratic fact-checking that undoubtedly kept Wynne busily answering correspondence from irate readers pointing out, for instance, that the Irrawaddy is a river in Burma, not Siam, and the knish a culinary invention of Russia, not of Germany. But, for better or worse, the *New York World* was, until 1924, when the *New York Herald-Tribune* began to run a competing daily version, pretty much the only place you could get your weekly cruciverbalist fix. After Arthur Wynne retired in 1918 and a young Smith College graduate named Margaret Farrar (then Petherbridge) was tasked with editing it, the *World*'s puzzle gradually began to take on the characteristics of the crossword as we know it today: symmetric, well enough checked for factual accuracy, resolute in the matter of eschewing two-letter words, and committed to the idea that no puzzle would ever be published that featured less than a seventy-to-thirty ratio of white squares to black.

It was with the publication of the Petherbridge-edited Simon & Schuster crossword book in April 1924, though, that things really began heating up, cruciverbally speaking. It should be remembered that the Jazz Age, which ran from the promulgation of the Volstead Act in 1919 to the Wall Street Crash of October 1929, was a time in which the American public was singularly susceptible to passing fads: bobbed hair (think F. Scott Fitzgerald's character Bernice), goldfish-swallowing, the ukulele, flagpole-sitting, the lindy—nothing was too frivolous to occupy the attention of a nation bathed in money and reveling in its newfound status as, arguably, the greatest military and economic power on earth. The crossword puzzle was simply nuts to a populace seeking distraction from the task of hauling their loot to the bank every Monday morning, and six months after Messrs. Simon and Schuster published their first ware, the country fell into the grips of a crossword fever.

In his brilliant book about the New York banking industry, *Where Are the Customer's Yachts? or A Good Hard Look at Wall Street*, the humorist and (I hope) inveterate crossworder Fred Schwed Jr. tells the tale of the bowl of nickels placed by the exit of a club car bearing sundry millionaires to Pennsylvania Station in 1929; it was there for the convenience of the nabobs, who were thus spared the necessity of having to reach into their pockets for the subway fare downtown. Schwed goes on to opine:

> There have been many explanations of the sudden debacle of October, 1929. The explanation I prefer is that the eye of Jehovah, a wrathful god, happened to chance in October on that bowl. In sudden understandable annoyance, Jehovah kicked over the financial structure of the United States, and thus saw to it that the bowl of free nickels disappeared forever.

Well, by late 1924, those same nabobs had also been spared the bother of having to lug a dictionary along when they took their trains from their homes in Oyster Bay or Chappaqua to the city and work: the Long Island and other New York–area commuter lines provided one in each of their cars. At the New York Public Library, a strict five-minute limit was placed on the borrowing of reference works, lest the fist-shaking mob lined up before the main desk in the reading room get too unruly while waiting their own turn at them. (Sort of like how the whole New York City library system currently imposes a fifteen-minute time limit on those using its computers, which makes doing puzzles on them an impossibility for most.) Priests and rabbis deplored the absence of parishioners from their services; spouses filed divorce papers against once-beloved partners who preferred doing crosswords to performing their connubial duties; two crossword-themed musical revues even appeared on Broadway, and both enjoyed six-month sellout runs.

Along the stairs leading from Will Shortz's living room to his home office upstairs are framed and glassed-over copies of a half-dozen pieces of crossword sheet music published between October 1924 and the conclusion of the Great American Puzzle Craze in roughly May 1925. Jon Delfin played some of these by way of Saturday-night entertainment at the 2003 Stamford event, and the five hundred–odd participants (an easy crowd, granted) roared their appreciation for the performance. In late 1924 the playwright and humorist Booth Tarkington sent Margaret Pether-bridge a letter blaming her and Simon & Schuster for ruining his year's work schedule. (It was signed "Malignantly yours," which one hopes, for her sake, was done in a spirit of fun, but the letter—it is quoted in full in Coral Amende's book *The Crossword Obsession*—reads a little too tartly, especially in the passage where it takes up the appearance of Petherbridge's *second* crossword book that same year.)

The Case of the Crossword Mystery

If you need further evidence of how thoroughly the country fell under the spell of crosswords in 1924 and 1925, I'd strongly advise you to buddy up to Will Shortz and wangle from him an invitation to his house in a pleasant suburban township just north of New York City. There you'll find not only the pieces of sheet music and the complete collection of twenty or so crossword publications (mostly in English, but in a handful of other languages, as well)— there are also crossword drink coasters, crossword postcards, crossword board games (the most famous of these evolved, over the course of the 1940s, into the familiar Scrabble), and crossword jewelry. In his library, though, you'll find the most remarkable puzzle phenomenon of all: the crossword mystery novel.

I estimated that Shortz owns around a thousand books specifically about crosswords and maybe several thousand more about puzzles in general, which I'd comfortably guess represents the overwhelming majority of publications in this particular literary niche. In fact his collection of books and magazines about puzzles numbers twenty thousand. The book about Japanese kana puzzles is neat, of course; Sandy Balfour's *Pretty Girl in Crimson Rose*, published in 2003, takes as its subject the (British) journalist's lifelong obsession with (British) cryptic crosswords, and it's the most consciously literary pick of the litter, though it's likely alien to the sensibilities of most stateside readers; but it's the crossword whodunits that really take the cake in terms of attracting and holding the browser's eye.

There's around a score of such creatures in Shortz's library (we'll revisit them in chapter 8), and after an afternoon's examination I'd say the best of them is *Crime of the Crossword*, by one John

Garland, put out sometime in the 1940s by an obscure and now-defunct London publisher (London: Columbine Publishing Co. Ltd., N.D.; if such a description sounds like something in a short story by Jorge Luis Borges, it's because crossword murder mysteries *are*, in fact, a subject recondite enough to warrant Borgesian analogies). As I read the thing, a typewritten note on yellow paper fluttered out of it and fell to the floor. The note was a description of the book, likely better than any I could come up with, and from its tone and content I suspected it was written by Will himself, which he confirmed after a minute or so of looking at it. I quote it verbatim, since it not only captures the book, but also something revelatory enough about Shortz himself. (For the record, a reprint publishing house might make a buck or two bringing *Crime of the Crossword* back; it really is quite good.)

A nicely-written story, with interesting characters, a fast-moving plot, and nice twists and bits of humor sprinkled through. The best example of this small genre I've read.

The crossword portion of the book occupies only the first 115 pages; what follows is a sequel to the story, in which the crook and the private detective meet again—interesting reading, but not having anything to do with the crossword.

Though the library catalogue of the British Museum gives the publication date of this book as 1940, the crossword portion of the mystery appears to have been written around 1925. Clues: The primitiveness of the crossword construction; the directness of the definitions (which show no sign of cryptic flavor); and a note in the text (page 37) that says that crosswords "are all the rage right now."

The puzzle is solvable, with a little help from an unabridged dictionary and gazetteer, and ties into the story nicely. The irregularity of the numbering does serve a purpose.

The reasons Shortz's précis is interesting, at least to someone writing a book about crosswords, are many: It shows that this form of puzzle has an identifiable phylogeny that allows one to infer, from internal data, roughly when and where a given example was constructed; it hints at how fundamentally different American and British crosswords are (or were to become over the decade or so following the writing of *Crime of the Crossword*); it serves as an example of how one needs to train one's mind in order to solve crosswords; it gives one an idea about how talented Will Shortz is as a writer (the copyediting niggle aside that he should not have hyphenated the adverbial construction "nicely written" in the first line of the note) and as an analytical thinker. All of these subjects I'll come back to later in this book; for the nonce, I'll just add that one more piece of evidence linking the writing of *Crime of the Crossword* to circa 1925 is that, along with the statement on page 37 mentioned by Shortz, there exists a brief passage instructing the murder-victim-cum-recipient-of-the-puzzle about how to solve it—a strong indication that the reader of the book would likely not have encountered a crossword before, which in turn dates the book to around the first full international flowering of this form of puzzle, in other words, around 1924 or 1925.

In *Crime of the Crossword*, the victim of the central murder is an importer of floor tiles (think grids), and the resolution of the mystery hinges on the detective's ability not only to rapidly learn how to do crosswords, but also to relate the pattern of tiles on a particular floor to the pattern of clues in an admittedly primitive and ham-fisted crossword puzzle.

Another novel, this one American, hurried into print ("crashed," as they say in publishing nowadays) to take advantage of the early puzzle craze, was Vincent Fuller's *The Long Green Gaze: A Crossword Puzzle Mystery* (New York: B. W. Huebsch, 1925). There's not much to say about this one, though the flap copy gives the general flavor of the thing. (Shortz's copy contains the original back matter, unsealed.)

ONE
Cross Word Puzzles with a Purpose: The reader can act as detective and solve the puzzles in order to solve the mystery.
TWO
An Irresistible Mystery Story: A strange murder, a curious theft, and plenty of other puzzles in the plot, whether you work the cross word puzzles or not.
THREE
Hidden Treasure! The answers to the puzzles, sealed in the back. See if you can wait till the end!
GO!

A slew of other detective novels (including one latterly written Nancy Drew mystery, *The Clue in the Crossword Cipher*) take puzzles as their central topic, but they all postdate the beginning of the crossword craze by at least a decade. *Crime of the Crossword*, written if not published sometime in England in 1924 or 1925, affords a neat and opportune excuse to turn to the fate of the crossword once it fell into the hands of the British: a story that says much about puzzles, about the differences between the ways John Bull and Jonathan Yank seem to view the world around them, and the ways in which national approaches to the crossword can act as a looking glass in which the differences between, and congruencies among, whole cultures can dimly be discerned.

The Crossword Crosses the Pond

Winston S. Churchill or Oscar Wilde or G. B. Shaw (or possibly all three) aphorized that Britain and the United States are two nations divided by a common language. For "Britain" in that formulation you could as easily substitute Australia or New Zealand, but you couldn't necessarily do so with Canada. Unlike in the United States and Canada, the British who migrated to the two antipodean nations took with them wholesale their native culture, which in neither country was diluted to any significant extent by influences either indigenous or, at least until very recently, imported as a result of mass waves of non–Anglo-Saxon immigrants.

By contrast, both the United States and Canada are cultural bouillabaisses. The linguistic patterns of the ethnically British who came to North America were deeply affected by concurrent or near-concurrent influxes of rival European languages, French in the case of Canada (and to a lesser extent of the United States, too), Spanish and African in the States. Moreover, in both countries the indigenous Native American nations left their cultural footprint on the mix, however lugubrious contact with Europeans turned out to be for them. Linguistically, ethnically, and culturally, the ultimately dominant Anglo-Saxon peoples were confronted with alien (in their eyes) competition that had to be assimilated or destroyed. They did not experience the unchallenged cultural dominance enjoyed—again, until quite late in the game—by British who migrated to the more separatist colonies south of the equator (including those in Africa and the Asian subcontinent).

Sweeping statements about the ways nations think and act are of course dangerous, but the fact is that crossword puzzles—and word games in general—are accurate barometers of cultural difference. Pick up a newspaper in Durban, Auckland, or Sydney and flip to the puzzle page. Overwhelmingly, it will be a British-style cryptic. Then pick one up in Ottawa or New York. Overwhelmingly, its puzzle will be the American-style grid featuring multiple crossed letters and noncryptic cluing.

Now, I can usually complete the *Times of London* cryptic—not in every case, and certainly not in the fifteen minutes it seems to take every British mother to complete, but much of the time. This isn't because I have some especially unusual talent for solving word puzzles (I don't), but simply because, probably as a result of having been stumped for so long by that Overlord clue mentioned in chapter 1, I've made a point of learning the six or seven rules that govern the construction of British cryptics. Give it to your average American or Canadian solver who hasn't learned the same rules, though, and that person will likely not get as much as a single clue. Conversely, give a *New York Times* puzzle to your average solver in Britain or Australia or New Zealand; that person, too, will likely be stumped. The question begs to be asked: Why should this be so?

The most likely reason is the two puzzles' hugely different underlying theories—I'm sorry I have to use this word in connection with what are essentially just amusing pastimes—about construction. If you grew up doing American-style puzzles, you'll have internalized the mechanism by which they operate. You'll also, chances are, be American (or Canadian), and so will have been swimming all your life in the sea of North American cultural references—its geography, its sports, its radio and television programs—that will be impenetrable to non–North Americans. American puzzles are primarily information-based and only secondarily wordplay-based. For instance, one clue in the April 17, 2004, *New York Times* puzzle by Brendan Emmett Quigley was "2002 upset," yielding SUPER-BOWLXXXVI. How many non-Americans would know, first, that

Superbowls are numbered with Roman numerals and, second, that the thirty-sixth was an underdog victory pulled off by the New England Patriots? (Quigley is from Boston, by the way, and a Patriots fan, so this was an intentional plug for his home team.) Any non-American who happened to solve enough cross-clues to yield the string LXXXVI would tear his hair out wondering what sport it refers to—has there been an eighty-sixth America's Cup yet?

Cryptics, again, are more wordplay-based than information-based. Easy clues (for example, the clue mentioned in chapter 1, "One of the U.S.," which, assuming that you knew at least one of the four letters, you'd have to be a dunce not to realize yields UTAH) are rare; most are much, much tougher, which is what makes cryptics the hardest word puzzles on earth to complete for all but the freaks of nature who can untangle them in ten minutes or less. This is true in part because they contain many fewer crosses—places where two answers intersect, so that finding one gives you an inkling of what the other might be—than do American-style crosswords. It's also due to the fact that most North Americans are as unfamiliar with the minutiae of British life and society as most British are with, say, what the NCAA is or which U.S. president built Monticello.

More to the point, the British, especially the English but also the Irish, have as a people a long and rich history, in both the print and oral traditions, of stringing together words unexpectedly for humorous or sarcastic effect. From Shakespearean puns ("the dribbling dart of love," or "country matters") to Cockney rhyming slang, the British are by and large more open to and adept at wordplay than are their North American cousins, a fact reflected in the dialogue of English comedy troupes such as Monty Python's Flying Circus and the Goon Show. This may be because, while modern-day North American English developed partly as a consequence of close contact with speakers of French and Spanish, among a handful of others, modern-day British English developed almost exclusively in the presence of nothing other than numerous English dialects.

In his memoir of serving in Burma with the 9th Borderers during World War II (*Quartered Safe Out Here*—it's one of the best personal recollections to come out of the conflict), the British writer George MacDonald Fraser provides an author's note about the Cumbrian dialect of the men he served with. By way of illustrating what it sounds like, he gives the Cumbrian version of the English sentence "Have you seen a donkey jump over a gate?": "Est seen a coody loop ower a yet?" The point is, except for "coody," each word in the Cumbrian sentence has a lexical analogue in its English counterpart, while the two sentences are grammatically indistinguishable. To an Englishman hearing it for the first time, the Cumbrian sentence would be gibberish; yet with a bit of practice he'd soon enough learn to make heads and tails of it. In a slightly different form, that last sentence could well enough encapsulate the mechanism by which one learns to solve British cryptics.

I don't believe the proposition is so off the mark that nineteenth-century industrialization followed by the huge troop formations of World War I threw together millions of Britishers, all speaking different dialects, and forced them to come to terms with the way everyone else spoke. (Though the Cumbrians, a fiercely independent and self-reliant people who, for instance, hunt fox for miles *on foot*, seem to have held out longer than most: Fraser is describing their dialect in 1945.) The British cryptic was developed around 1930 and was an instant hit; it's still wildly popular all over the Commonwealth today (Canada aside, and assuming Australia remains part of it for very much longer). Perhaps it would have enjoyed less spectacular success had Britain's linguistic history not predisposed so many people to solving it—and had the average Brit not taken such historic delight in co-opting American inventions and transmuting them into impenetrable Englishisms, such as calling elevators "lifts" and delivery trucks "pantechnicons."

Puzzling for Peace

So, if the crosswords that appear in North America and the British Commonwealth are so different even though the same tongue is spoken in both, what can be inferred, in terms of comparative culture, from the crosswords produced in lands that speak different languages entirely?

Before the question can even be taken up, a couple of points need to be addressed. First, how well or how badly you do on crosswords in a language or dialect other than your own is no measure of your competence in that language or dialect. Plenty of people can whip through a *New York Times* puzzle in ten minutes, yet still have a half-completed *Times of London* cryptic dating from late 1998 lying on their desk; by no means does that imply they're anything less than competent speakers of BBC English or American English. (A better measure is if you can understand the rapid-fire delivery of the evening news in another country well enough to explain to a citizen of that country all the nuances of what has actually been said.) Second, crossword styles vary: British cryptic grids contain few crossed answers, while American puzzles are just the opposite; French puzzles are symmetrical but contain relatively more crossed answers than their counterparts in the U.K.; Italian puzzles tend to be open (again, meaning they have a high proportion of white squares to black) and pun-filled, though rarely are they cryptic; Russian puzzles are symmetric but often come in odd shapes, though they overwhelmingly favor a high percentage of crossed clues. (These are broad generalizations; many, many exceptions are to be found in each case, and I can't talk about crosswords done in languages I can't read.) Third, crosswords are disposable amusements, not weighty documents, so they tend to reflect the popular culture of the moment as much as anything else; to have any hope of doing them, you need to be deeply immersed in that popular culture. All that said, doing foreign-language crosswords can yield certain insights about the relationships between cultures and between languages.

In addition to being a writer I'm also a translator of books from the French, Russian, and Italian. One thing I've noticed that has as far as I can tell yet to be taken up by academic linguists, although I'm sure many other translators have pondered it, as well: The compressibility factor varies with each original and target language. For instance, I've found that about 110 pages of French yields 100 in English; 105 pages of Italian yields 100 in English; Russian and English are pretty much on a par with each other. No one translates British English into American English, but I suspect if they did they'd find their American text a tad shorter than their British one; at least that's what the line of analysis I seem to be pursuing—that compressed languages seem to be associated with American-style crosswords and looser ones with British-style cryptics—would indicate.

Although French is technically my best language in terms of speaking it, I couldn't get through a puzzle in the tongue to save my life. I can get through Italian puzzles with relative ease, even though Italian is my worst language in terms of speaking it. Although my Russian is functionally that of a hypereducated Russian twelve-year-old in about the year 1882, I can usually inflict a fair amount of punishment on the puzzle that appears in the daily New York–based *Novoe Russkoe Slovo* ("Since 1910"), though I get stumped by the more contemporary clues.

It makes sense that I can't do French puzzles, since they're done in a language that seems, at least in my experience, the least congenial to English translation, and they're aggressively Gallic in their jokes and references. Jean Rossat, a well-known French puzzle constructor (or *verbicruciste*, as the term is perversely rendered in and around the City of Light), at a crossword festival in 1986 unveiled the Grille du Condor ("Condor Grid"), an enormous thing containing 14,528 squares and a seemingly infinite collection of the sort of fill you find in weekly magazines such as *Paris Match*: two-letter words, lots of unchecked letters, inexplicable (to non-French speakers) puns and jokes—in short, the stuff that would make a stateside crossword editor blanch. The Grille du Condor, though, was a media sensation, and Rossat found himself catapulted from relative obscurity—his constructions until then had mainly appeared in a provincial newspaper called *Le Courrier Savoyard*, where he was working as a reporter—into nationwide prominence, which he has enjoyed ever since. If anything, then, the crossword bug is international: The styles of puzzles may vary across borders, but the impulse to solve them doesn't. (In 2003, Rossat was the keynote speaker at the Twenty-sixth American Crossword Puzzle Tournament, which says something interesting about how apolitical the world of puzzling is. The tournament was held in March, as usual, as the drums of war in Iraq were beating throughout America, and a motion had just passed in the House to change the term "French fries" to "freedom fries" as an insult to the country that most adamantly opposed armed conflict. At the tournament, Rossat was lionized: Though the United States was to invade Iraq three days after its conclusion, all the contestants wanted to hear about was how French puzzles worked, and if they were as popular in France as they are here.)

It would take a mixed convention of cognitive behaviorists and linguists to unravel why crossword puzzles, even those produced in nations as close as Britain and the United States, are so deucedly difficult for anyone to solve who isn't a countryman of the people who build them. But perhaps crosswords in other languages and from other cultures should be a mandated part of international studies programs in every university and military college around the world. The kids would have to work hard, granted, but maybe the eventual result would be—finally—something like a global entente: No statesman would ever consider waging war against a country that happens to be home to his favorite puzzle constructor.

Britain versus America

Every crossword puzzle ever made in the Western world falls somewhere, structurally speaking, between the wholly keyed American puzzle and the nearly unkeyed cryptic puzzle. What this means, again, is that American-style puzzles require that every letter appearing in them has to be connected to at least two others, while British-style puzzles allow—in fact they prefer—there to be as many unchecked letters as possible.

The most frustrating thing for solvers of American-style puzzles is a cross between two words or phrases with which the solver is unfamiliar or doesn't know how to spell. Many people, for instance, have never heard of Sonja Henie, the Norwegian star of the 1928, 1932, and 1936 Olympic skating events who is the darling of American constructors because her last name offers a fine opportunity to act as a cross for up to five other words. Say the "n" in the name crossed with the answer to the clue "Famed British villanellist Wystan." If you don't know your early twentieth-century Olympics figures or your mid-twentieth-century British imagist poets, and hence that the answer to the cross clue should be AUDEN, you're cooked. (If, as I suspect, we all are wont to misspell or misuse certain words, one of my verbal *bêtes noires* is Henie—to me, she's invariably "Hedie.")

Something like the same problem can stymie would-be solvers of British puzzles. For his 2003 book about cryptics, Sandy Balfour chose as a title the phrase "Pretty Girl in Crimson Rose" for very good reason. Once you've applied your store of cryptic know-how to that clue, you get REBELLED—because "crimson" can be "red" and a synonym for "pretty girl" can be "belle," so if you place the latter within the former, and then think about what that extraneous "rose" can also mean, "rebelled" is what you come up with. For the most part, solving cryptics demands that you know not so much a huge grab bag of facts as a small set of strategies for deciphering them—yet British and American cryptics are still mutually impenetrable.

In *Pretty Girl in Crimson Rose*, Balfour, however, writes about what one solver thinks is the best cryptic clue ever written, which if true means that British puzzles are on occasion as determined by specific, local cultural conditions as are their American cousins. In the following passage, which is part of an extract from the book that appeared in the *Guardian* in 2003, "Araucaria" is the nom de puzzle of the British newspaper's crossword constructor (or "setter," as they say in England); Jeffrey Archer is the British novelist, politician, and peer who in the 1990s was tried for, convicted, and sent to jail for charges of lying in court. I have retained the *Guardian*'s British punctuation.

Araucaria wrote the clue that Nick Smith in a letter to the Guardian on January 21 2001 claimed to be "the best crossword clue ever". Consider two pieces of information that would have been readily available to Guardian readers such as Nick at the time. The first is that in 2000, 13 years after he told it, Jeffrey Archer's lie about Monica Coghlan came back to haunt him. The second is that, before his subsequent trial and conviction, Archer retired from the public eye and took refuge in the Old Vicarage, Grantchester.

And so to the clue: "Poetical scene has surprisingly chaste Lord Archer vegetating (3, 3, 8, 12)". The answer is The Old Vicarage, Grantchester, a "surprising" anagram of "chaste Lord Archer vegetating", or as Nick Smith put it to me, "the most perfect clue, probably the best ever".

While *Guardian* reader Nick Smith may think this the best clue ever, most if not all American readers would be extremely challenged in terms of solving it. Some might recognize "surprising" as cryptic puzzle-speak indicating the answer will be an anagram of part or all of the words in the clue. Few would know about Jeffrey Archer or the legal pickle he found himself caught within. Even fewer—again, if any—would be aware of the Old Vicarage, Grantchester, or of its significance to the whole proceedings (it involves a reference to a Rupert Brooke pastoral poem, FYI). So although cryptics in general can be thought of as less hermetically sealed to non-British people as American puzzles are to non-Americans, they are not always so; on some occasions, in fact, there would be a greater chance that a randomly selected Englishman could make his way through a *New York Times* puzzle than you or I could ever hope to solve a *Guardian* one.

The Relative Characters of American and British Puzzles

The British opted to make their version of the crossword harder than the American one for a variety of reasons, most of them cultural, but some of them perhaps economic. As a general rule, while

British puzzles are harder to solve than American ones, they're also easier to construct—you as the builder don't need to agonize about coming up with stacks of three fifteen-letter answers, for instance, or undergo the drudgery of making sure that every letter in your puzzle connects to at least two others (and that all the resulting words are in the dictionary). This is why, when you go to the American Crossword Puzzle Tournament, you'll see the participants flocking around constructors and spotting them drinks at the bar— or, more lucratively for the constructors, buying their books. For the maker of a cryptic, structure and layout are the easy bits; the hardest part is making the clues work. For this reason, the editor of a puzzle in a British newspaper tends to be the most prolific or even sole creator of the puzzles that appear within it.

Of late, the growing popularity of "quick" puzzles—the American-style constructions that began to appear in British papers over the last decade, most notably in the London *Times*—seems to show that a convergence is developing between the world's two dominant crossword forms, especially since American puzzle makers have, over the same period, displayed an increased willingness to incorporate into their creations wordplay of the sort more commonly associated with British crosswords. (I initially called this phenomenon "cryptic creep." One day I mentioned the term to Will Shortz, whose doubtful reaction to it—no one wants to be a cryptic creep—led me to retool it. These days I've been calling the convergence "cryptic drift.")

Luckily, the appearance of the quick puzzle in England has not cast the cryptic off its throne, though one hopes it will increase the number of Britons who do crosswords. I say "luckily" because around the cryptic puzzle has developed the phenomenon of the solitary and pseudonymous puzzle maker. Since cryptics are easier to construct than American puzzles, you don't need legions of freelance contributors, overseen by one all-powerful editor, to make sure one appears in your newspaper every day of the year. All you need is one guy reliably cranking them out for you (who might be the editor himself), which both fosters very different crossword styles across the British press and gives people the chance to personally and genially hate the classically pseudonymed demons who think up the tortures a British solver is subjected to daily. I have it on very reliable authority—actually, it was pointed out by the person who copyedited this book—that an episode of the BBC *Inspector Morse* crime series ("The Setting of the Sun") revolves around crosswords. According to a Web site my editor referred me to (a writer's life is sometimes an easy one), the episode opens with the inspector hosting an awards dinner for a crossword competition, and during the meal one of the participants is murdered; Morse, who constructed the puzzle the competition centers on, in the end discovers that the killer has used it and the dinner as his alibi. The same copy editor also mentioned that crosswords appear in a Lord Peter Wimsey mystery (another BBC crime series, this one based on the mystery books written by Dorothy L. Sayers). The larger point I'm trying to make is not just that I'm lazy and editorially fortunate; it is rather that there exists a very close, almost intimate bond between British cryptics and the people who solve them, and this is known to and sometimes exploited by British television writers. The same bond is absent in the United States—it is hard to imagine, for instance, Detective Sipowicz on *NYPD Blue* busting the perp thanks to his crossword sensibilities, and even harder to imagine an American television audience staying tuned in long enough to watch it happen.

American puzzles are generally far less quirky and whimsical than British cryptics, even if some of the constructors whose work appears in the *New York Times*, such as Brendan Emmett Quigley and veteran Maura Jacobson, have a distinct signature style that one can, with a bit of experience, readily recognize. In general, though, it would take a remarkably discriminating solver to guess, without looking at a puzzle's byline, which constructor is responsible for a given grid. Solvers of British cryptics instantly know, on the other hand, which person, or at least which person anonymously working at which paper, can be blamed for them. This makes sense: If an individual is responsible for creating 365 puzzles a year, his "hand" quickly becomes highly recognizable to the regular solver. (And British puzzle makers tend to be extremely prolific, with some regularly supplying material to as many as three or four dailies at a time.)

For this reason, and because of the very subjective nature of writing cryptic clues itself, the relationship between the solver and the constructor in England is much more intimate than it is in America. A recurrent feature of British puzzles is in fact the reaction to them you find in the letters-to-the-editor section—in the United States, such an eventuality is practically unheard of; the "Election Day" puzzle that appeared in the *New York Times* on November 5, 1996, is indeed the only American puzzle in modern crossword history I know of that generated a spate of reader mail. Conversely, anyone looking into the history of the cryptic is struck by the letters editors seem to receive every time their paper's old constructor is replaced by a new one. Most of these letters are either bitter reproaches or paeans of praise—again, reflective of the strange personal intimacy that characterizes the relationship between English solvers and constructors. Many of them, though—it seems to be a cottage sport for some solvers—contain speculation, based on the puzzle's content and form, about the character and habits of the constructor. "He has had an inadequate legal training of which he is ashamed, attended Harrow and not Eton, and is fond of long walks and dogs"; "He's a man of the cloth and a recent widower who drinks." (I made these two up, but they catch the general spirit of the thing.)

The respective histories of American versus British puzzles tell us a lot about the people who make and solve them—indeed, one of the points of Will Shortz's "enigmatology" is to identify how a puzzle can reveal things about the times and cultural context under which it was conceived. It sounds like a cliché, but the cryptic reflects a sensibility that is elitist, introspective, fond of humor and wit, and a bit naughty; the crossword's sensibility is plain-dealing and democratic (okay—*relatively* plain-dealing and democratic).

The way we do crosswords teaches us something about our collective nature—but then we already knew that Englishmen and Americans are more alike than any two other people in the world, except that one is the introvert in the family and the other the extrovert. What the history of puzzles tells us, however, especially of late, is that Britain and America are in fact growing ever more alike—because the nature of the puzzles we do is converging. To some that's a good thing, to others a bad one. As long as enough of us are simply doing our crosswords every day, however, I won't venture an opinion one way or the other.

Chapter 3

■ PUZZLE NEOPHYTE
■ SEEKS PUZZLE MENTOR
■
■
■
■

Anyone wanting to attend the American Crossword Puzzle Tournament and do halfway well at it is confronted by the basic question: What on earth do you do to prepare yourself for it? When covering the event for the *Boston Globe* in March 2003, I'd wanted to talk to someone other than Will Shortz or his tournament organizer and amanuensis, Helene Hovanec, or anyone other than the principals of the main puzzle venues in America today—the crossword editors of the *Los Angeles Times*, the *Wall Street Journal, New York Newsday*, the *Boston Globe*, the *Philadelphia Inquirer*, even the *New York Sun*, the fledgling conservative paper of the low circulation that was fortunate enough, in its first days, to recruit as its puzzle editor a young fellow named Peter Gordon, whose anagrammatic pseudonym, Ogden Porter, is known in solving circles as a particularly tough constructor.

Color me a lunatic, but my first thought when the question arose for me was, Find yourself a Virgil who will guide you, à la Dante, through the circles of the crossword Inferno, and make sure this person is not a highly paid, deeply entrenched representative of "the business," as its practitioners ironically term the commissioning, editing, and publishing of crossword puzzles in early twenty-first-century America. That was why I called up a friend at St. Martin's Press, the New York–based publishing company that peddles the bulk of reprinted puzzles—those seventy-five-page-long booklets you find in airport news kiosks or on the rotating rack at the rear of your local bookstore and that add more to the bottom line of the companies that print them than any other type of publication appearing in their semiannual catalogs—and asked him who an ideal crossword Sherpa might be. The answer was instantaneous: Brendan Emmett Quigley.

There's a special kind of power that attaches to being a reporter, even a very occasional one such as myself, covering a large event devoted to one highly specialized activity. First, the people you talk to don't really think of you as an individual; with your notebook in your hand, you're the reified representation of whatever impressive-sounding newspaper you're stringing for. Second, as they speak, people are simultaneously self-conscious, trying to see what you're writing down, and calculating the odds of getting their name in print, all of which effectively prevents you from being the subject of their attention (this makes reporting the ideal job for the morbidly shy). Finally, because you're a reporter, just about anyone you ask will lead you to the person you really want to see—they do so, I suspect, in the hopes that some part of your conversation along the way will be quoted in your piece. But this wasn't quite what happened with Brendan at the American Crossword Puzzle Tournament in 2003.

You'd think a crossword competition would be a quiet and understated sort of affair, given that it features the largest collection of introverts this side of the last Kafka family reunion, but it was hard to pick out a solitary figure, much less one you've never laid eyes upon, from the milling mass of puzzlers all chatting away furiously. As I didn't precisely specify in chapter 1, it took the photographer, Joe Tabacca, approximately six seconds, after we walked through the doors leading into the Stamford Marriott Hotel's Grand Ballroom, to pick Brendan out from the crowd of five hundred or so preparing to launch into that year's first heat in the tournament.

"I think that's our guy," Joe said. "Over there, about a third of the way from the left side of the room, at the middle table. The one with the red baseball cap."

"Brendan never said he'd be wearing a baseball cap."

"Yeah, but look at his muttonchops. They're red. And he's really thin, like you said."

I looked hard at the person Joe was pointing out; even with glasses my eyesight is understandably nowhere near as acute as Joe's, and I couldn't be sure the figure I was trying to focus on was Brendan. At that moment, the individual we were talking about stood up, turned around, glanced at us, and came loping over through the crowd—it was my first experience of Brendan's Argus-like and rather uncanny ability to know when he's being talked about. This was maybe because, as I was quickly to learn, he so often *is* talked about, at least in the context of an international crossword tournament. Like a film star or famous sports figure, he's developed a sixth sense for knowing when other people recognize him.

Now, crossword tournaments are fundamentally different from arena sports or celebrity photo opportunities. Perhaps because the stakes are so low (the tournament's highest purse prize is four thousand dollars, and there are no other similar contests currently in existence), it's not an extremely competitive undertaking, which may in part also owe to the fact that there's such a tremendous disparity between the relative skill levels involved: If you don't finish among the first ten placers in your first three years of trying, you probably never will come close to doing so—at least that's what the tournament's records indicate—and consequently will never have a rat's chance of a stab at the grand prize. At the same time, though, for most of the participants the point isn't winning the grand prize. The point is to do better in the standings this year than you did the last time around, and to mingle with people who share with you the belief that the game is worth more than the finish. In fact, many attendees have told me they feel a twinge of disappointment when the grid in front of them is entirely filled in, because that means the pleasure of challenge is over and done with. It's fun to merely take part in a crossword tournament and to bathe in the presence of so many other people who share your enthusiasm for the game; simultaneously, there's very little likelihood that you'll ever be a member of that rarefied club of people—as innately gifted at their game of choice as the starting five of a professional basketball team—who can come close to the hope of placing first, second, third, or even twentieth. The chance of victory is not what brings most people to Stamford every March. The draw is the mere joy of participation.

At the Twenty-sixth American Crossword Puzzle Tournament, Brendan wasn't even trying—he was just there to do the puzzles and schmooze, a not-uncommon behavior in the decidedly lax competitive setting at Stamford. As I was very soon to learn, talking to him is like having a discussion with a particularly intelligent but unusually hyperactive hummingbird (assuming that hummingbirds talk). There's a solidness about him—the kind of sheer comfort in the occupation of one's own space that characterizes high school football stars or popular small-town dentists—that belies his lankiness. He is intensely self-deprecatory but at the same time thoughtful and a stickler for factual accuracy, a combination that produces, when he's talking, a cataract of theses followed up immediately by antitheses that can leave the listener lost and helmetless in the jungle of Quigleyesque discourse, not knowing precisely in what direction—

directions, really, with Brendan—the conversation is trending. It's sort of like reading one of those history books penned by East German scholars during the Cold War, in which sober pronunciamentos of fact are inevitably shrouded in a mist of dialectic hedging whose only purpose is to give the writer an out should, sometime down the pipe, the authorities decide to change the party line.

The first time I encountered the Quigley dialectic was while interviewing him after the second Saturday-morning round of the 2003 tournament. I asked him what the attraction was that Stamford held for him, and he replied, "It's the only place in the world where you can talk about crosswords for two days straight without feeling like a complete freak." I was writing the quote down in my notebook when he waved his hand in the air and said, "Nah—don't run that. It's just what I say to everyone who asks." The quote appeared in my *Globe* piece on crosswords anyway—no use wasting a perfectly good throwaway line—but immediately I thought to myself, "What's with this retortive style of expression, anyway, where you say one thing and then immediately take it back? And does Brendan's propensity for it bear any relationship to the fact that he constructs the most consistently difficult puzzles that appear in the *New York Times*?" I supposed that, in the unlikely event I'd ever write about crosswords again, I'd want to talk to Brendan about them and the people who do them—it was a reasonably sure bet he'd be game to talk. And if he was, well, I'd have somebody around to give me both sides of the equation, which is the lazy researcher's Holy Grail.

If It's Friday, It Must Be Brendan

It wasn't until several months after the 2003 tournament that I spoke to Brendan again. In the intervening stretch of time I had found myself at something like loose ends, with a major bout of writer's block stymieing a project I'd been working on, a whisper of low-grade depression making an ever-present background noise, and necessity pointing its bony finger toward a long series of free-lance book-editing jobs and translations whose rewards would be far more financial than spiritual. I'd been sufficiently convinced by the high spirits and atmosphere of cheer at Stamford, even in the face of impending war, that there must be something therapeutic about drowning oneself in puzzles. My response in the face of adversity was to break out the plastic and subscribe to the online *New York Times* crossword puzzle. (For the first few years, an online subscription cost $19.95, and then the *Times* wised up; I guess someone in corporate development figured that puzzlers are puzzlers, that an extra fifteen bucks a year wouldn't turn too many of them off, and that the loss of the people who were offended by the massive price hike would be more than made up by the many hundreds of thousands of dollars in additional annual revenue. Someone in the Times building, it's not unfair to surmise, now sits in a newly painted vice-president's office, thanking his or her gods every day for crossword puzzles.)

When I subscribed, there were approximately 2,300 crosswords in the archive. I knew that on good days, when the writing or editing or translating was going well, I probably would do no more than three or four. On bad days, when I *woke up* feeling like the protagonist in a Solzhenitsyn novel (sometimes, mercifully, *The Gulag Archipelago*; other times, *Cancer Ward*; in either case, though, definitely somewhere around page 687), I figured I'd do up to ten. I decided to never do a Monday and rarely a Tuesday puzzle, since they were too easy to bother with. What the numbers added up to was this: Using the archive, I could hedge for up to a year against continuous bleakness; in the happy event that things didn't turn out for the absolute worst over that period, I'd end the year with maybe a few hundred puzzles yet to go, an outcome I'd be more than glad to celebrate with the shelling out of another thirty bucks and change.

So, there I sat in my Brooklyn Heights apartment one blisteringly hot afternoon in late spring 2003, waiting for my *Times* account to open, the air conditioner going full throttle against the muggy, sweltering heat and not putting up much of a fight against it; the computer was whirring its little fan like an electronic dervish, I was shirtless and dripping, the cat was lying, prostrate and sloe-eyed, shedding copious amounts of fur on a manuscript I had just set down, and it was obvious to both of us that a dropsical nonagenarian waving at us with a concert stub would be a better cooling mechanism than my battered Haier (which, to be fair, hadn't wholly reawakened yet from its winter hibernation). And then, like the sudden and blissful descent of an arctic front, my user name and password yielded the first of those thousands of providential crosswords.

Within a few days I'd reached far into November 1996, missing Jeremiah Farrell's "Election Day" puzzle only because it was printed on a Tuesday, one of the days I was mostly eschewing—and a big mistake it was to skip practicing the first and second puzzles of the week, I was later to discover, since there's an art to doing the easier puzzles as much as there's an art to doing a Friday or a Saturday, and knowing it is important to scoring high in the first few rounds during a tournament. Within a few weeks I was knocking at the door of January 1999, and I had started thinking about the crosswords I'd done thus far and come to certain conclusions.

The first was that, to a degree I hadn't really thought about before, crosswords are highly specific to the cultural and temporal circumstances under which they're constructed. (I touched on this when I was talking about the differences between British and American puzzles in the last chapter.) Before, for instance, her death in

August 1997, Princess Diana was a staple of the *New York Times* puzzle—that combination of two common consonants and vowels made the name a cinch for constructors struggling with a particularly thorny five-letter fit. Since her fatal car accident in Paris, though, Princess Di has largely been absent from the *Times* crossword. In a Fred Piscop grid dating from February 18, 1997, one of the few Tuesdays I actually did, I was unaccountably disturbed when I ran across the 10-Down clue, "Prominent Manhattan sight," which yielded TWINTOWERS. Having witnessed firsthand the destruction of the World Trade Center, and having lived for three months through the consequences of its collapse, I filled in that answer with something approaching physical nausea; as I did so, I knew that nothing like that clue would ever appear in the *Times* puzzle again. More benign from a psychological point of view was the brief absence from the puzzle of the Concorde SST after one of the aircraft crashed outside Paris in 2000; the plane and the clue returned soon after, but both were to suffer again in 2003, when the whole supersonic transport fleet was mothballed forever. (Nowadays, a clue for the supremely useful S-S-T consonant combination would be "Former fast flyer" or something.)

The *Times* puzzle, of course, appears in what they like to call in the publishing business a "family" newspaper (I've always wondered what a non-"family" newspaper would look like—I suppose they mean those city independents in which naughty ads appear on the back pages), so the crossword can't use obscenities or refer to depressing subjects such as STDs, cancer, or self-immolation. It does its best to avoid words and topics that might conceivably offend anyone reading the paper itself—a factor that, given a circulation in the millions, must keep Will Shortz up at night. Which means that death, pain, illness, sexual deviance, and similar themes are mostly out. I'm not, in fact, sure why the latter is all so necessary, although

I suppose that, when you have a franchise as popular as the *Times* crossword, it's better to err on the safe side, though any child who can fight his way through your average grid is probably mature enough to handle the occasional louche bit, while the more socially conservative elements of the American population who would take umbrage at references to homosexuality or atheism (or "agnatheism," which is my preferred term for spiritual rationality) are unlikely to want to so much as physically touch a copy of the *New York Times*, much less flip through to the C section and attempt its crossword puzzle.

The second thing I noticed—this is where the fact-geek side of my character emerges—is how phenomenally good Will Shortz is at calibrating the difficulty level of the puzzles he prints. I noted down the respective times it took me to finish the several thousand puzzles in the *Times* archives, which is easy enough to do, since the applet used to deliver them over the Web has a built-in clock. Discounting Mondays, which I never did, and Tuesdays, which I rarely did, more than 90 percent of my puzzle-completion rates fall within the following ranges: Wednesday, six to seven minutes; Thursday, six to eight; Friday, seven to fifteen; Saturday, ten to seventeen; Sunday, fifteen to twenty-four. (I threw the raw data away; in a small apartment, 1,900 Post-it notes actually take up a fair amount of living space.) Yes, there is an element of luck to doing crosswords, in the sense that sometimes you're in phase with what the constructor is trying to do while at other times you're not. In the aggregate, though, I'd have to say that Will Shortz really knows his business; you may think a given Friday is harder than a given Saturday or vice versa, but the data—for instance, the statistical results compiled from American Crossword Puzzle Tournament records—show again that, on average, a solver will do a Friday more quickly than he does a Saturday, a Thursday more quickly than he does a Friday, and so on back to the top of the week.

Constructing and doing crosswords are similar in the sense that you're never going to be that good at either unless you practice. (Of course, if you have that odd set of analytical and mnemonic tools at your disposal that makes for the best of solvers, you're going to do well in a tournament anyway—the same sad but incontrovertible fact that governs the standings in chess, math, and Scrabble tournaments.) To do well solving crosswords, you absolutely need to keep a running mental list of "crosswordese," the set of recurring words that constructors reach for whenever they're heading for trouble in a particular section of the grid. It's quite wonderful to see how well Shortz had done at removing from the crossword lexicon the hoary old favorites—GNU, ADIT, ANOA, and the like—that made the working days of previous *Times* puzzle editors that much easier. Still, a rule of thumb to all would-be solvers (even competitive solvers) is to make a mental note of as many three- and four-letter vowel-heavy words as you can. As in Scrabble, these represent the game's meat and potatoes; unlike in Scrabble, the actual words will be torn from the living language, not from any official dictionary, and may involve acronyms, abbreviations, variant spellings, capitalized letters, or any or all of these in combination. To solve a crossword, you need to be constantly attentive to the tricks a constructor will pull—for instance, using RANDR for "rest and recreation," LTYR for "light year," or TSGT for "Technical Sergeant." And to do that, you have to pay close attention to the body of material from which the constructor is pulling the words he'll use to fill his grid— which, for better or worse, includes everything in the world, barring total obscurities that no solver could be expected to know. (Like the good justice's definition of pornography, you'll know these when you see them, and you'll probably write an angry letter to Will Shortz if you do.)

The third thing I noticed—this is, again, after doing several thousand puzzles in a matter of months, which certainly sets the mind to thinking in terms of large, stable patterns—is that getting through a grid hangs largely on your ability to recognize and sort together within your memory things that belong to the same category or order of things. In the most basic sense, we do this every day: When someone says "road," we know they could potentially be referring to anything from a back alley, to a boulevard, to a highway. What a good crossword puzzler does, though, is lump into that same category equivalent terms he may have read about but not actually experienced—a fast solver knows that "*calle*," "*strasse*," and "*rue*" are words he might be called on to use when confronted by, respectively, clues like "Pedro's driveway leads to it" or "An Audi parks on it" or "Swann's way?" The thing is, if in some book or other you run across a word that's unfamiliar to you, like "reebok," you need to look it up and associate it in your mind with something else before heading on to the rest of the sentence in which it appears; a crossword puzzler will think not only of other brands of sports sneaker, but also of associated words, such as "gemsbok" and—sigh—even "gnu." In the fifth round of the twenty-seventh American Crossword Puzzle Tournament, this sort of associative thinking spelled, for me, the difference between emotional breakdown and license to gloat. If you get the knack of thinking associatively, it's actually a useful mental tool to have at your disposal in pretty much any situation. Once you've trained yourself to think in this way, you'll find yourself, almost uncannily, pulling out the right and appreciated word whether you're speaking with a diamond cutter, an auto mechanic, an expert in medieval political theology, or a Jain priest. What it comes down to, you see, is trivia—but trivia stored in the right mental cupboards, from which you can readily retrieve it.

The fourth thing I found was that, apart from the intraweek difference in difficulty levels, very few *New York Times* puzzles bear the stamp of sheer individuality. This is largely because Will Shortz has a consistent editorial policy from which it's very, very difficult to try to budge him. (Constructors know what Will's rules are and follow them closely; even so, they never know when their grids will appear in print, and consequently they cannot know to what extent he will change their fill and cluing.) Even solvers who have been doing the *Times* puzzle for decades are unlikely to look at the name of the constructor; to tell the truth, it doesn't really matter. It matters very much to other constructors, of course: A lean grid with thirty or fewer black squares in it and unexpected fills buttressed by unhackneyed cluing will earn the constructor a dozen laudatory messages on crossword chat boards. To the general run of solvers, though, a puzzle is just a puzzle; if you can complete it without using a reference work or an Internet search engine, you think "Woo-hoo!" and then just get on with the rest of your day.

But I found, over the course of doing the archived *Times* puzzles and recording my speed on them, that there was one constructor's name I associated with what an actuary would call a significant deviation from the mean. Of all the puzzles I did in far more time than my average for a specific day of the week, most could be ascribed to the same fellow; a couple of other constructors threw me off my game some of the time, but none did so with the same perverse consistency.

By this point—let's call it August of 2003—I had come to look on the name "Brendan Emmett Quigley" with the sort of respect an Indus River Valley tribesman might once have shown toward a Macedonian hoplite. Like the tribesman circa 320 BC, though, my awe toward my potential foe was tinged with a glimmer of hope. I mean, I knew he was a fearsome constructor, but I'd also seen his posted ranks in five previous American Crossword Puzzle Tournaments, which were okay but not wildly impressive: 165 out of 258 in his rookie year in 1997; 217 out of 286 in his next showing in 2000; 149 out of 322 in 2001; 274 out of 412 in 2002; 327 out of 495 in 2003. (This last ranking isn't quite fair; Brendan left the tournament before the seventh heat, for which he scored zero, which is why he told me he wasn't competing that year.)

I knew I wanted to attend the Twenty-seventh American Crossword Puzzle Tournament, which was coming up in nine months. I didn't necessarily want to focus on one of the top scorers at Stamford, since no single solving style is representative, and in any case even the best solvers can't tell you why, apart from the fact that they practice a lot, they consistently lead the field. So instead, I thought, I'd deviously try to glean from Brendan the skinny on how to beat top-drawer crossword constructors at their own game.

Coffee and Cream

"When a Brendan puzzle comes in," said Will Shortz to me several months after the 2004 tournament, as we were sitting and chatting in his comfortable book-lined study, "it's like strong coffee taken black; when it appears in the paper, it's strong coffee with cream."

What Will means is that Brendan's puzzles are beautifully conceived in terms of design and execution: Brendan consistently dreams up grid patterns that are original and pleasing to the eye and fills that are replete with unexpected tidbits drawn from deep within his extraordinarily retentive mind, and the combination is pleasurably deadly. At the same time, though, Brendan isn't quite as exercised by the cluing aspect of crossword construction; he admits that he becomes bored with a puzzle once the grid and fill have been worked out, and spends as little time as possible on the grunt work of coming up with clue questions that will allow solvers to decipher the puzzle.

"When I saw the first one he sent in," Will explained, "I immediately knew it was something. But then I looked at the cluing and did a double take—it was filled with misspelled words and plain errors. I called Brendan up and he admitted that he hadn't used any reference work—he hadn't even cracked a dictionary—to make his puzzle." As he said it, Will stared off into the middle distance, his brown eyes tinged with what looked like contemplative disbelief.

"Do you get some sort of comfort out of building grids?" I put out the question late one winter night, as Brendan and I were in the middle of one of the epic phone conversations we had fallen into the habit of having, given that he lives in Boston and I in New York. I asked the question because—well, because he can sound so *worried* sometimes.

"Fuck it, no," he replied after a moment's hesitation. "A crossword, including the grid, is the document of a moment—it's a cross section of whatever I'm doing and thinking at the time. It's just that I've turned thirty and I have more angst . . . more angst than . . . there's this girl I'm seeing sometimes who calls me Woody Allen, but then again she's pure AA material."

"All right, then. Will says that when he first sees one, it's like strong coffee taken black. Does he mean that the way you think, the way you see things, is somehow responsible for how difficult your puzzles are?"

"Yeah—Will does a lot of work on my stuff in the *Times*, but even then it usually runs on a Friday or Saturday. So, I guess I'm an outsider—sometimes I feel like I'm outside of *everything*. I don't mean to make the puzzles hard. You know, I'm not an asshole—it's just that I devour stuff and regurgitate it in the puzzles. It's like *Jeopardy!* on acid."

On another occasion that I can't precisely identify—my notes about it appear in a section of my steno pad devoted to another topic entirely—Brendan waxed fine about the theory of puzzle construction. I'd been, at the time, wondering what other sort of activity was comparable to the creation of a *Times*-worthy crossword. Looking at Will Shortz's roster of some three hundred contributors, I realized the bulk of them were not exactly prolific: There are a few one- or two-timers, a large number whose average appearance in the paper is around five, and a much smaller subset who can count thirty or more puzzles to their credit. In terms of my anecdotal observation, this pattern of distribution almost exactly reproduces what you find in the world of published poetry—a lot of people have a handful of world-class poems in them, a few have one or two, and a few have a career's worth. Will believes that if you can do one great puzzle, you can do any number of them. But that's not the case with Jeremiah Farrell, the Harper Lee of crosswords, who hasn't published one since "Election Day" in 1996: It was so good that he hasn't yet dared to construct another. I asked Brendan to weigh in on the issue.

"Something that takes the same time and energy as a crossword? I don't know. The smartass in me wants to say 'Crossing the street.' All I can tell you is, if it's too easy to make, you won't be able to sell it. A good crossword should be hard to build, because if it isn't, it'll be too easy to solve. There's a reason people don't really like those Dell crossword books where all the puzzles are basically manufactured by a computer. The idea of making a crossword based on constrictive tricks, like not using one letter of the alphabet—it's just not that hard for the solver to figure out. You're not hitting one out of the ballpark when you do that. You always want a difficult construction. I don't know if a poem works the same way."

To explore whether Will Shortz is in fact the cream to Brendan Quigley's coffee, I decided to take, at random, one Quigley published in the *Times* in 2004 and another published somewhere else—in this case, in the *New York Sun*—and compare them. The *Sun*'s puzzles, for the record, are harder than the ones that appear in the *Times* by an order equivalent to about two days in a seven-puzzle-a-day format; a *Sun* Monday, in other words, is roughly equivalent, in terms of solving difficulty, to a *Times* Wednesday. (Also for the record, Shortz once wondered aloud in my presence what sort of audience Peter Gordon is hoping to attract—the *Sun*'s circulation is currently about fifty thousand, which yields a potential puzzling subpopulation of about one-tenth of that, while the increased level of difficulty in the puzzles effectively eliminates the newbie solver from even attempting them. As far as I can tell, Gordon is hoping to create a subscription-based puzzle keyed to the most avid of solvers, although it's too soon to predict whether he'll be able to pull it off; as of 2004, he hasn't. But the *Sun* puzzle has only been around for two years.)

The *Times* puzzle appeared on Saturday, April 17: A seventy-word fifteen-by-fifteen featuring two fourteen-letter horizontals, two ten-letter verticals, and only thirteen three-letter answers. It's a tough puzzle to crack; only by a miracle, I suppose, was I able to get it in 11 minutes 41 seconds, but that was with one square in error (for "Plant used to prevent erosion" I filled in AXWEED instead of AXSEED, which made my answer to the cross at 33-Down, "Sheepish excuse lead-in," WEE instead of SEE). One of the reasons Brendan's puzzles are so tough, again, is that he tends to pick up intellectual shiny things—words such as "axseed" and "uracil"— and put them into his grids. Another reason is that tendency of his to project his momentary state of mind into the grid, which produces, in this puzzle, the extremely hairy answer to 55-Across, which I mentioned in chapter 2. There the clue that yielded SUPER-BOWLXXXVI was "2002 upset victory"—Brendan had been watching the game while working on this puzzle. He'd also included three music-related clues that are impenetrable to tin-ear sorts like me: "Gibson of pop" (DEBBIE), "1982 Toto hit that won Record of the Year" (ROSANNA), and "Rapper Sandra Denton's stage name" (PEPA). On top of Brendan's fondness for compound answers that can be clued in literally dozens of different ways (DAYONE, TWOPHASE, NAMEDROP, ILLHUMOR, INLUCK, etc.), these fills tempt the potential solver to throw down his pen or pencil the moment he has finished his word count: There's simply no easy way, unless you're creepily in sync with Brendan's thinking, to find a break in the pattern.

In the same grid, though, the experienced *Times* solver immediately picks out Will Shortz's edits to the cluing. "English sum?" at 23-Across (IAM—think of "cogito ergo sum") is a classic Shortz difficulty maker; in a Monday or Tuesday puzzle, the same answer would have been clued as something like "Seuss title Sam _____." At 26-Across, "6 letters" for MNO (think telephone dial pad) is a similar Shortzism—the idea being that you clue three-letter answers harder as the week goes on, since they're the window through which most solvers hope to sneak into the puzzle. "Like a cat's existence?" (NINEFOLD), "Look into?" (XRAY), and "Paper pusher's words" (EXTRAEXTRA) all look to me like Will-style cluing; at least they're analogous to similar formulations longtime *Times* solvers have encountered often before, and certainly they provide the grappling hooks you need to scale the wall Brendan has deftly thrown up in front of you.

The *Sun* puzzle dates from Friday, August 20; it, too, is a fifteen-by-fifteen, but this time the word count is slightly higher, and there are only eight answers three letters long. Again, to a fuddy-duddy like me, the presence of so much contemporary culture in the puzzle, as well as its use of so many compound answers that can be clued in so many ways, acted as an efficient deterrent to my initial efforts to crack the thing—in the end, this Friday crossword took me just under seventeen minutes to solve, although this time I did so without making an error. The three-letter answers are tough if you're not thirty or younger and into sports and music. I had no problem with "Never, in Nürnberg" (NIE), "Chosen number?" (FEW), "Name that is Hebrew for 'lion' " (ARI), or "Simply not done" (RAW). I was stymied by "Dashboard Confessional's musical genre" (EMO, short for "emotional," the type of late-punk rock pioneered in the 1980s by the band Hüsker Dü) and "Center of Houston" (YAO). The first letter marking the intersection between 49-Across ("B## equivalent") and 49-Down ("Construction site sight") eluded me for a while, since I don't know musical notation and for a long time refused to think that a nonabbreviated clue could yield an abbreviated answer (the two were, respectively, DFLAT and DOZER). The top-left or northwest quadrant had two loosely clued lulus stacked one on top of the other that took me at least a minute to decode: "Acronym that describes many desktop publishing programs" (WYSIWYG) and "Homecoming provision?" (HOTMEAL). In both cases, the clues aren't inherent, as we used to say in high school debate, to the answer; "wysiwig"—"what you see is what you get"—was a programming-industry catchphrase popular in the early 1990s that is by no means limited to desktop publishing, while many people come home, much of the time, to no cookery at all, especially if they're single.

So, in a sense, yes—Will is the cream to Brendan's coffee, in terms of making a raw Brendan construction something that fits roughly into the schema of the *Times* crossword puzzle. His *Sun* puzzle was eminently satisfying to finish even if Peter Gordon isn't as stringent an editor as Will Shortz is in matters of cluing; that in fact may be why *Sun* puzzles are, day for day, harder to complete than *Times* ones. Will Shortz presides over the ne plus ultra of American crossword institutions at the *New York Times* and thus has rigid standards that come close to taming the wild constructing mind of Brendan Emmett Quigley; Peter Gordon presides over the upstart *New York Sun* puzzle, where he can afford to allow his contributors a freer rein.

Some of us like our coffee black; some of us like our coffee with cream. But some of us—the few and the proud—like our coffee no matter how it's served up, just as long as it's not decaffeinated.

Crosswords and Woody Allen

Brendan and I sit at a corner table in the Soho bar that used to be my favorite, back when I lived in the neighborhood and spent a lot more of my time in bars than I do now. He's in town only briefly, because he's due in a couple of hours in Weehawken, New Jersey, where college buddies of his share a house. Before us are a couple of pints of Bass Ale and a dilemma.

Brendan had come bearing a tale of woe: His recent ex-girlfriend, a high-strung sort by the sounds of it, is weighing heavily on his mind, and he's wondering if his problems finding a decent woman reside in the great mass of available womanhood or in the particularities of his own personality. It's an interesting problem, compounded for crossword puzzlers by the fact that what they do day in and day out is set solitary problems for themselves that they solve in solitude and, except for at the American Crossword Puzzle Tournament, rarely celebrate but in solitude. Crossword puzzles, in short, tend to be attractive to people who are comfortable being alone with themselves; even if they're married and have twelve kids and a great job and a lively social life, they can still approximate the hermitic existence for a ten- or twenty- or hundred-minute period every day when they're working on a puzzle, and they very much look forward to doing so.

The dilemma is this: Given that doing crosswords is in a sense such an intimate activity, conditioned at least at the hard-core level by the solver's intimate familiarity with the workings of the constructor's mind ("constructor" in the generic sense, that is), is it either legitimate or wise, when you're talking about your much-beloved hobby with someone who feels about it the same way you do, to speculate about the personal psychologies of the characters who inhabit the crossword world?

Because that's what hard-core solvers—the kind who do fifteen puzzles a week or more and make it a point to attend the American Crossword Puzzle Tournament every year—do. In competition, it's of intense interest to you to know who the constructor of the next scheduled crossword is; in all likelihood, you'll have done many puzzles by that person before, so you'll have internalized the general pattern of that person's approach to the task of actually making and filling in a grid. By now you'll have a sense of what to expect when you open up the *New York Times* to the daily puzzle and see Brendan's byline right there next to Will's: You know the puzzle will feature a strange mix of contemporary trivia and eclectic historical information, and you can be sure that most if not all the three-letter answers in it will be clued in unexpected ways. (Before Brendan, the e-m-o triplet in a crossword was always in some way a reference to the comic Emo Phillips; there's a middlingly famous medieval villa in Italy of the same name, but I don't think anyone has used that fact as a clue yet.)

I want to stress here that I'm talking about a very specific subset of the American crossword world: fanatical solvers of the *New York Times* puzzle who are familiar with the work of the most prolific members of Will Shortz's stable—in other words, the few hundred or so Americans who in their affective commitment to puzzles come close to the level of fanaticism displayed by British fans of British cryptics. Members of this subset naturally tend to perk up at the sight of a favorite constructor's name. Still, puzzles aren't fine old Bordeaux wines; you can't, by nose and taste, say with any confidence that (barring a byline) this puzzle is a Frank Longo or that one a Merl Reagle. A Brendan puzzle is by and large recognizably a Brendan puzzle to me even before I read his byline, for instance, but I couldn't say the same thing about a Cathy Millhauser, Stanley Newman, or Michael Shteyman puzzle; all I could say about a production by any of the latter is that it's good, fun, challenging, and professional, and thus likely to be by one of the *Times* stars. These caveats aside, it's still true that American puzzles are far less recognizably *by* a given constructor than are British cryptics. I'd venture a general rule with respect to *Times*-style American puzzles: Knowing who constructed one helps you solve it if you've solved enough puzzles by that person before, but solving one won't tell you who constructed it.

If you're a crossword addict trying to determine how to solve more quickly the puzzle in front of you, whether it's by Brendan Quigley or any of the three dozen or so constructors who currently dominate the "crossword biz," to what extent does your knowledge of the people themselves help you get through their puzzles? I believe—and I think Brendan was relieved to find this out—the answer is some, but not nearly enough to warrant the effort of armchair-psychologizing them. I've done a lot of editorial work for Random House, for instance, and in a publishing enterprise small or large it's impossible for even a freelancer to avoid hearing the scuttlebutt that permeates the place from the messenger room in the basement to the big corner offices on the top floors—as Evelyn Waugh would tell you if he'd ever written about it, book publishing constitutes one of the biggest and most active rumor mills humanity has ever devised. It's for this reason that I know that one of my favorite constructors, Stanley Newman, the *New York Newsday* puzzle editor and former head of Random House's puzzle division, has a reputation for alternating between charm and irascibility in the blink of an eye (which is a neat piece of information to have under your belt when you see his name in the byline position of the puzzle you're about to do; you're fairly sure you can expect equal doses of humor and mind-numbing challenge). But as I raise my arm to the waitress for refills, I know the personal lives of constructors and editors isn't a topic I really want to talk about; I sense, also, it's not something Brendan is eager to address. (In chapter 10, we will meet the top-scoring man and woman at the 2004 Stamford tournament and try to figure out why they're both so incredibly fast and accurate in competition; for now, let's keep Brendan as our Sherpa to the Mt. Everest of crossword constructing.)

"Crossword puzzles aren't the thing I want to be *known* for," he says once the waitress has scuttled off again. "I mean, I know I'm weird by almost anyone's standards, but so's pretty much anybody who constructs. You can't sit there for hours on end thinking about the puzzle you're doing, earning maybe three, four bucks an hour, without being weird. It's not like we're on TV; it's not like I'm *looking* for people to talk about me. I don't think Will or Stan are, either. For Christ's sake, we're just making puzzles."

Brendan himself got into the business by chance. He'd never so much as looked at a crossword, as far as he can recall, before he was about twenty. Over the summer of his junior year at the University of New Hampshire, he was temping for a law firm in Boston by day and playing in obscure indie-rock outlets by night. Then the crossword obsession hit him by surprise.

"We didn't have much to do most of the time—we were just warm bodies the lawyers liked to have around. At one point the office manager came around and said we couldn't listen to the radio, which is what I did just to get through the afternoon. So instead I decided to do the *Times* puzzle every day. I wasn't any good at first, but then started getting it. Pretty soon I was photocopying it and making up my own fills and clues. Over the next year at school I kept at it, and after I graduated, when I was twenty-two, I sent Will my first puzzle. I sent him my second one a couple of weeks later. He published the second one first and the first one second, but he still thinks the first one I sent him was the first one he printed."

Eight years and some 250 published puzzles later, Brendan is now one of the brightest figures in the crossword firmament, hailed on crossword-oriented Internet message boards when a puzzle of his appears in the *Times* or the *Sun* or *Newsday*, a book of his puzzles is out from St. Martin's Press—but he's unhappy with himself. I mean, there's no way he'd ever want to have or be good at a real job at a real office; no aspiring rock star would. (From Will Shortz himself through Peter Gordon and Stan Newman and so on, none of the other current big names in American crosswords would, either, I suspect; at least none of them seem to have traditional day jobs.) Once Brendan called me from his cell phone while he was driving around in his car, lost on his way to a catering job in Jamaica Plain, Massachusetts; we talked for an hour or so about crosswords, and I suspect that some Brahmin matron found herself one canapé server short that night. Somebody really ought to reward Brendan for his crossword work more generously than does the *Times*, with its $100-a-pop weekday-puzzle payment rate, or St. Martin's, with its royalty-free crossword-book policy in which the author makes $3,000 and the company a hundred times as much, or the occasional matron who may be unaware that this slacker kid she's yelling at for being late to her party is in fact the person responsible for the half-hour of joy she experienced that morning getting through her daily crossword—probably the most pleasure any man afforded her since that memorable cotillion in 1962.

Then again, some rich young heiress might like to squire about on her arm a skinny, red-headed, baseball-capped crossword genius with the Boston version of a Woody Allen's charm, and at the same time know she's making tens of thousands of devoted solvers happier now that her odd, self-torturing beau is making more puzzles than ever.

"I don't know, man," Brendan would say about this fantasy. "I think I'm giving up on women. Or at least, they'd be better off giving up on me. Right now all I have is puzzles."

Chapter 4

A crossword
pilgrimage

The Marriott Hotel in Stamford is an unlikely mecca. If, like many residents of New York City, you don't own a car, you can make the journey north by train in just forty-five minutes. You'll alight at Stamford's newly constructed five-story glass-enclosed station and take the stairs down to street level. With luck, you'll find a cab waiting at the curb. Without luck, you'll have to walk five blocks to the hotel. On the cold and windy night of March 12, 2004, I had no luck and so hoofed it.

Downtown Stamford is a study in contrasts between corporate optimism and urban blight, with futuristic-looking insurance company and bank headquarters set haphazardly down among a tarmac-and-concrete tangle of shuttered buildings and with a maze of on- and off-ramps. (Interstate 95 runs through the middle of Stamford's downtown, a relic of the Le Corbusier craze of the 1950s that similarly bisected the other Connecticut coastal cities of Bridgeport and New Haven.) The wide, empty streets and darkened parking garages reminded me that it was Friday evening, and the employees of Union Banque Suisse, whose corporate headquarters are located in the building next door to the Marriott, had long since left for home in the suburbs. No one else was abroad. The I-95 underpass, with its rotting sidewalks, potholes, and puddles—the latter inexplicable, since it hasn't rained in a week—is not pedestrian-friendly; nor, for that matter, is downtown Stamford as a whole. In the dark it was all sort of forbidding, especially for a lone walker with a trundle bag, who is apparently a rare enough sight to attract the attention from a high proportion of passing automobiles. In the light of a weekend day, the scenery is merely depressing; nestled amid the surrounding landscape of vacant parking lots and deserted office complexes, the Marriott, to the people staying there, might as well be a moon base or Antarctic research station.

I never thought that arriving at a giant chain hotel could seem like coming home, but it did for me as I walked out of the cold night air and into the Stamford Marriott that evening. The first time I had been here, Joe, the *Boston Globe* photographer, and I had arrived at the hotel—by taxi—on Saturday morning, just in time for the first three heats of the weekend's seven-puzzle ordeal, and, as soon as we hit the lobby area, we were overwhelmed by a wave of almost palpable hyperactive geekish energy. I've never been to a Shriners meet or a Democratic or Republican national convention, or, for that matter, any large gathering of folks enthusiastically waving the same banner, so I don't know if infectious enthusiasm is always a hallmark of such occasions. The scene that greeted us as we forged into the Stamford Marriott lobby was like something out of a Hieronymus Bosch drawing (minus the devils and other nasty stuff). There was a mind-boggling amount of puzzle-themed clothing: One woman was done up in a head-to-toe outfit consisting entirely of crossword patterns; a skinny, bearded man in a bandanna wore a giant no. 2 pencil on his head; a petite brunette was walking around in a T-shirt whose front read REAL WOMEN DO IT IN PEN. Hipster kids (comparatively speaking, given the crowd) clustered together, smoking cigarettes; and, scattered here and there, subdued-looking members of the hotel staff looked on, probably wondering what they had done in a previous incarnation to deserve being caught, right now, in the dead center of this logophiliac maelstrom. Within the first few seconds I began to regret I was there not as a participant but as an observer, so immediately was I smitten by the sheer fun of it all; when I glanced at my photographer, I noted that he bore the slightly awed expression of someone who doesn't quite know what to do with a wealth of possibilities suddenly and unexpectedly dropped in his lap. In terms of human color, there was simply too much there to shoot all at once.

It was with this memory in mind that I walked into the ocher-and-brown-schemed hotel lobby as the Twenty-seventh American Crossword Puzzle Tournament got officially under way. I shook off the cold March air I was not to feel again for forty-eight hours and hauled my bag up to the check-in desk.

A Word of Advice to Puzzle-Tournament Attendees

Like millions of other people, I'm uncomfortable in a crowd; the prospect of being the center of attention, or anything remotely like it, in a group of people is the stuff of nightmares for me. In my innocence, I figured there might be a slight possibility I'd do well enough at the tournament to actually, on Sunday, have to compete, before the whole gathering, in one of the three sudden-death finals. (Division A, the hardest, is open to all; Division B is for people who haven't won a Division A or B title within the last seven years; Division C is for those who haven't placed in the top 20 percent in the last three years. It seemed reasonable that, having practiced so much, I'd have a chance at the Division C finals.) Division D is for contestants who haven't finished in the top 40 percent during the past three years. Division E is for contestants who haven't finished in the top 65 percent during the past three years. (I would have just made D, it was to turn out.)

I knew that if it actually came to standing up there, solving away at a big board in front of five hundred–plus crossword freaks, I'd likely dissolve into a puddle of utter panic. I don't know when I developed this tendency toward stage fright (as a debater in high school I often had to perform before large crowds, and it never seemed to bother me then), but I have, and it's awful, especially since I actually *like* to talk to a crowd of people. (For a couple of years in the 1990s I worked at a then-fast-growing investment firm in New York, and one of my jobs there was to tell large groups of new hires about the dos and don'ts of both the securities industry and the company now handing out their paychecks. In theory it should have been fun—there's nothing like making stocks-and-bonds jokes to a glassy-eyed audience—but in practice all it meant for me was misery.) As a hedge against possible success at the American Crossword Puzzle Tournament, therefore, I had decided to turn, as so many others do in similar circumstances, to a chemical shield against the anxiety such success would arouse in me.

Up in my room at the Stamford Marriott, I swallowed one of the little pills my mother had pulled out of her medicine cabinet and slipped me a few months before, when I had been home for the Christmas holidays. (She's a little agoraphobic, too, though possessed of medical resources superior to mine.) The pills were something called Ativan, and I'd been holding off trying one until this evening; I figured I'd test both the effectiveness of the stuff at damping my social unease and its potential effect on the puzzle-solving parts of my brain. As it turned out, that was a big, big mistake.

I don't know how to characterize my state of mind as I entered the vast ballroom where the weekend's contestants were already gathering for two hours of Will Shortz–hosted "warm-up puzzles and entertainments." "Coleridgean" would encapsulate it, I suppose; I was tooling around within a great cloud of mellow goodwill, marveling at the lack of contingency of it all, wondering only why the ballroom floor should apparently be covered by some sort of rubbery substance half a foot thick—that, of course, was the Ativan. There were a couple hundred people in the room, chatting or doing puzzles while waiting for the fun and games to begin, and the low hum of conversation provided a pleasant aural contrast to the harsh soullessness of the vast, impersonal room.

"Hey, man," a voice said to me. I looked up and standing before me was Brendan Emmett Quigley—it was odd, I thought, that the first person to address me personally at the tournament should be he, the only crossword-puzzle constructor of my acquaintance and my guide in this strange new cruciverbalist territory.

"Hey, Brendan," I think I said. "Where you sitting?"

"Uh . . ." He glanced around with a preoccupied expression that, along with his cropped red hair, lankiness, and almost perennial baseball cap, is his trademark look. "Not here. I'll be at the bar. Gotta talk to some people."

"Okay, then. Maybe later."

"Yeah, I'll catch you then."

As he walked off, I noted he was being closely trailed by two or three twenty-something young men, one of them with a video camera on his shoulder. The trappings of fame, I thought to myself, even in a world as small as this one.

I sat down at the first unoccupied seat I found and took stock of my surroundings. Neither Will Shortz nor the night's two featured speakers—veteran constructors Patrick Berry and Mel Taub—were at the podium at the front of the room yet; it was just before eight o'clock, when the festivities were slated to begin. Through the haze, I realized my first impression—that half the people in the room or thereabouts were chatting, the other half doing puzzles—was seriously off the mark. *Most* of the people were quietly doing puzzles: either the ones included in the tournament-registration packets we'd all just picked up or the ones appearing in the crossword books that were for sale in the halls outside the vast room.

This is when I noticed the first of several themes that would mark this particular weekend. By and large, the contestants at Stamford appeared unhealthily consumed by puzzles. The seven that made up the main tournament should have been enough for even the most gluttonous cruciverbalist—as you'll see, even I, who'd been doing an average of ten a day in the months leading up to Stamford, would begin to get good and tired of crosswords by around the end of the fourth heat. But all around me on this night, folks were contentedly scribbling away, allowing nary a moment's pause between the completion of one and the beginning of another. After each puzzle in the competition, I'd find out the next day, roughly half the contestants would get up and leave the room for whatever reason—to compare notes, to grab a smoke, to walk off the adrenaline (which, believe me, builds up over the course of four and a half hours spent solving difficult intellectual problems under the awful pressure of the clock). Some merely needed to escape for a few minutes the oppressive drabness of the virtual Astrodome (without all the cheery fake turf) we were stuck in all day long. The other half, I'd discover, would whip out their newly purchased puzzle books and get cracking on them until the next round began.

In chapter 1, I mentioned that in the *Boston Globe* piece I wrote about the 2003 tournament, I compared a dedicated solver at Stamford to a chocoholic at the annual convention of the National Confectioners Association. At the moment, it seemed the right image to use, but now, sitting in that huge room and under the influence of a pill that, if anything, made me *more* introspective than usual, I began to get a little creeped out by the truth of it. By no means all, but certainly a large proportion, of the folks around me simply had crosswords on the brain.

"I go on jags myself sometimes," Will Shortz later said to me when I asked him about this phenomenon. "If something really catches my attention about it, I'll do a whole book straight." One of the people sitting and doing puzzles on that Friday night was memorable-enough-looking—he was very large, very tall, very wide, very florid, probably in his late sixties or early seventies, and a retired lawyer if I've ever seen one—that I recalled him when he sat down at my table for the awards lunch on Sunday afternoon. It turned out that he was, like me, a first-timer at the tournament; it also turned out that he didn't particularly enjoy doing crosswords under a time constraint.

"Then why come to the tournament?" I asked. "I mean, couldn't you just have asked Will to send the puzzles to you?" (Instead of physically attending the Stamford tournament, you can also, for a token fee, either "attend" electronically or have the organizers mail you the seven crosswords afterward.)

"I just like puzzles."

"If you don't mind my asking, are you married?"

"Yes."

"Does your wife do crosswords?"

"Oh, no. No."

"She'd find all this a bit . . . strange?"

"Yeah. She doesn't understand—I just like puzzles. I like it here."

The fact is that some people understand the desire to do puzzles while others just don't. Yet the affinity for crosswords obviously runs deep in the general population—why else would millions upon million of puzzle books be published and purchased each year? The odd thing, again, is that nothing particularly identifies the person who is more likely than another to enjoy puzzles, except for the fact that he constantly solves them—the professor of English you'd expect to like them doesn't, while the fellow who comes to clean his office does; the editor hates them, while the musician can't get enough of them. The passion for puzzling, like heads for figures or ears for music, recognizes few social or economic bounds; it can thrive in the most unexpected places yet refuse to show its face where you'd lay good money it was certain to do.

My suspicion, which I touched on before, is that the impulse to make or solve puzzles has an ancient pedigree. Back when humanity lived not in organized societies but in isolated bands, a certain survival premium would be placed on those small groups that counted among their numbers individuals who could pick up on patterns no one else noticed. Where most would see a sun-dappled forest edge and nothing else, some would see the tiger lurking there, its camouflage veiling the deadly threat it represented; where most would see a picture of strangers walking innocently along the opposite mountain ridge, some would see a group of warriors plotting to make off with the clan's womenfolk. Nowadays we don't need to worry overly much about hidden tigers or about protecting the clan's mothers and daughters. However, at one time the ability to correctly pick the threatening pattern out of apparent randomness could mean the difference between life and death. I don't think it's unreasonable to suppose that humanity over the millennia selected for this skill, much in the way that it has selected for resistance to diseases or the ability to carry a tune, both of which have a greater impact on the survivability quotient of the group than over that of the individual. Not everyone needs to have these skills or attributes: In the human division of labor, you need only a few scouts, a few hunters, a few healers, a few bards, a few people with green thumbs. With those people around, everyone else can get along with their daily business, much in the same way that the world today needs only a few professional athletes, a few doctors, a few mathematicians, while the rest of us troop on doing whatever it is we do from sabbath to sabbath. People who simply can't help but do puzzles may be acting out, in a modern form, a behavior imposed on humanity by the ineluctable laws of selective adaptation; they can no more avoid doing crossword puzzles than someone with sickle cell anemia can catch malaria.

It may be that Shortz's tournament is so popular simply because it *does* afford crossword enthusiasts the unique chance to do just that—binge on their favorite obsession—without having their spouses suggest divorce or their kids complain that there's no dinner on the table. Here, dinner is always on the table, courtesy of the Marriott staff and whatever plastic is in your wallet, and no one will mind your solving a puzzle as you're quietly eating.

Puzzling in Xanadu

I'd just been riffling through the registration packet, wondering which of the puzzles inside I might want to tackle first, when Will Shortz walked to the podium and got the Twenty-seventh American Crossword Puzzle Tournament off to its start.

I was falling deeper into the throes of the Ativan (I'm not sure why doctors' offices aren't thronged with hopheads claiming social anxiety disorders) and feeling very much like a character out of *Fear and Loathing in Stamford*; one thing I could be sure of was that I was going to perform as well, during this first night's fun-and-games session, as a post-operative Stepford wife.

My complete inability to get more than halfway through either of the two puzzles handed out in the course of it gave rise to an interesting thought. Now, to someone who doesn't have the specific set of skills it takes to do crosswords, it's difficult to explain what they're all about. You can say that puzzles are like variations on a theme in music, but the metaphor, though close in some respects, is too broad. You can say that they're like math problems using words, but they're not—pure math puzzles, like sudoku, have a large, distinct audience of their own. To someone who doesn't have a large vocabulary, a grab bag of trivial information available at his mental fingertips, an eye for patterns and symbolic relationships, not to mention a sense of humor generous enough to make room for the corny, crossword puzzles will never be much fun. But let's turn the thought on its head: If you are a cruciverbalist and want to know what it's like suddenly *not* being one, try the following experiment.

Get yourself a copy of Saturday's *New York Times* puzzle and set it aside. Do not have dinner. Go to a bar and order a Campari and soda; drink it. Order a dry gin martini, up, and drink it. Repeat with a vodka and grapefruit juice, a whisky sour, and a rum and Coke. If you have the constitution for it, ask the bartender every now and then for a tequila shooter. Stumble home. (Note: If you're driving, hand the car keys to a friend.) If there's a Heineken in your fridge, down that, too. Do not drink any water, juice, or hydrating substance whatsoever. Go to sleep. When you wake up, groan piteously, then head to the kitchen table, where you'll have left the puzzle the night before. Attempt it.

You can do that, or you can take Ativan and then try an "oral clue" puzzle by Patrick Berry and a puns-and-anagrams puzzle by Mel Taub. Neither is an experience you'll want to undergo twice, if you have any pride in your crosswording abilities.

The Berry puzzle was meant to be a team activity, but given my mental condition and the fact that Brendan Quigley was AWOL at the hotel bar, likely getting toadied no end, I decided to sit out the social side of the event and merely observe—and a damned good idea that turned out to be.

Berry's was an "oral" puzzle because, well, the clues were read aloud; the point was that each was a close homophone of another, real clue that yielded the correct answer. For my part, I guessed only one of these: SINGERS as a result of "Aquires membership," which, homophonetically, is "A choir's membership." "Used finesse," yielding SHAMPOOED, was, in my opinion, too simple and not really in the spirit of things, but I missed it anyway. My favorite was OREGANO for "Urban pizza joint" ("Herb in pizza joint"). "Been in a cold place"—CRISPER, "Bin in a cold place"—was clever, but problematic to those of us who pronounce "been" with a long "e" and not short "i" sound. After ten minutes of this, I was wondering if it weren't time already to go find Brendan at the bar.

Mel Taub's puns and anagrams, though, soon had me thinking about more radical actions than fleeing into the taproom—such as catching the train and heading back to New York forthwith. Not only was his puzzle phenomenally difficult to someone whose intelligence level has been chemically reduced to that of a sick wombat; it was also timed. Psychologically speaking, it's a heck of a lot more disconcerting to be racing a clock that isn't adding the seconds and minutes, like a proper red-blooded timepiece, but rather *losing* them, so your progress goes from the cheery heights of 30:00 to the ghastly abyss of 00:00 in many fewer heartbeats than you'd think possible. It doesn't seem quite fair, especially when you've got a whole quadrant of the puzzle to check to see that the clock is indeed reading 10:00, only to realize with a thrill of horror that the one and the zero have been transposed, and, gosh, you've only got a minute left before the crows of failure will be settling down on your shoulders. For the first time in ages, I realized, I wouldn't be finishing a puzzle in time.

You wouldn't think thirty minutes could pass so swiftly—well, maybe you would if you've ever showed up half an hour early for a dentist's appointment to have your wisdom teeth pulled—but I suppose that's why Will scheduled the weekend's hardest puzzle for Friday evening. It gave those of us who had never puzzled competitively before our first opportunity to battle the implacable clock (a lesson I did not, as events were to bear out, entirely absorb), and it reassured the nervous that the worst of the weekend had passed without causing any damage, since the night's challenge represented no judgment on our solving skills, at least not in official scoring terms. And thank Christ for that, I thought glumly.

The clock—the real one, not the infernal backward-counting digital banner of death—now read ten. Next on the tournament schedule was the grim-sounding "10:00–11:00 PM Wine and cheese reception," which my instincts told me to avoid. It was time, instead, to belly up to the bar, order whatever dinner the Stamford Marriott offered at that hour, and find out exactly what sort of creature these puzzle people were, at least the ones who liked heartier fare than warm Chardonnay and soggy Brie. Plus, with the Ativan still coursing through my system and my intellectual processes consequently still disrupted, I figured that a couple of Sam Adamses and a chat with the more party-oriented tournament-goers would be just the thing for me. Overall the night's lesson was valuable: If you ever have to choose between maintaining mental clarity or staving off a social neurosis, go for the mental clarity—your throat may be dry, your palms sweaty, and your knees aquiver, but at least you won't find yourself getting beaten at crossword puzzles by every reasonably bright six-year-old in the house. In other words, there would be no more Ativan for me this weekend.

Kudos for Constructors

As a particular subsection of the business-traveling class knows all too well, hotel bars in provincial outposts are pretty much all alike—the wood paneling, the sleepy waiters, the carpet whose color you might describe as "orange" only if you were under the influence of some powerful and exotic hallucinogen (or at least something as powerful as Ativan).

On this Friday night, though, the Marriott taproom presented a very unusual sight. Yes, at the drinking trough was a scattering of people who were obviously regulars—Stamford's downtown area isn't exactly hopping in terms of nightspots, barring a handful of windowless taverns. By a factor of at least ten, though, the regulars were outnumbered by puzzlers: very excited and very loud puzzlers. And this is perhaps the time to mention a peculiar feature of the crossword demographic: Puzzlers tend to be more animated than the rest of the population, or at least the segment of it as represented by the patrons of hotel bars. At the risk of drawing too great a conclusion from too small a group, you could see it the moment you stepped onto that ocher-yellow-reddish carpet—the regulars whose drinks the bartender wordlessly refreshed were distinctly less enthusiastic than the crowd of fifty or so crossword-tournament attendees carousing among them.

Unless they're being followed around by guys with video cameras or are wandering past with a giant pile of their books clutched in their arms, constructors are extremely difficult to pick out from a crowd of random puzzlers. As a broad generalization, you could say that they tend to be males in their middle age (or just past it) who build puzzles as a sideline to a career that has something to do with math. But then Frank Longo (thin, youngish) or Cathy Mill-hauser (petite, female) comes to mind and blows the sweeping generalization to the four winds. Constructors fall into no discernible age group, either; the 2004 tournament was graced by the presence of Michael Shteyman, a prolific *Times* contributor who was taking the weekend off from being a pre-med junior at Johns Hopkins, as well as that of Frances Hansen, the eighty-four-year-old grande dame of the tournament (who, sadly, passed away later that year). The only things that can universally be said about them is that they're very friendly, extremely fond of puzzles and word games, and are apt to spend long hours talking about crosswords, but those same descriptions apply to pretty much everyone who goes to Stamford as participant, judge, or hanger-on—or indeed as host or master of ceremonies. In a nutshell, constructors are a lot like solvers.

Like puzzlers, constructors tend to look younger than they are. In 2003 I interviewed Jay Kasofsky, the one person who has attended every American Crossword Puzzle Tournament to date. I figured at the time that he must have gone to his first one at about the age of twenty-five; as it turns out, this fiftyish-looking fellow is a long-retired high school history teacher from upstate New York who's gracefully nudging toward seventy. Ditto with Will Shortz himself—people who see the fifty-something puzzlemaster on his weekly train trip into the city to pick up his mail at the *New York Times* and record his segment on National Public Radio would think they were looking at, maybe, a newly minted literature professor heading in to

New York University for his Friday seminar. Will, like many of the participants in his annual crossword tournament, is preternaturally well preserved.

There seems to be something about doing crosswords that keeps people young, or at least keeps them thinking young. Years ago someone published a study about nuns in North America and their susceptibility to Alzheimer's. The study found that there was a direct correlation between the complexity of the sentence structures in a piece of writing done by a given nun when she was young and her likelihood *not* to develop the disease in old age. In other words, nuns who expressed themselves in something more sophisticated than mere declarative sentences—those who used nuance, a complicated vocabulary, metaphors, similes, and the like—tended to be significantly more resistant to the disease, as they aged, than their sisters who displayed less of a tendency toward written verbal pyrotechnics while young. The study seems to buttress my conviction that doing crosswords is something like drinking from the Fountain of Youth.

For sheer anecdotal evidence that doing crosswords is the equivalent, in mental health terms, of what running twenty miles a week confers upon your physique comes from the euphoniously named Marilyn Munro. Marilyn, whom I first met while covering the 2003 tournament, was until 2000 the other Jay Kasofsky—she'd been, up to then, a participant in every American Crossword Tournament since the program began in 1978. A self-described Rhode Island housewife, she soldiered gamely on through some twenty-four competitions, usually placing somewhere in the comfortable middle of the standings, but always seated next to Jay. (They describe each other as "crossword best friends.") Just before the twenty-fifth tournament, though, Marilyn had a serious stroke—it was something of a miracle that she even survived. She didn't make it to Stamford in 2002, although she was back, sitting again next to Jay, for the twenty-sixth in 2003, placing 481st out of the 495 registered entrants—which, when you think about it, is pretty impressive, though I'm not sure how the final fourteen finishers felt about getting outscored by a septuagenarian stroke survivor. (Marilyn was there for the 2004 competition; her friends had set up a place for her by one of the exit doors, in case anything should happen to her, but when I saw her she'd somehow made her way to the front of the ballroom, where she sat, next to Jay, at the same table they'd occupied for more than twenty-five years.)

It's probably absurd to make a really broad generalization about a population otherwise as heterodox as crossword puzzlers, but they do seem more lively and curious about the world around them than, say, the people you meet waiting on line at the Department of Motor Vehicles. I don't know precisely in which direction to credit this fact; maybe the nervous energy you need to do well at puzzling tends to overflow in social situations, or maybe something in the disposition of someone drawn to solving crosswords also drives them to, I don't know, walk twenty miles a week or something, and when they're marooned in Spaceship Marriott they talk instead. Then again, perhaps the crossword gene codes for both puzzle-solving skills and giddy excitability.

Standing among the impressively large crowd at the Stamford Marriott bar when I walked in were Brendan Emmett Quigley and a veritable Who's Who of contemporary star constructors: Rich Silvestri, Bob Klahn, Jim Page, David Kahn, and Peter Gordon were the few of many I actually recorded in my notebook. (That Ativan pill was, of course, still wreaking its mental mayhem, and a lot of my notes now look like those webs you see spiders making in cautionary sixties-era documentaries about LSD abuse.) Sure, there were some nonconstructors drifting about. But Friday night at Stamford is all about the constructors, who come early to talk shop together; Saturday night is when they collect their kudos from the unwashed masses. (In 2003, as I arrived at the Marriott early on Saturday morning, I met a woman standing outside, waiting for a cab back to the train; she'd published five puzzles in the *New York Times* and had come up only for the previous night, just to talk with Will and other constructors. She confessed to a horror of actually competing in a puzzle tournament and refused to give me her name for fear it might appear in print—but then again, spend ten minutes in the world of crossword people, and you'll collect enough examples of neurotic behavior to warrant putting out a new edition of the *DSM*.)

Brendan, it turned out, had spent the last two hours up in room 807, where a mysterious group calling itself "the Cru" ("the Crew," of course, but also the first syllable of the word "Cruciverb," the title of the online crossword discussion group to which they all post messages) was having its annual wine party. Back in the taproom, David Kahn was showing Brendan his new collection of puzzles as I walked in. Brendan turned to me, thumping his finger on one of the puzzles, and said, "Jesus Christ! Look at this!"

The gimmick of Kahn's book was that all the puzzles in it were themed around Major League baseball. The one Brendan was looking at was called "Cooperstown," and it took me a couple of seconds to realize what he was so excited about—the only letters you needed to complete the puzzle were "C," "O," "P," "E," "R," "S," "T," "W," and "N," which is both clever in conception and devilishly difficult in terms of building a grid that actually works. Talk about your gimmicky writers like Georges Perec, who produced his novel *La Disparition* without using the letter "e"—well, puzzle constructors perform similarly amazing tricks every day, and the harder they are to pull off (and to pull off a puzzle, you have to make solving it feel natural, which means that puzzlers working on "Cooperstown" should complete it without even being aware that in doing so they're using only eight letters of the alphabet), the more likely they are to elicit, on Friday night at Stamford, outbursts of wonder and admiration from fellow constructors.

Around midnight, Rich Silvestri, Brendan, and I were talking about our favorite puzzles. Mine, again, was the infamous Jim Farrell "Election Day," which appeared in the *New York Times* on November 5, 1996, and the answer to whose clue "Tomorrow's headline?" could be either BOBDOLEELECTED or CLINTON-ELECTED, depending on your choice of BAT or CAT as the answer to the clue "Black mammal" and so on through six other clues. Will Shortz says it was the most controversial grid he's ever published, with the letters he received about it evenly divided between angry Democrats and angry Republicans, all of whom decried the newspaper's gall at making a blatantly partisan political prediction (Farrell, a retired professor of math, now devotes his constructing abilities to creating puzzles for the blind). Silvestri's was one by Randy Ross entitled "Initial Occupations," in which the initials of some famous person's name yielded the first letters of each word in a double-barreled job description (for instance, "D. H. Lawrence" producing DESIGNATEDHITTER). Typically, Brendan didn't have a favorite—or, rather, he had lots of favorites and refused to choose among them.

"I like Frank Longo a lot, but it's all really kind of impersonal with puzzles. Bob Klahn's grids are great, yeah. And every time I see a David Kahn I think, 'Gee, I wish I'd have thought of that theme.' When you're talking about that level of focus, you just have to respect *every* puzzle these guys do."

Not bad, I thought—even after four beers (I was paying, and thus counting), Brendan was still his same insufferably fair and equitable self, far more likely to praise than to damn and yet at the same time unwilling to commit himself to something so absolute as a statement of extremes: such as, for example, citing a puzzle that might just happen to be his favorite.

"Yeah," said Silvestri, a stocky, fiftyish fellow with an ash-colored Santa Claus beard from behind which two brown eyes peer out in a fashion that can only be called mischievous. "What it comes down to is that a crossword should be fun to do, and that's all there is to it." As a day job, Rich teaches math at a community college on Long Island; he has published more than fifty puzzles in the *New York Times*, the overwhelming bulk of them under the editorship of Will Shortz. When I asked him why he hadn't been as prolific under Will's predecessor, Silvestri only said, "Well, Maleska and I didn't see things the same way"—a tactful way of skirting the issue of Maleska's hostility toward the new wave of constructors who began, as of about the mid-1980s, challenging the stodgy sort of crossword-making (no brand names, few puns, little wordplay) that Maleska and, by consequence, the *Times* preferred throughout his nearly twenty-year tenure. It's difficult to imagine Eugene T. Maleska's group of constructors swilling down the suds while talking a mile a minute about one another's creations; it's difficult enough to imagine Maleska wanting to even *meet* a constructor in person, much less a score of them, all comparing notes. Under the tenure of Will Shortz, new-wave constructors have found their niche—in fact, you'd now have to look very hard to find any working constructor who isn't part of the new wave. (Master solver and longtime constructor Stanley Newman, who is currently editor of the *New York Newsday* puzzle, once replied to a question from a reporter about the Maleska–new-wave struggle with the terse and telling "We won.") As I thought about it, I realized that the atmosphere in the Stamford Marriott bar was in fact celebratory:

Imagine a bunch of Young Turk scientists who have just completely changed the paradigms of their field, bearding their elders at their world annual conference, and you'll understand what I mean. These guys had won the battle against an ancient, moribund, and, under Maleska, close to tyrannical crossword tradition, and it showed tonight in their unfettered enthusiasm. They were here to relish their creative freedom, which still tasted fine after their decade and a half of reveling in it.

Though they were the revolutionaries of America's ninety-year-old crossword tradition, the constructors in the Marriott bar were, in terms of puzzling, dyed-in-the-wool conservatives. About half of those I have spoken with do their constructing the old-fashioned way, which is to say by hand on graph paper, though the younger ones use computer crossword programs that do things like set up the grid and suggest fill words. Silvestri, for instance, does all his puzzles by hand; Brendan Quigley uses a computer program, but his obsession with the structure of the grid means he spends so much time tweaking any given one that he might as well, in the end, have produced it manually. I had a brief chat with veteran *Times* constructor Jim Page along these lines that resulted in my first nagging suspicion that my six months of pretournament practicing had not, in fact, done much good in terms of preparing me for the competitive ordeal that loomed in the very near future.

I asked Page what he thought of a very odd phenomenon I had noticed while doing the daily *Times* puzzle online. The *Times* premium crossword site allows you to do all sorts of things, such as solve with a friend via remote connection and the like, but primarily it has a built-in clock, which is a very useful thing if you're interested in training yourself to speed-solve. The top-ten best times for the day's crossword are posted in a vertical sidebar on the upper right hand of the solving page. The times posted there, I noticed on my very first visit to the site, are all ludicrously fast: on the order of a minute for weekday puzzles and a minute and a half for a Sunday. Since I know from experience and observation that the minimum time required for even a Monday-level puzzle by the very best solver is two and a half minutes, and since the site is set up in such a way that a given account has only one chance at posting a time, it was obvious that people were using one subscription account to download and print out the puzzle; once it was solved, they'd use their second account to speed-type in the answers and thus post a time limited only by their ability to key quickly. It's sort of like Rosie Ruiz at the 1980 Boston Marathon—you can't really get your mind around why someone would want to so blatantly and obviously cheat and to so spectacularly fail at doing so.

"I mean," I asked Page, "what conceivable satisfaction could someone get out of it? It's not like anyone would believe that ElizaJ or whoever did a Friday puzzle in fifty-seven seconds."

Page looked thoughtful. After a moment he said, "I don't know—maybe, to some people, the satisfaction is worth it. Just seeing their screen name posted there. What I *do* know is that everyone does puzzles faster on a computer. The thing that counts is how fast you do them on paper."

I took a nervous gulp at my beer, processing the implications of what Page had just said. Suddenly it seemed much less important to figure out why someone might want to cheat (and pay for two *Times* subscriptions) simply to get their user name high up on a list no one pays any attention to anyway. Far, far more troubling was the fact that the last month of my training regime had consisted of doing puzzles online instead of on paper. With a feeling of sick dread, I realized that it takes far less time to click on the key for "m" than it takes to write the letter itself—I'd completely overlooked, therefore, the fact that I'd be writing, not typing, in competition, and that the fast times I'd scored in practice and was so proud of were about as useful to me in this situation as a bikini would be to a polar bear. For the last month, in other words, I'd been living in cloud-cuckoo land—disaster was beckoning with all the insistence of a Jehovah's Witness knocking at your front door.

Meet Omar McAron— or Aron Corman, After Beers

Given the hour, the pace at which the bartender seemed to be placing frosty new bottles of beer in front of Brendan and me, and the Ativan (seems to contraindicate nicely with Sam Adams, that stuff), it seemed almost inevitable that we should all try anagramming my name into something reasonably approaching one you might find in a city phone book. The impetus for this was, really, Peter Gordon, the crossword-puzzle editor of the *New York Sun*, who as "Ogden Porter" is also one of that paper's most prolific constructors. (It's sort of fun to read the byline "Ogden Porter/Edited by Peter Gordon" and wonder how many people think it strange that editor and constructor share the exact same complement of letters in their names.) I had read Stefan Fatsis's book *Word Freak*, about his adventures climbing his way up the ranks of international Scrabble competitors, and so knew that in that weird environment people tend to anagram for fun. There's something of a convergence here between Scrabblers and crossword aficionados, if only because the latter know that approximately 1 percent of the answers they'll be asked to produce in a given year will involve rearranging the letters in a clue (unless, that is, they're British, in which case the proportion will be much higher). What was a bit alarming on this night was the gusto with which five of the most famous and accomplished constructors currently alive attempted to transmogrify my name into a reasonably workable alternative—it may not sound like a fun thing to you, but it's a real hoot to these guys.

I don't know if it was the beers on top of the Ativan on top of my long-standing admiration for the oeuvre of musician Frank Zappa, but the best I could come up with was "Moon Carma," which isn't even an anagram of my name. I don't know who came up with "Omar McRoan"—my notebook for this stage of the weekend is covered with writing in at least three separate hands, plus an unidentifiable stain that appears to be the remains of a spilled Guinness Stout—but it led the pack until Peter Gordon came over, looked at the scrawled-over page, and jotted in "Aron Corman." (To a puzzler, "Aron," as in "Elvis Aron Presley," is a perfectly acceptable variant on the name "Aaron." A puzzler would also likely know that "Aron" is the correct spelling of the word in Arnold Schoenberg's opera *Moses und Aron*, though not because that's the German form of the name; Schoenberg, a superstitious sort, wanted to avoid having thirteen letters in the title of his opera and lopped one "a" off "Aaron" to achieve his numerical ideal.) In any event, if I ever need to take a powder and live on a tropical island under an assumed name, I'll have to thank Peter for the one I'll use, even if I realized afterward that the name is an anagram of mine only to a person wearing beer goggles. (I'm assuming that Interpol agents don't read books about crossword puzzles.)

As I paid up—it was two in the morning by now, and my handwriting was no longer legible, and the bar was about to close up for the night—I asked Brendan what my chances were for the following day. He set his mug on the counter and looked at me with an expression of pity.

"You're gonna get crushed. But don't worry about it—my first time, I came in dead last. Even with the divisional flights, you're gonna get crushed. Crushed."

On that sobering note I headed up to my room, where I phoned the front desk for a wake-up call at seven in the morning. Brendan's prediction was still echoing in my ears as I settled into bed. Well, fine, then, I thought to myself. I may get crushed—and I was confident enough that I wouldn't—but I vowed to myself that at the very least I'd do as well as, if not better than, Brendan Emmett Quigley. Looking at the bar bill, I thought it would be a tragedy if I didn't.

Chapter 5

HOW NOT TO prepare
for competitive solving

If you ever need a moment of pure existential unease, I'd strongly recommend sitting, alone and slightly hung over, groggy after five hours of fitful sleep, a copy of *Gravity's Rainbow* by Thomas Pynchon before you and trying to choke down a breakfast of dry omelet and tepid orange juice in the eight A.M. emptiness of the Stamford Marriott Hotel's in-house restaurant while contemplating the four-hour, six-puzzle ordeal looming ahead, courtesy of the Twenty-seventh American Crossword Puzzle Tournament. At least I'd slept off the Ativan.

Brendan Quigley's prediction of the night before, that I'd fare miserably in this day's competition, had metamorphosed over the past hour from a statement that I thought laughable into a presentiment of truth as inalterable as a message from the oracle at Delphi. Brendan himself was not yet in evidence; he would drift down from his room an hour later. Except for Laura Bauer, a colleague from my hedge-fund days who first told me about this tournament, and Daniel Okrent, from whom I'd rented a house in the Berkshires a decade earlier and who had recently been tapped for the unenviable job of public editor at the post–Jayson Blair *New York Times*, I knew no one else in the premises except, very cursorily, Will Shortz himself. Neither Laura nor Dan were anywhere in sight; *Gravity's Rainbow*, ordinarily a book I read every two years or so, offered, in my mental and physical state, no succor today. It would have been nice to take a brisk precompetition stroll outside, but it was still unseasonably raw for southern Connecticut this time of year, my coat was upstairs in my room, and in any case there isn't much, in downtown Stamford, to walk *to*, unless you want to pick something up from the CVS pharmacy a hundred yards down the street from the hotel's back door. So, instead, I decided to take a closer look at the day's schedule and at the list of the five hundred preregistered contestants. (Another fifty or so showed up as walk-ins.)

From eleven to twelve forty-five, we would be having our go at three puzzles: a fifteen-by-fifteen (time limit fifteen minutes), a seventeen-by-seventeen (twenty minutes), and a nineteen-by-nineteen (thirty minutes). The first would obviously be a standard Monday- or Tuesday-type daily puzzle; if I couldn't do it in six minutes at the outside, I'd eat the nearest hat I could find. The twenty- and thirty-minute puzzles seemed likely gimmes, as well: From my months of practice, I knew I averaged around twenty-three minutes for Sunday *Times* puzzles, which are usually twenty-one squares by twenty-one. The next three puzzles were slotted for between two-thirty and four-thirty in the afternoon: another fifteen-by-fifteen (twenty minutes), a seventeen-by-seventeen (twenty-five minutes), and a nineteen-by-nineteen (thirty minutes). So it looked like puzzles four and five would be harder than your standard *New York Times* daily, while six would be, in terms of size and difficulty, roughly equivalent to puzzle three, the last one in the morning session. The sugar from the orange juice and the protein from the omelet seemed to be doing their stuff, because all of a sudden I felt my head clearing and the prospect of total disaster receding—not quite over the horizon, but at least close enough to it for comfort. The final puzzle, at nine A.M. on Sunday morning, was a twenty-one-by-twenty-one with a time limit of forty-five minutes. That cheered me considerably, since it had been at least a decade since I'd completed a Sunday *Times* crossword in more than half an hour. I began to think that I wouldn't do so badly after all, Brendan Emmett Quigley and his predictions of doom notwithstanding.

Then I cast my eye over the word count of each puzzle once again in an attempt to determine which of them would have a theme or not—since, generally speaking, the fewer words in a puzzle, the more likely it is to have a unifying principle. If a given puzzle does have a theme, identifying it in as little time as possible gives the solver a significant edge, if he can spot it early enough to take full advantage of it. By that measure, it looked like puzzles one, two, and three, with respective word counts of 78, 98, and 128, would be clued more easily than puzzles four, five, and six, which though the same size as their morning counterparts had slightly lower word counts: 76, 96, and 120. The seventy-six-word fourth puzzle, I read in the registration packet, also featured a hundred-point bonus answer. So it looked as if the morning puzzles would each be a question of pure filling, while the afternoon puzzles would take a fair bit of mental gymnastics to solve—unless you cracked, within the first minute or so, the gimmick the constructor used to base his puzzle's architecture upon. Guardedly, I began to think my overall prospects for the day weren't actually that bleak. In the course of solving a few thousand *Times* puzzles in the months before the tournament, I'd found that my strong suit was themed puzzles with relatively low word counts. And while it was impossible to tell from such scant evidence how tough each of the seven puzzles would turn out to be, it seemed from the preliminary indications that I wouldn't do too badly, if only my head would keep clearing and if Lady Luck condescended to give me at least a weak smile once or twice over the course of the tournament.

Next I turned to the list of registered contestants that had been handed out with our tournament schedule, my idea being to figure out from it what proportion of them, based on the two- or three-word biographies they had provided in their entry forms, were mathematicians, musicians, or other assorted quantitatively minded types—because those were the people who, historically, do well at the American Crossword Puzzle Tournament. I was hoping against hope that, this year, they would be far outnumbered by people less likely to stand so stolidly between me and the brass ring. Here, too, the prognosis looked good: Only about half of the entrants seemed to be symbol-and-pattern-recognition types, with the rest a patch-work collection of teachers, editors, journalists, business consultants, lawyers, and the unthreatening like. In the "can-it-really-be-true" column I placed one excursion-boat captain, one professional legal skip tracer, one out-of-work actor, and one aerial photographer; in the I'm-so-funny column, there was one "modern-day esne," one "amateur professional," one "NASCAR dad," one "cat attendant," and one "aspiring indie-rock god" (this last was Brendan Emmett Quigley). I had to say that the competition didn't look all that tough—except for the fact that they were all solvers motivated enough, and presumably good enough, to devote a weekend out of their year to the recondite activity of correctly completing cross-word puzzles within time limits that would have more casual crossword-attempters wailing for Mother.

At this point that first morning of the tournament, I began to feel positively hopeful. In retrospect, I'm very, very sorry I didn't take that long walk around downtown Stamford instead of spend-ing a full hour building an intellectual sandcastle that, as the adage says of battle plans and the shock of first contact with the enemy, was foreordained to collapse the moment any degree of stress was brought to bear upon it. But now none of my hopes or fears mattered; a crowd of contestants was gathering around the doors leading into the Stamford Marriott's Grand Ballroom, and in the middle of it was a slightly bleary-eyed Brendan Quigley beckoning me toward him. I don't know how it happened, but an unspoken agreement seemed to have been struck between us that we'd compete not only against the tournament at large, but also against each other. Fed and reasonably revived from the night before by a couple of cups of coffee, I figured that at the very least I'd beat Brendan at his own game and on his home turf. So it was with something approximating optimism that I took my seat beside him just as Will Shortz was walking up, once again, to the podium in the middle of that cavernous hall.

The Ordeal: A First Taste

A competitor in a crossword tournament has three enemies to face: the genius of puzzle constructors; the vagaries, vicissitudes, and inconstancy of his own mind; and the clock. At the 2003 tournament, a big problem was the clock: The Stamford Marriott staff had misplaced the gigantic analog one that had been used to time heats for umpteen previous tournaments, and it took some minutes—and much impatient grumbling on the part of the assembled contestants—for it to be located in whatever storeroom the hotel used to house Brobdingnagian timepieces that were pulled out only one weekend a year.

In 2004 the old analog device had been replaced by a digital one, which as we filed in and took our places ominously read 15:00, the time limit for the day's first puzzle. Once the room quieted down, Will Shortz launched into the annual ritual of reciting the scoring rules, whose central importance has been internalized by all seasoned competitors, but whose significance is generally lost on a rookie attendee.

A first-timer at the competition who overlooks the basic rules is making a big mistake, however, since managing your time is perhaps the single most important thing you have to do if you wish to place anywhere near the top of the puzzling heap at Stamford. You get 10 points for every correctly filled-in answer across and down. You get 25 points for every full minute you complete a puzzle before time runs out; however, you also lose 10 points for every incorrect or unfilled-in letter in the puzzle. (There's no such things as negative points, though; if you make more mistakes than the time you post under the limit, you simply score 0.) A complete and error-free solution to a puzzle earns you another 150 points. In the day's first puzzle, for instance, there were seventy-eight answers; if you got all those correct, you'd score 780, plus the 150-point complete accuracy bonus, plus 25 points for every full minute you solved the puzzle under the fifteen-minute limit, for an eventual score of anywhere between 930 (if you used the whole fifteen minutes) and 1,330 (if you solved the puzzle correctly in under three minutes). Puzzle four in the tournament also featured a bonus answer worth 100 points.

What this means—and what I didn't fully realize in the heat of competition—is that, at the American Crossword Puzzle Tournament, you're better off striving for a full and complete solution than going for the time bonus. The trade-off between time and accuracy is a somewhat counterintuitive concept to master, especially when you see the fastest solvers turning in their puzzles before you've even got your pencil properly sharpened. But you'll never have a hope of doing well at Stamford if you don't keep it in mind at all times. Since a complete and correct solution is worth 150 points, if you finish filling in a grid with, say, six minutes still left on the clock, you're better off spending up to five minutes checking your answers to make sure they're all correct than you would be turning in the puzzle the second you're done. If you finished puzzle four—the one with the 100-point bonus answer—with four minutes left on the clock, you'd be better off using three of those minutes to figure out the bonus than to hand the solution to a referee immediately, or with just a minute or two spent fruitlessly chasing after the bonus. Not only that, but you have to keep an eye on the clock at all times; if you finish fifteen seconds into a given new minute, it's pointless to hand your puzzle in at that moment, since you'd just be wasting forty-five seconds of free potential checking time for no gain in return.

I'll stress that, for a rookie solver, keeping all of this in mind under competitive conditions is extremely difficult; not only are you concentrating on solving puzzles under the gun (puzzles, mind you, that perhaps 90 percent of your fellow citizens couldn't complete if you gave them a week in which to do them), but you're also unconsciously pressured, timewise, by your out-of-the-corner-of-the-eye awareness of how many of your fellow contestants have completed a puzzle before you and already scurried out of the hall. It takes a significant amount of mental discipline to actually check your solution two or three times before you turn it in, since the temptation to *look* as if you're among the fastest solvers is very powerful.

Only when you've entirely internalized the idea that "wasting" a minute or two checking a puzzle is superior, as a strategy, to handing it in at the first opportunity will you maximize your chances of placing well in a given heat. Yes, it's unnerving to see the same ten or twenty people raising their hands, every round, in less time— even half—than it takes you to solve and check the very same puzzle. The point is, those people are oddities and quidnuncs whom you'll never match in a race against the clock; therefore, your goal shouldn't be speed, but the 100 percent accuracy you absolutely need if you have any hope of making one of the divisional championship berths after everyone's scores over seven puzzles have been tallied. Even the best and fastest solvers make silly mistakes, after all, so if you concentrate on not doing the same, and you're really lucky, you might just find yourself in the running for a crack at a title.

With a solid grasp of the title requirements, if not necessarily of how to use the clock to my advantage, I sat beside a silent and tense Brendan while the day's first puzzle was being placed, facedown, before each of us. In my tournament notes, I find the scribbled sentence, "Who's the girl standing next to Helene?" Maybe twenty seconds after I wrote it, all contingency—all contingencies involving pretty young women unexpectedly encountered—vanished. Will Shortz had just shouted out the "Go" command, and my world was suddenly reduced to one fifteen-square-by-fifteen patch of pure puzzling hell (which you too can experience merely by flipping to the tournament puzzles reprinted at the back of the book).

The First Half of a Grueling Day

Actually, the initial puzzle of the tournament wasn't bad at all—described as a "warm-up" exercise on the sheet placed before us, it was a straightforward Monday- or Tuesday-level crossword by Michael Shteyman. I was glad of that, too. His grids are elegant and clever, which is unusual for a constructor who is so young; remarkably, he had never made a puzzle in English (or even spoken a conversational sentence in English) before he and his family emigrated to Baltimore, Maryland, from St. Petersburg, Russia, in 1997. Michael ("Misha" to his Russian-speaking friends) is unquestionably a phenomenon: A slight, dark-haired, elfin-looking fellow, he works like a maniac at his university classes and publishes puzzles with a frequency that I, at least, find sort of alarming, especially since English is unquestionably his second language. (Imagine moving to France or Germany or Japan today, with the barest grasp of a tongue you'd learned only in school, and becoming one of those nations' preeminent puzzle builders within four years: You'd probably be pretty proud of yourself if you could manage to pull such a stunt off.)

Misha was kind to us contestants: His easy puzzle was themed— the clue at 7-Down read "Familiar phrase that contradicts 17-, 38-, and 59-Across," and it clued handily as NOIFSANDSORBUTS, a clutch of conjunctions that each reappeared in the three respective answers CATCHMEIFYOUCAN, STARSANDSTRIPES, and LIFEISBUTADREAM. Knowing intimately the constructor's native land, I was amused to find, tucked away in his grid, three Russia-related words: TASS, DUMA, and USSR. (I thought I detected another Russian theme in the answer KRAUT for "Cabbage, on a wiener," but then again you'd have to know that Russians are fond of cabbage, if not of Krauts.) In my notes I scribbled "Completed in 7—Quigley in 5 or 6," which turned out later to be true: Brendan scored 1,155 on this puzzle and I 1,130, meaning that we'd both aced it, though Brendan got 25 more points for the minute less than me it had taken him to complete it. The other lesson about the American Crossword Puzzle Tournament is that you need to develop a Zen approach to solving: Again, I usually finish a Monday- or Tuesday-level *Times* crossword in three to five minutes, if I do one, but in this case I choked and almost doubled my usual time, largely thanks to jitters. I realized I should have practiced these easiest of all puzzles, as well; because I hadn't, I took more time on this one, and so scored at least 50 points less on it than I should have.

There's a fifteen-minute break between heats, and during it I went up and introduced myself to Shteyman—probably, I thought, the only time that day he'd have someone blubbering congratulations to him in his native tongue (which turned out to be true: Months later, when we began the first of several phone conversations about puzzles, he said, "Oh, yes—the one person there who spoke to me in Russian"). We chatted a bit—Misha was clearly moved by his first starring role at the American Crossword Puzzle Tournament, and thought the sight of five hundred–plus solvers doing his puzzle was "pretty cool"—and then I returned to my seat, the referees came by again, placing facedown before us the day's second puzzle, a twenty-minute Fred Piscop production called "A Comedy of Errors." In my notes are two items: "Need luck!" and "Cute girl as judge—can't catch her name, as her tag is always hidden." Just before Will Shortz sounded the starter's gun again, I pointed her out to Brendan, who was back in his seat beside me. He looked at her, looked at me, and said: "What are you, Humbert Humbert? She's, like, twelve, for God's sake."

"She's not twelve—she's twenty if she's a day. Man, just look at her!"

Brendan did. The young woman in question sported various attributes you could never in your life mistake for belonging to an adolescent.

"Yeah, maybe. You're still a letch."

I was about to reply when Will let out his distinctive "Ready . . . go!" Once more the world instantly reduced itself into a square filled with black-and-white boxes, and silence fell on the great hall. This time it was me and five hundred others against the clock and the mind of Fred Piscop—constructing legend, chief scorer at the American Crossword Puzzle Tournament, and the known perpetrator of some of the worst puzzling tricks ever to frustrate and annoy and thrill generations of solvers.

But this puzzle, too, was straightforward, with the themed entries—DROPPEDWEIGHT, FLUFFEDAPILLOW, BOOTEDHIS-COMPUTER, SCREWEDUPABULB, and BLEWHISCORNET—all incorporating rough synonyms for making a mistake. Brendan completed it in twelve minutes; it took me thirteen. His score of 1,380 beat my 1,355 by 25, which at this point gave him a 50-point lead in our little undeclared head-to-head battle. Again I felt as if I should have worked more quickly, especially when compared with the time—nine minutes—it took me to correctly fill in Piscop's Thursday-level puzzle when I did it again, months later, in the quiet of my Brooklyn Heights apartment. In chapter 1, I admit, I said that a filled-in crossword is a dead letter, but this isn't entirely true. One of the notable characteristics of most American-style crosswords is that you can do them again a few months later (a year or two is better) without experiencing the shock of re-recognition you would if you tried, for instance, a British-style cryptic puzzle twice within the same span of time. The generic nature of a typical American fill, in other words, allows the repeat solver to unremember, given a minimum lapse of three months or more, the specifics of a particular puzzle, which is rarely the case with a cryptic. There are exceptions—I could never look at the 1996 *New York Times* "Election Day" puzzle with the same virgin eye I first encountered it with, and so still remember how to solve it in the shortest possible time—but in general American puzzles don't have the individual character that British puzzles do, the hook that enables you to remember forever the gimmick the constructor used to build it. This makes American puzzles almost infinitely repeatable as entertainments or time-passers, if only you allow enough time between the first solving and its reprise many months or years later, which may in part explain why American-style puzzles are so commercially successful, while cryptic puzzles aren't. You may have solved all the puzzles in Volume

78 of the Simon & Schuster crossword collection way back in 1986, only to pick up the same book in an airport newsstand in 2005 and still use it to get you through a transpacific flight lasting fifteen hours. Try to do the same with a *Times of London* collection of the same vintage and you'll be stridently calling for the cocktail tray three hours out of LAX. American puzzles aren't as clever as British ones, but they're less memorable, and so more apt to appear fresh if you see the same ones after a long enough interval of time. Crosswords are sort of akin, to borrow a line from Graham Greene's *Travels with My Aunt*, to the collected novels of Sir Walter Scott: by the time you finish the last one in the set, you've forgotten enough about the first that you can return to it again with pleasure. And so on it goes until, on your day of reckoning, you're only halfway through your thirtieth rereading of *The Heart of Midlothian* when the Grim Reaper comes a'collecting.

Before the next heat began, I had at last a chance to read, if only partially, the name tag of the attractive young referee who was now passing out the day's third puzzle at the table in the Stamford Marriott ballroom occupied by me and Brendan, among a few score others. It should give you some idea of how absorbing the solving of crossword puzzles can be that, less than halfway through the tournament, my first thought upon espying the few letters I could read against the young woman's quite generous *poitrine*—"BRE" were the first three out of what I assumed was a total of four—was their potential role in a hypothetical crossword puzzle. Instead of leering like a satyr at the woman herself, I was thinking about how that specific configuration of letters might show up in such words as "aBREaction" or phrases such as "BREwersyeast" or "LaBREatarpits" or—but before I could make my way further through the possible alphabetical configurations, Will Shortz was at the podium again, and three seconds later we solvers were flipping over a puzzle by

Merl Reagle called "Re-Fills." Once more nothing mattered apart from the piece of paper in front of me, the black-and-white squares upon it, and the microseconds before I'd be, once again, entirely in their thrall. And trying to master them before Brendan did.

At nineteen squares by nineteen, pun-filled and delimited by a potentially punishing time frame of thirty minutes, "Re-Fills" was a beast of a crossword puzzle. Its trick was to use, by way of a partial clue, a homonym, or near homonym, of an entirely different word or phrase. In a typical crossword puzzle, for instance, the clue "Agnus _____" would usually elicit DEI, a classic constructor's favorite; in this case it yielded MOOREHEAD, since the actress's first name, Agnes, is a homonym of the Latin word for "lamb." Other potential solving pitfalls included "Bona _____" (CONTENTION), "Fleur-de-_____" (EVERGLADES), "_____ Saud" (THEMARQUISDE), and my least favorite, "Mai _____" (NOSEISCOLD). Experienced puzzlers will recognize each homonymic clue as part of a standard crossword "fill," the set of often-seen words and phrases that represent, for constructors, a jumble of convenient letter combinations offering all sorts of possibilities for stacking three or more words on top of one another—hence the pun in the puzzle's title. I managed to get through it in twenty minutes, scoring 1,280 for the perfect fill plus 250 for the ten minutes under time in which I completed it; Brendan finished a minute ahead of me again, but this time he missed one letter and so lost 20 points for two incorrect words, 25 for the one incorrectly filled-in square, and the 150-point bonus for an errorless fill. In my notes I wrote that I thought he was at least 75 points ahead of me; in reality, I was ahead by 4,015 to 3,870. I wished I'd known that then, because I would gladly have rubbed it in. The sad fact of the matter is that the victory would have been empty—troubles, bad troubles, were about to descend on me, and in battalions, not single spies.

Crosswords and the Mystery of Sex

Over the break for lunch, Brendan and I split up, he to go get mobbed by adoring fans (in terms of which constructors appear more often in the photos page of the American Crossword Puzzle Tournament Web site, Brendan wins hands down), me to grab something to eat. I thought of taking a walk around Stamford in the hopes of finding a café, but again the weird gravitational pull of the Marriott kept me indoors—looking back at the tournament weekend now, I realize that the hotel may as well indeed have been, for all that anyone actually exited it, surrounded by an atmosphere of pure methane. So I had a burger and a beer at the hotel bar (it was the last food I was to consume for the rest of the weekend), where I was joined by a building contractor from Pennsylvania—I didn't write his name down, but think it was Gary—to whom I eventually mentioned the pretty judge.

"She's somebody's daughter," said Gary.

"Well, I figured that."

"No—I mean somebody big in the puzzle world."

"Oh." The glum thought struck me that perhaps it wouldn't be wise to hit on someone who might turn out to be the chief scorer's beloved offspring, at least not mid-tournament.

This got us talking about sex, or the lack of it, at the tournament, a subject Gary seemed to have strong views about.

"It's all really about sex, a lot of it."

"How's that?"

"Think about it. You have all these people who wake up and say to themselves, 'Gee, I feel like filling up little holes with something today.' You'd think they'd get it, but apparently they don't."

"I don't know if anybody's getting anything here. Maybe I'm

not seeing something, but it doesn't exactly feel like Plato's Retreat here."

"Yeah? Just look around," Gary said, reaching for a mozzarella stick.

I pondered his words as I paced the hotel lobby, waiting for round four to start. There was definitely something to what Gary had said—not necessarily that sex was involved, even in some exquisitely sublimated way, but certainly some sort of obsessiveness was. For my part, I already felt wearied by the day's competition; and, yes, part of it was that I had practiced so much doing puzzles on a computer screen, not on paper. But people all around—in the hotel restaurant, on the sofas in the lobby, even in the tournament hall itself—were avidly filling in grids, as if they had some sort of craving for puzzles that was not satisfied by the six we were officially completing that day. The trade in crossword-puzzle books was as brisk as ever; there wasn't a hard copy of the *New York Times* to be had in the whole place, though someone had kindly left a photocopied stack of that day's puzzle on a table near the entrance to the Grand Ballroom. If you didn't watch out, you could trip over clutches of people feverishly solving away while sitting on the lobby floor.

I very much doubted that the constructors, rock stars that they were at this event, were getting any, either—because, let's face it, most are on the far side of fifty, and all would place high on any nerdishness index you could devise. Eggheads, as a group, just don't tend to be Lotharios (which is probably *why* they're eggheads). Brendan was single and more eligible for groupie adoration than any other constructor there, but he wasn't exactly getting mobbed by the girls. There was a group energy of the sort you might associate with a mass mating ritual, sure; but nobody was ripping off their clothes in the Marriott taproom. They were too busy doing or talking about puzzles.

I wondered if sex weren't in fact somehow involved in all this, although at a level even more subtle than that of sublimation. If you accept my theory that the impulse to solve puzzles might represent the archaic remnant of a survival strategy coded into humanity a hundred thousand years or more ago, you could also carry it a step further to try to explain why things like sexual perversion exist today. Imagine being one among twenty in a Neolithic band; you would have wanted to create as many offspring as possible, simply because you could never be sure how much of your genetic payload would, given predators, enemy humans, and unexpected cliffs, live on into another generation. In our large, organized, hierarchical society, on the other hand, the individual needn't worry so much about procreation as such. If your home is in a big city with running water and sewers and enough food around for everyone, you can afford to spend a greater proportion of your innate sexual energy on things that are fun for you, such as doing it while wearing a bunny suit and fireman's boots or solving ten crossword puzzles a day. In other words, the vast amounts of intellectual energy expended on puzzles at Stamford, it strikes me, is at best a distant behavioral cognate of the sexual activities most of us know go on behind barred doors every day (or night) in Anytown, U.S.A. After all, it's easy enough to associate all obsessive activities with an underlying sexual impulse, but I doubt such a connection holds true with the solving of crossword puzzles. A grid is after all only a grid, and it would take a truly pathological mind to conflate it with anything else.

No. What was going on—what makes the American Crossword Puzzle Tournament such an unusual event to observe, let alone take part in—was loads of pure, red-blooded, all-American obsession, the sort of thing you'd come across at, say, a Bakelite collectors' meet or a high-profile celebrity trial. It's a circus atmosphere, really, although in this case the participants are simultaneously the audience *and* the performing seals. There is a manic quality to the goings-on, granted, but the point is, no one would come here with the specific purpose of trying to get some pani-pani on the side. (Except for me, of course, if half a chance arose, but thankfully it never did: The prospect of having my scores toted up by the irate father of a seduced Bre-something was not one I relished.) The people attending the tournament were there to indulge in their ruling passion, and none but Gary and I were going to read into their cruciverbalist frenzy anything but pure and innocent ludic self-gratification.

Brendan and I returned to our seats (he'd spent part of the lunch break having a dip in the hotel pool) a few minutes before the round-four puzzle was handed out—an open fifteen-by-fifteen by Patrick Merrell with a word count of seventy-six, which would make it equivalent to a Wednesday *New York Times* crossword. The puzzle's title was "What is the answer?"; within it were four clues as to what this "answer" was, and figuring it out won an extra 100 points for the solver. Anyone familiar with kids' word games should have guessed that the answer was, well, "What"—all you do is transform the interrogative sentence into a declarative one. The four clues were "Hint #1 to solving this puzzle," "Hint #2 to solving this puzzle," "With 29-Down, where hints #1 and #2 will lead you, and "See 67-Across." Following these leads, you ended up with "four," "grid," and "corners," and the four corner squares in the grid contained the letters "w," "h," "a," and "t"—"What." I really, really wished I'd figured this out at the time, but I didn't.

Both Brendan and I finished in eight minutes. I made a strategic error of the highest order by failing to figure out what the bonus answer was—I don't know what I wrote in the little space left for it at the top left corner of the page, but it certainly wasn't "what." A larger issue emerges here: how absolutely critical it is to keep in mind that accuracy is far more valuable a factor than time. The "what" answer was worth 100 points; I should have spent up to three minutes—risking a mere 75 points of lost time—nailing it down. (When I did the puzzle later at home, I got it in ten seconds.) I also should have checked my answers to the puzzle itself, making sure that the grid was correct in its entirety, since it wasn't: I had answered 56-Down, "She, in Brazil" with ESA instead of ELA, which made 60-Across, "Followers," into the nonsensical TAGASONGS instead of TAGALONGS. Had I spent one minute and 25 points checking my down clues against my acrosses, I would have spotted the error and earned the perfect-fill bonus of 150 points. Instead I scored 740—10 points for the correct 74 words out of a total of 76—plus 275 points for finishing eleven minutes under time (actually, 300 points for twelve minutes less the 25-point wrong-letter penalty); Brendan scored 1,310. I figured he was still 75 points ahead of me, which was now close to true: Brendan 5,180, me 5,120.

After this heat, just out of curiosity, I went back into the Grand Ballroom when there were just under four minutes left on the clock. About a third of the contestants were still at their places, scratching away furiously or staring ashen-faced into the middle distance, depending on how they were faring with Merrell's puzzle. When the clock ran down to 00:00, most of this last third were still there; this pattern pretty much repeated itself all tournament long, with the top, middle, and bottom thirds leaving or staying, as the case might be, in the same regular and predictable order no matter the difficulty of the puzzle. As one woman headed out of the room after time was called, I overheard her complaining about the conversational roar made in the corridor by the earlier-finishing contestants. "It really, really isn't fair," she said. In fact, the source of the noise was the brisk trade in crossword books, T-shirts, and the like the tournament sponsors were carrying out just on the other side of the ballroom doors: The noise the woman was complaining about was the din of commerce.

If the third grid in the tournament was a beast, the fifth was a monster. Created by Stanley Newman, puzzle editor of *New York Newsday* and the then-fastest solver in crossword history, it was a ninety-six-word seventeen-by-seventeen with a time limit of twenty-five minutes called "Compound Fractures." As you'll have noticed by now, the Stamford event is a warm, friendly, and laid-back affair—you couldn't gather together a nicer bunch of people unless you were organizing an international convention of flying nuns. In the wake of Newman's puzzle, though, it came perilously close to turning ugly.

As you'd expect, the people who attend the Stamford tournament can at times lose perspective when talking about puzzles with nonpuzzlers. I learned this a few months after the 2004 event, when I was talking on the phone with Will Shortz. I told him I'd just been bitterly complaining to a friend because, for the first time in close to a decade, I hadn't managed to complete a Sunday puzzle in less than half an hour. (This particular one took me a humiliating thirty-two minutes.) "Well," Will responded after a pause, "I don't expect you got much sympathy from your friend." He was right; I didn't, and deservedly so. My point, though, is that when the Grand Ballroom at the Stamford Marriott is still *two-thirds* filled with the fastest solvers on the planet as the clock is cascading into the low single digits, whatever constructor responsible for their collective ordeal had better use that remaining time to check out of the hotel and head for higher ground.

The conceit of "Compound Fractures" was that five of its long across clues—three seventeen, two fifteen letters long—were close to nonsensical terms that happened to sound like the names of chemical compounds. For instance, 73-Across, "Thirst for knowledge," clued out as CRANIUMAPPETITE; 19-Across, "Prison riot participant," yielded PANDEMONIUMINMATE; "Plant pest" at 22-Across turned out to be the almost incomprehensible GERANIUMTERMITE. When I talked with Will and Stan about it much later, both expressed reservations about the puzzle—"I do admit it was a bit arch," Will said—but the fifth grid at Stamford is traditionally the hardest, and both men thought "Compound Fractures," despite its faults, fit the bill.

My first lucky turn on the road to solving this particularly gruesome puzzle fell in the southwest corner of the grid, where the 66-Down clue was "Life-jacket stuffing" (five letters), which I knew, for reasons I'll explain later in the book, was a tropical plantstuff called "kapok." The first vowel of that word corresponded to the first vowel in the answer PANDEMONIUMINMATE, which in turn made it possible for me to figure out both that infernal answer and the theme of the puzzle overall.

The cluing was *hard*, but for whatever reason—maybe getting KAPOK was all the encouragement I needed—I was on Stan's wavelength. I later told him that the reason I'm not a doctor today is largely because I couldn't get through organic chemistry in college, and so I am sensitive about things that merely looked like the compounds that have kept me from enjoying an income of three hundred thousand dollars a year ever since. Most others in the Stamford Marriott ballroom *weren't* on his, or his puzzle's, wavelength. I managed to finish with seven minutes to spare on the clock; Will Shortz himself picked up and marked the time on my puzzle, which was odd, since I was halfway across the hall from where he usually stationed himself, and when solvers started raising their hands he rarely had the chance to stray more than a couple of feet from his habitual post. When I stood to leave, I was shocked: It was twenty-three minutes into the twenty-five-minute heat, and three-quarters of the contestants, Brendan included, were still working hard at the puzzle before them.

I did better than Brendan this time—965 to his 890—but I had made a crucial error that kept me from fully capitalizing on my connection with Stan. At 39-Down was the clue "Narita Airport client," and, not knowing offhand the name of any Japanese air carrier but JAL, I guessed that ADA would do. I was wrong. The correct answer was ANA, which corresponded with the across clue ("1928 Winter Olympics star," which was Sonja HENIE, not "Hedie," as I mistakenly wrote down—you'll recall why). As it was, Brendan and I were now functionally tied, with overall scores of 6,085 for me and 6,070 for him, with only two more puzzles to go before the finalists' round. I practically somersaulted out of the ballroom to await the end of the heat.

"Heat" in this case was never a more apposite word. When you look at the results columns from the 2004 tournament, the first four all kind of look the same, with the averages clustered fairly tightly around figures anywhere between 1,000 and 1,200. When you look at the results for puzzle five, all you see is a long, dismal list of 400s, 500s, and 600s, with a classic bell-curve scattering of higher and lower scores to either side—an indication that the unprecedented had happened and that close to half the contestants had failed entirely to complete Stan Newman's puzzle. There was so much grumbling when it was all over that I suggested, I think only half jokingly, to Will that he might want to tell Stan it would be a wise idea to make himself scarce for a while. Newman may or may not have intended to make this fifth puzzle quite as impossible—it was "mean," to use the characterization he himself later proffered—as it was; what I do know is that, for a couple of hours, a whole lot of people at Stamford were extremely interested in having a word or two with him. None of them was smiling.

The sixth and final puzzle of the day was a straightforward nineteen-by-nineteen by another longtime *Times* constructor, Maura Jacobson, whose fondness for groan-inducing puns is legendary among crosswords fans. "Clothes Call" was a 120-answer grid with a time limit of thirty minutes. Of course, all the puns—double entendres, actually—had to do with items of apparel, so it was a safe bet that this one would be a pure horse race in which whoever could write fastest would win, since it doesn't take long to figure out a clue such as "Hat for a woman having her hair set?" (answer: ROLLERDERBY) or that the answer to "Analyst's lingerie?" will be FREUDIANSLIP. Nonetheless, I again screwed up one single square in the puzzle, again forfeited 195 points, and again Brendan finished before me—this time by two minutes—and turned in a perfect fill. Once again, I hadn't checked my across answers against my down ones. In this case my mistake was 24-Across, "High hat," a four-letter word that I filled in with the noun SNOB; had I only checked against the down clue—"Baseball's Felipe" for ALOU—I would have known to fill in the across clue with the verb SNUB instead. This is the sort of sloppiness that can make a grown man weep.

Though my jotted totals at the time placed me ahead of him (no one calculates for errors), Brendan finished the sixth puzzle correctly in nineteen minutes to earn 1,825 points; I finished in twenty-one, with one mistake, to earn 1,580. At 7,895 to 7,665, he was safely and irretrievably ahead of me overall. I had detected a distinct coolness emanating from him since the Stan Newman debacle, and certainly couldn't help but notice a renewed cheer about him now that he'd obviously trumped me (he didn't know by how much) with the Jacobson puzzle. At the same time, I still thought I'd aced the Newman, and I had no idea I'd made stupid mistakes in the Merrell and Jacobson puzzles, so I looked forward to the posting of everyone's respective standings at the end of the day. I very, very much hoped it would be an inconsolable Brendan who repaired to the hotel bar after digesting the results to fortify himself against past misfortunes and the upcoming evening's rather forbidding-looking "social" events.

As you may have guessed, that was not the way things turned out.

Chapter 6

ATTACK OF THE

HIGH SCHOOL GIrLS

If the 2003 American Crossword Puzzle Tournament found its Achilles' heel in the Case of the Missing Analog Clock, the 2004 event almost met with utter disaster because a few local high school girls apparently didn't know how to read a digital timepiece. As a consequence, the unfortunate young women earned for themselves a permanent, if not laudable, place in crossword history.

Some of us sensed at the very outset of heat six that something was amiss. We really started worrying the moment when Will Shortz announced that a half-dozen girls from Stamford's Westhill High School had been hired to help out in the tabulation room all day (the rumored recompense was thirty bucks and lunch), and he'd promised them that in the sixth and final heat of Saturday's competition they could pick up contestants' puzzles when they raised their hands and mark down on them their completion times—Will's idea was that the girls would appreciate seeing in flesh and blood and action the solvers they had as yet known only as impersonal columns of numbers.

You could almost feel the wave of unease spread through the crowd—not because it was high school girls per se who were helping to score our efforts, but simply because it was a changing of horses in midride with no clear reason why it was necessary. But we participants forged on and handed in our puzzles when we were done (mine and Brendan's were picked up and marked by Will himself, thank heavens), and, in the excitement generated afterward by the announcement that the tournament standings based on the first day's competition had been posted in the lobby, most of us forgot all about the young ladies from Westhill High.

If you suddenly announced you were going to pay people a thousand dollars, cash, to accept an ingot of gold from you, I doubt the crush at your front door would be greater than the one before those five pieces of paper posted on the north wall of the Stamford Marriott's lobby. When I finally made it through to the front, I noted with some dismay my position—184th out of five hundred or so—and with some satisfaction Brendan's: merely 172nd. It did seem somewhat odd that Brendan was ahead of me, since I'd figured Stan Newman's fifth puzzle had given me the edge on him. Of course, I also felt a slight hope that Brendan had made at least one mistake on the sixth puzzle, so there was the glimmer of a chance that, once the full day's results had been tabulated, I might perhaps come out ahead after all. The next day's puzzle, the seventh and last in terms of open competition at the tournament, would settle the issue. And, luckily, it was a twenty-one-by-twenty-one, or Sunday-size, grid with a time limit of a generous forty-five minutes. Since I usually get through a Sunday *New York Times* puzzle in anything between seventeen and twenty-five minutes, I figured I'd be able to overtake him—if I had my full seven hours and didn't stay up too late.

After enduring a few minutes of—I hope—good-natured ribbing and gloating from my favorite crossword-puzzle constructor, I repaired to the hotel bar (Brendan floated off to some other cruciverbalist revel in a room upstairs), where I ordered a beer and ran into my lunchtime interlocutor Gary, the contractor from Pennsylvania. I didn't quite catch where he stood among the pack—the subject was the hot topic of the evening, much like SAT scores are around the time college boards send back their entrance-exam test results—but we did talk about the obvious front runners.

"Jon Delfin's looking good," I said.

"Yeah, but my money's on this skinny black-haired kid. Always times out first—or he did in half the heats today, as far as I could tell."

"What about Al Sanders?" I asked. Al Sanders was ranked first after the initial five rounds; I sat at the same table as he at the next day's preawards lunch and came to know him a little better. A man of proverbially few words, he described himself as a project manager from Colorado—but I got the sense that, if I ever ended up working for him, a few of his spare, slowly enunciated words would be capable of demolishing whatever positive notions I had about my work ethic, competence, and ability to do anything but waste everybody else's time. Al, at that lunch, didn't seem a fun guy.

"Nah," said Gary. "Sanders will choke at the board. He always does, every year."

Like Ellen Ripstein until she won the tournament in 2001, Sanders is the Susan Lucci of the crossword world—a person who perennially is runner-up for, but never winner of, the grand prize. (Just in case you don't have a subscription to *Soap Opera Digest*, the prize Lucci never won until 1999 was an Emmy Award for best daytime television actress in the United States—she'd been nominated for it eighteen times before.) Since he began attending the American Crossword Puzzle Tournament in 1999, Sanders has placed fourth once, in 2000, and third four times, in 2003, 2002, 2001, and 1999. ("Al should set up a whiteboard at home and practice on it," Will

Shortz later said to me. "He needs to learn how to win the finals, because he clearly dominates in open competition." From Will's words, you can foresee that Al failed to win again in 2004.)

At this point, suffering from a surfeit of socializing and feeling a little wiped after the day's puzzling, I returned to my room to shower and read some more *Gravity's Rainbow* before heading back downstairs for the new round of fun and games scheduled between eight and ten-thirty: A quiz contest hosted by constructor Mel Rosen and his wife, Peggy, a group solving of a "crossword mystery" concocted by Margaret Petherbridge way back in 1946, a photographic tribute to her by Will Shortz, and finally a cavalcade of personal reminiscences about crossword-dom's grand old lady by a list of people long enough to seem like the Golden Horde's order of battle. For the record, I wouldn't recommend that anyone attending the American Crossword Puzzle Tournament take along Thomas Pynchon's magnum opus to read during the event; passages early in the book evoke life during World War II at "the White Visitation," a fictional psy-ops center on the Kentish coast of England staffed by a bizarre collection of mind-readers, Ouija-board fanatics, statisticians, Ouspenskians, spirit-channelers, and superannuated brigadiers who in the aggregate come uncomfortably close to approximating the crowd you mix with in March at the Stamford Marriott.

At any rate, I reluctantly forsook the quiet of my room and headed back downstairs, where Brendan was nowhere to be found— yet another wine-soaked Cru gathering was to blame, I supposed. I drifted into the Grand Ballroom, which was just beginning to fill up with tournament participants looking forward to the evening's scheduled entertainment. I noted that few of the cool kids—the younger constructors like Brendan and Misha and the under-fifty crowd of solvers who hung around them—attended; the only one I spotted was Peter Gordon, who took a seat near the most convenient exit. Then Will Shortz walked to the podium and spoke the words that confirmed the darkest fears of all of us who had felt that shudder of dread when he had introduced the high school girls at the outset of the sixth heat. What he said went something like this:

"Hello, everyone. I'm afraid to say there's been a slight problem with the scoring in the last round. It turns out that some of the high school girls we invited to pick up puzzles and mark down finishing times recorded, in some cases, not the minutes remaining on the clock, but the seconds. What that means is that some of the times recorded actually exceeded the forty-five minutes allotted for the round, and we have no way of telling, from the puzzles that were picked up by them, what the real times were. So we're going to pass around pieces of paper and ask you to write on them your name, your contestant number, and the time you remember finishing puzzle six in."

To say that the crowd broke into a quiet murmur of dismay would be a pronounced understatement—it was more like the sort of noise you'd hear from the floor of the House of Representatives if the majority leader announced that congressional franking privileges had just been suspended. The point is, I had the sense that contestants at the American Crossword Puzzle Tournament are prone to think, even under the best of conditions, that the scoring process, though overseen by the highly respected *Times* constructor Fred Piscop, is not necessarily all that reliable. (Indeed, while finishing up my *Boston Globe* article about the tournament the year before, I checked the final standings as reported on the tournament Web site to buttress a point I'd made that the fastest finisher I'd seen then—a Boston-based freelance textbook editor named Katherine

Bryant—had not placed better than sixty-fourth out of five hundred; in fact she'd placed thirteenth, which was adjusted in the standings only after my article had gone to press. Thus far in the 2004 tournament, I'd been slithering in and out of the various venues in the hopes of avoiding her.) I'm not saying that the scoring team at Stamford doesn't know its job, because it does. What I am saying is that scoring three thousand puzzles, each with its own idiosyncrasies in terms of handwriting style and relative legibility, in the space of a couple of hours is labor-intensive and naturally prone to at least a few errors.

I duly filled in the piece of paper placed before me, noting just that both my and Brendan Quigley's sixth puzzles had been picked up and marked by Will Shortz himself—no possibility of unorthodox scoring there. But you can believe that the subject of post–fun-and-games taproom conversation later in the night was mostly about the sad decline of high school educational standards—an observer ignorant of the fact he was in the middle of a crossword-tournament crowd could be excused for believing he'd stumbled into a particularly activist meeting of the National Education Association. And "high school girls" instantly and permanently entered the cruciverbalist lexicon in the same way as, during World War II, "snafu" did that of the common G.I.

Once the commotion died down, Will introduced Mel and Peggy Rosen. Mel Rosen is a constructor whose trivia-heavy grids have been appearing in the pages of the *New York Times* since the days when Will Weng was the paper's puzzle editor. He and Peggy live on Marco Island, in Florida, and every week they and a few friends host a trivia contest at a place called "The English Pub" in nearby Naples. The night's first event, then, was a fifteen-part challenge in which we contestants had to figure out whether such questions as these were true or false:

Steve Jobs and Steve Wozniak chose "Apple" as the name for their garage-built computer as a sales ploy because they wanted to sell it in schools. They picked the name so they could use the slogan "An Apple for the Teacher." What's Up, Mac: True or false?

Members of the band Duran Duran have recently confessed that—just for the fun of it—they used to compete in Duran Duran lookalike contests . . . and they usually won. Duran Duran–like Duran Duran: True or false?

Forensic scientists have discovered that when someone tells a lie, the stress increases the vascular pressure in the liar's nose, causing it to become measurably larger. Pinocchio Effect: True or false?

In 1895 Gelett Burgess wrote the lines "I never saw a purple cow / I never hope to see one / But I can tell you anyhow / I'd rather see than be one." Almost everyone "of a certain age" has heard those lines. What most people don't know is: Twenty years later, embarrassed and dismayed by the notoriety of that little bit of nonsense, Burgess wrote "Ah, yes, I wrote 'The Purple Cow' / I'm sorry, now, I wrote it! / But I can tell you, anyhow / I'll kill you if you quote it!" Rueful Sequel: True or false?

The answers are, respectively, false, true, true, and true; out of the overall fifteen, I scored eleven correct, which put me by a count of hands into something like the top thirtieth percentile among the people in the room; only one got all fifteen correct. I repeat close to verbatim four of Mel and Peggy's questions not just to brag about my potential for doing okay, should I ever find myself of an evening at a pub in Naples, Florida, but to convey how pencil-necked the crowd at the Stamford tournament actually is: We ate this stuff up, and found in it the perfect emotional antidote (in the short term, at least) for the bombshell Will Shortz had dropped on us not twenty minutes before. Mel and Peggy mentioned that, by tradition, the patrons at their local tavern would occasionally yell out "Switzerland!" in response to particularly unanswerable questions, so of course it was shouted out two or three times during the course of the proceedings—those who come to the Stamford tournament can be counted on to provide cheesy commentary. In a sense, it's why they're here in the first place.

I stuck around to watch but not participate in Margaret Petherbridge's crossword-puzzle mystery. When, at long, interminable last, Will gave the signal for her descendants to introduce themselves—and there were endless numbers of them, children, grandchildren, great-nephews and nieces, so much so that one began to wonder how she ever found the time aside from producing offspring to edit as many puzzles as she did—I gave it a couple of minutes before discreetly slipping out to the refuge of the Marriott bar. I figured I could catch the photomontage tribute later, after a fortifying beverage or two.

Crosswords and Fertility

The first person I ran into after ordering a beer in the crowded taproom was the only one I'd been assiduously trying to avoid since I arrived on Friday evening—Katherine Bryant, the editor from Boston. I should mention that the piece I'd written for the *Globe* had the singular misfortune to run immediately after the United

States declared war on Saddam Hussein's Baathist regime in Iraq. At the last minute, it was edited into a much shorter version than the one I had sent in—it's a sad thing, but foreign invasions tend to take precedence, in newspaper editors' orders of priority, over humorous human interest reportage such as the covering of crossword tournaments. (Go figure.) One of the unanticipated effects of my piece's last-minute abbreviation, however, was that certain passages within it that were retained in the final printed version assumed a disproportionate weight; one of these, I am very sorry to say, was a description of Katherine racing out of the first heat in the 2003 tournament, after something like three minutes and change, shaking with adrenaline from the excitement of the bout. I used a Thoroughbred racer metaphor to capture the image, which would have been unremarkable in a thousand-word article; in a four-hundred-word piece, though, it kind of stood out, which was why I was loath to talk to her on this occasion—you don't want to run into a top-drawer crossword solver after you've gone on record not only misrepresenting her actual past performance but also intimating that she resembles, in effect, a horse.

I really didn't have to worry, though. If there's anything you quickly learn at a crossword-puzzle tournament, it's that most anyone attending will give you the benefit of the doubt, even when you've done them the disservice—in their hometown newspaper, to boot—of comparing them to an ungulate (though at least to a highly fleet-of-foot member of that animal order).

"Don't worry about it," Katherine said. "It was a neat little piece in the *Globe*—you made the tournament sound fun."

"But I said you came in sixty-fourth."

"Yeah, I know. There was a screw-up in the early postings. You can't be blamed for that. I knew where I placed, so it didn't matter to me."

"I didn't mean to compare you to a horse, either. I mean, that's just the way it came out. It was meant to be a compliment, and I'm really sorry it ended up not sounding like one. Really sorry."

"You're competing this time?"

"Yeah."

"How did you do on the fifth puzzle?"

"Okay, I think. I beat Brendan Quigley on the times. That's really the only bar I've set for myself—beating Brendan."

Katherine Bryant looked away from me; the expression in her eyes just before she focused on something at the other end of the room can only be described as pitying.

"He's a great constructor," she said after a diplomatic pause. "I don't think he's ever done that well in the standings, though."

Brendan, in fact, doesn't generally do that well in competition—again, it's the National League–pitcher syndrome, where very few constructors consistently outperform nonconstructors. There are some exceptions—Stanley Newman and Jon Delfin immediately leap to mind—but in each case these are people who were solvers first and only later became constructors. Newman, in fact, gave up competing at the American Crossword Puzzle Tournament after winning it in 1982 and then coming in second and third, respectively, over the next two years; he came to realize that he preferred, and made much more money, selling grids and, later, editing them—puzzle editors are indeed among the very few in the crossword business, again, who actually make a living at it. Jon Delfin took first prize seven times before publishing a crossword in the *New York Times* in 2004. (In that year's standings, he came in a humiliating second.)

Katherine and I chatted on for another few minutes, discussing, among other topics, the Brooklyn Navy Yard, a historic industrial zone of about four hundred acres in New York City that I'd recently become familiar with only because my younger sister had just taken a job there as the Navy Yard Development Corporation's chief archivist. Crossword people are generally folks who have a lively interest in trivia, so Katherine, being no exception to the norm, listened attentively as I answered her query about the place's history, which stretches from the 1790s to the present and includes, among other factoids, that it was the place where the USS *Maine* was built in 1898. Katherine and I parted on pleasant terms—I was still, however, fairly sure she wouldn't mind throwing a chair or something at me—and went off on our separate ways. She rejoined the crowd of young people with which she had been attending the tournament for the last five years. After finishing my second beverage, I went back to the Grand Ballroom, in which the next scheduled event was the photomontage tribute to Margaret Petherbridge Farrar, followed by a recollection of her long, long career as crossword-puzzle editor—it had started in 1919 and lasted until just before she died in 1984.

I have to admit I'm no great partisan of lifetime tributes or of festschrift books in which a dozen scholars publish their collected twenty-page memoirs about their beloved but now sadly passed-on colleague in the field (if you ever work in academic publishing, you will rapidly come to dread the moment your editor in chief asks you to oversee the production of this sort of book), but the Farrar presentation at the Twenty-seventh American Crossword Puzzle Tournament was, by any measure, a remarkably sadistic version of a painful but seemingly inescapable ordeal. Yes, Will Shortz deeply respects and admires Farrar and wanted to take this opportunity to honor her and her life. At the same time, I'm not sure he's aware that the rest of us—even when "the rest of us" means a gathering of crossword-puzzle maniacs—might not share completely in his conviction that every past detail about an admired and beloved predecessor's life is worthy of two hours of our time. I may be an ungrateful crank wholly unrepresentative of the way the rest of the crowd at Stamford felt in March 2004, but I can also say that most of the eyes I looked into were definitely glazed after ten o'clock.

Looking at Will Shortz in all his emceeing glory, obviously tickled pink by the fact that he could present so much crossword-puzzle history in flesh-and-blood form to so many avid fans of the institution, I felt profoundly guilty—I mean, I adore crosswords, too, but not so much that, under the circumstances, I could come close to approximating his passion for the subject's more obscure bits of technical and historical arcana. That's why, although I felt downright bad as I once more stole my way from my seat near the front center of the room to one of the more inconspicuous rear exits, I also experienced an overwhelming sense of relief. Because I knew the cool kids at the tournament weren't bathing in the wondrous presence of so many of Farrar's offspring. No—the cool kids couldn't care less; they were downing beers in the hotel bar.

The Perils of Overintellectualizing Crossword Puzzles

As I walked into the taproom, no doubt with a pronounced skulking to my gait, I almost careened into the attractive proctor I'd noticed in the course of the day's puzzle solving. She had changed outfits—jeans and white turtleneck had been replaced with a rather fetching blouse-and-skirt ensemble—and the transformation underscored what Brendan Quigley had noted but I hadn't (I've got to have that eyeglass prescription updated), that she was obviously quite, quite young.

But also nice and uncommonly mature, as it turned out; we got to talking, and in the course of the next five minutes I found out that she was a junior in college, a great lover of crossword puzzles, of course, and the niece of Helene Hovanec, the woman who had, since its inception in 1978, been Will Shortz's partner in crime in organizing the American Crossword Puzzle Tournament. Bree, as Helene's niece turned out to be named, had agreed to act as a proctor at the tournament because she was daunted by the prospect of competing with a large crowd of fanatical cruciverbalists—an interesting echo of the woman I'd met waiting for a cab outside the Stamford Marriott that Saturday morning the year before, who similarly was intrigued by the event but not especially eager to vie head-to-head against such opposition. It's true that the people who go to Stamford are very, very good, as a group, at solving crosswords and, for that matter, all manner of complicated word games. However, as Bree found out—as anyone who ventures a foot inside the hotel lobby on a tournament weekend soon does—you'd be hard put to find a collection of people anywhere who are as open, generous, kind, and interested in knowing about you as the Stamford puzzlers. The fact that everyone here is so friendly takes some of the pressure off; as you sit down for a heat, it's a comfort to think that the two hundred or so people who'll solve the puzzle faster and better than you are genuinely sympathetic to your plight. Bree told me she'd probably compete the following year; then, after exchanging a few more pleasantries with me, she sauntered off to do whatever it is Brees do on late Saturday evenings in huge, impersonal hotels located in the blighted centers of postapocalyptic southern Connecticut towns.

I had just ordered a stiff scotch and soda and was settling down at the bar with *Gravity's Rainbow*—Brendan and the crowd I'd run with the night before had yet to make their appearance, though the place was packed with a hundred or so other crossword-tournament attendees—when two women in their mid-twenties (I gathered) seated beside me struck up a conversation with me. (Outside of New York, the sight of someone reading at a bar is rare enough to excite comment; if you're single and aren't in New York and want to meet other people, I'd recommend it as an icebreaking tactic. Don't attempt this in the city itself, though: Your competition will be heavy, and most of the other readers will likely be more attractive and more successful and richer than you.)

The two women had an interesting enough story. One of them, Stephanie Parsons, was, like me, a rookie attendee at the tournament. The other, her friend Christina Kelly, was a video filmmaker recording Stephanie's adventures at the tournament for a documentary she was planning to make about it. Both hailed from Park Slope, the relatively recently yuppified section of Brooklyn where people new to the city often find their first apartment, or at any rate did about five years ago. Since I'd lived there for a number of years before the baby pram–and–Volvo set discovered it, we got to talking about the astounding and sudden transformation of the area from quiet urban backwater to absolute warren of hip bars, upscale food stores, and expensive clothing boutiques, not to mention ever more outrageous rental rates. Soon enough, though, I fell into ranting about my pet theories with respect to crossword puzzles. Now, normally, if anybody started talking to you about the more theoretical aspects of a word game late Saturday night in a hotel bar, you'd probably smile, nod some, and quietly ask the bartender if this weirdo could be removed from the place. But this was Stamford in March—Stephanie and Christina, bless their hearts, were actually interested in hearing what I had to say on the subject.

I'd been thinking, naturally, rather intensively about crossword puzzles—there's no way you can work your way through nearly two thousand of them in the space of six months without either going bats or attempting to impose some sort of rationality on such a bizarre way of spending all your time. Additionally, when you're spending a considerable amount of time with crossword-puzzle constructors, you tend to begin waxing theoretical about the minutiae of their daily activities whenever the opportunity arises.

Specifically, what I had really focused on was something that sounds like the stuff of a Ph.D. thesis advisor's nightmares: the congruence between crossword puzzles and one way of conceptualizing the writings of the Russo-American author and poet Vladimir Nabokov, whom I've long been fascinated by and who is familiar to people because of, in this order, the novel *Lolita*, butterflies, chess problems, and literary word games. As an undergraduate, I had convinced the then-visiting (now tenured) Yale professor Mikhail Alexandrov to let me attend his graduate seminar on Nabokov, the chief aim of which was to explore how the writer's literary oeuvre could be analyzed in terms of the interplay among aesthetics, ethics, and metaphysics within it. (I know, it sounds daunting and probably irrelevant—but it was Yale and we had to do something with our time.) I had theorized, after a day of fighting my way through ten or more *New York Times* puzzles in a row, that the same three elements as they operate in art and literature correspond to the way that the grid, the fill, and the cluing operate in crossword puzzles: The grid is aesthetic for obvious reasons, because the frequency and placement of black squares versus white make up the difference between an elegant and an inelegant puzzle; the fill is ethical because it has to adhere absolutely to certain practical rules; the cluing is a puzzle's metaphysics, since it represents the interface between the puzzle and its potential solvers—the means by which the disorder of nonsolution is transformed into the order of one complete and correct solution.

I hope that it was weariness from the day's tournament activity and the couple of rounds of drinks we'd gone through—and not utter boredom—that Stephanie and Christina both sported thousand-yard stares as I explained the theory in elaborate detail. In any event, Christina said, as they stood up to head back to their rooms, that she'd like me to appear in her video: Would I mind meeting her at seven the next morning to do the taping?

I agreed, of course, though had I known that my late-night intellectual gymnastics would transmute, come the bleary dawn, into weary platitudes, I would have slept in instead. Looking back now, I suspect that Christina Kelly is a master at using purposefully vague directing to elicit the comical truth from her interviewees, and this is borne out by what I ended up saying in her film. As you read it, imagine me feeling, after four hours' sleep, as if my brain had been exchanged for two quarts of motor oil, and struggling valiantly to make my way through sentences in which I had forgotten, after two or three successive clauses, whether I'd used a verb yet. I include only the initial "um," though in the tape there is an alarmingly large number of them:

> Um, the difference between the average solver—and I'm an average solver—and a superb solver is that the superb solver is both visually and symbolically oriented and able to pick up patterns in the cluing very, very quickly.

The next person who appears in the video is Tyler Hinman, the 2003 B Division winner who would, in 2004, place twelfth overall at the tournament. What he says, in sum, is about the opposite of what I did: That the best solvers hunt and peck for answers but simply do so more efficiently than anyone else, and grand theories about puzzling be damned. It's a funny juxtaposition; the whole film is funny. But, yes, I'm looking forward to the day I meet Christina Kelly again, because I'm eager to talk to her about my small role in her film—perhaps as eager as Katherine Bryant had been to meet me again after she read my *Globe* piece.

No more than ten seconds after Stephanie and Christina went up to their rooms, Brendan, another gaggle of admirers in his wake, showed up in the bar. Within moments, the rest of the previous night's collection of two-in-the-morning anagrammarians materialized again, this time with the addition of constructors Peter Abide and Jim Jenista, and once more the bunch of us closed down the bar at three or so in the morning.

The one thing I remember before belatedly tottering off to my room was explaining to Brendan what I'd expounded not an hour earlier to Stephanie and Christina, all the stuff about grids and fills and cluing and aesthetics and ethics and metaphysics. Brendan pondered for a second before setting his last beer of the night onto the bar counter and turning to face me.

"Marc," he said, swaying slightly but looking me straight in the eye, "you're talking about crossword puzzles. It's really not that complicated. They're just *games*."

Chapter 7

THE LaST
PUZZLE

It's nine in the morning on Sunday and I'm seated beside Brendan Emmett Quigley in the packed Grand Ballroom of the Stamford Marriott, waiting for the proctors to hand out the seventh and last regular-competition grid of the Twenty-seventh American Crossword Puzzle Tournament. As in the five prior heats, all the faces around me are familiar; the participants at Stamford don't tend to switch places much, which makes them, after only one day of competition, feel like veteran riders of commuter trains, who likewise tend to come to a rapid and permanent collective agreement about seating arrangements. For a reason that escapes me, I'm not feeling all that well, physically: Sometimes there's an odd tinniness when I hear someone speak, and my balance doesn't seem to be as reliable as it usually is. Thus far this morning, I've been interviewed by a filmmaker, in my turn have interviewed a half-dozen crossword constructors and tournament-goers, drunk two or three large cups of hotel coffee, and tried but failed to rise to the challenge of eating breakfast. I realize I've in fact not eaten anything since lunch Saturday.

Worst of all, Brendan is smiling beatifically. The standings after the first five rounds have been posted and, contrary to my calculations, he's ahead of me, still placing 172nd out of five hundred as compared to my 184th. I thought that my routing him in the fifth puzzle would have resulted in precisely the reverse situation; scores from the sixth have not yet been factored in because the high school girls' problems with recording times have forced a late retabulation, but he did better than I on that one anyway. The puzzle we're about to be handed is a standard Sunday-style twenty-one-by-twenty-one composed by Mike Shenk, the editor of the *Wall Street Journal* puzzle, with a time limit of forty-five minutes. So my hopes are sanguine that the smile on Brendan's face could reverse directions once the final standings are posted—if only I can clip a minute or two off my Sunday-puzzle average time now.

The level of intellectual and nervous energy in the giant room is palpable; everyone knows roughly where they stand in general competition. The top 100 or so will be trying to claw their way far enough up the tournament ladder to qualify for divisional laurels; 398 participants in the lower 80 percent of the field are clutching at the remote but hopeful prospect that this last puzzle in the tournament will be, for them, the sort of home run that shoots them high enough in the standings to warrant bragging rights; of the two remaining attendees at the 2004 event, one is simply hoping the crossword gods will be kind enough to let him beat the other, the smirking red-haired constructing genius in the chair beside him.

At the same time, everyone knows that gathered in this cavernous chamber are the best of the best, in crossword terms—even placing last in the tournament means something, because who else, scratching their hesitant way through a Friday *New York Times* puzzle on the seven-fifteen train into the city, would willingly attempt the same puzzle under the awful pressure of a clock set to a twenty-five-minute limit? The least competent, least quick solver among the throng waiting impatiently around you would still leave in the dust about 90 percent of the general population who've ever taken a stab at filling in a crossword—most likely the one that appears weekly in *TV Guide*. You get the impression, waiting for this last *New York Times*-style puzzle of the tournament to be placed facedown on the table in front of you, that the intellectual wattage in this place is high enough to juice all the light bulbs in any medium-size city you could care to name. (The person who could figure out a means to do that is probably, in fact, sitting within your eyesight at this very moment.)

Then the analog clock by which all our lives are ruled turned nine, the scheduled hour to begin the last crossword of the tournament. As the giant digital timepiece in the Marriott Grand Ballroom flipped from "00:00" to "45:00," Will Shortz's voice called out the iconic "Go!" This seventh and last puzzle was entitled "And the last shall be first"; with a word count of 140, it was likely to be a breeze. At Will's cue, I flipped over the piece of paper that bore it and set to work.

"And the last shall be first," I quickly figured out, was an indication that each of the theme answers was a phrase in which one or more consecutive words ended and began with the same letter, one of which was to be dropped from the fill. The clue for 16-Down, for instance, was "Source of some student funds," and the answer was PARTIMEMPLOYMENT; the clue for 71-Across was "Procrastinate," and the answer was LETHINGSLIDE. I worked my way counterclockwise through the grid starting from the upper-left corner (the "northwest," in crossword parlance), so it wasn't until I was very nearly done with the thing that I encountered, in the northeast at 22-Across, the clue "The USS *Maine* was built there." I let out a quick laugh, which must have surprised the solvers working in the same part of the room as me; crosswords are frequently witty and sometimes quite funny in a cornball sort of way, but as a rule never what you would call knee-slappers. The answer to 22-Across was BROOKLYNAVYARD—the very topic I'd raised in my mea-culpish talk with Katherine Bryant the night before. With twenty-four minutes left on the clock, I was about to raise my hand to call over one of the proctors when I noticed that one of my answers—DEKA at 38-Down as an answer to the clue "Ten: prefix"—looked weird to me; the standard spelling in English is with a "c." I switched the letters and noted I had only five seconds before the clock was going to tick over to twenty-three. Brendan and I raised our hands at the same time—a dead heat of twenty-one minutes, which ain't bad for a Sunday *Times* puzzle, and I knew my fill was error-free.

For about fifteen seconds, that is. As we left the room, Brendan said, "I don't know if it quite worked, that 'k' in DEKA."

"No, it didn't, not in English, anyway. I changed it back to a 'c' at the very end."

"So you think that SKIMPS spelled with a 'c' is English, too?"

I must have blanched; at any rate, Brendan was looking at me cockeyed.

"What," I asked, a catch in my throat, "was the cross clue again?"

"I think it was 'Practices parsimony.' "

"Oh, hell."

Because Brendan was right—DEKA may have been iffy, but using a "c" in SKIMPS was definitely out. Or at least I'd never seen it as a variant spelling, and, ever since I was a child, I've paid pretty close attention to issues of spelling in English.

"Dammit," I said. "There goes 150 points."

"You mean 170 points"—because I'd lose ten each for the misspelled SKIMPS and DEKA. It was to be only cold comfort, a few weeks later, when Will Shortz told me that, aside from the devilish fifth puzzle, this particular cross in the seventh tripped up more than a third of the contestants; it helped, in other words, to separate the wheat from the chaff, standings-wise. The reason that comfort was cold is that, I thought bitterly to myself, the better solvers *hadn't* made the same mistake. The better solvers, as Stanley Newman would tell me, tend to do more than merely glance over their completed grids to make sure they haven't left a square unfilled—the better competitive solvers practice checking each across clue against each down clue, because they've completely internalized the fact that the 25 points you lose to that careful examination is more than offset by the 150 points you earn for turning in a perfect fill. I still don't think DEKA was a wholly fair answer; on the other hand, if I'd spent five more seconds thinking about it instead of refusing to cede another full minute to Brendan, I would have realized that, compared to the spelling of SKIMPS that my last-second change produced, it was a no-brainer to go with the "k." I also learned the lesson that all of us learn all the time, but that few of us (the happy few who place high in crossword competitions) manage to assimilate: that your first instinct in any situation is usually the correct one.

By this time, the two-thirds of the attendees who had still been rooted in their seats as Brendan and I finished that last puzzle were starting to file out of the Grand Ballroom. I decided to take a walk in the bracing air outside—I was still fuming about SCIMPS—and in the main lobby of the hotel ran into Katherine.

"Hey, thanks!" she cried out.

"For what?" I'd completely forgotten about the Brooklyn Navy Yard.

"Where the USS *Maine* was built—wasn't that just amazing? We were just talking about it last night."

"Yeah, it really was. Say, you don't think 'skimps' is ever spelled with a 'c,' do you?" I was hoping she thought it was, in Chaucer or Caedmon's Paraphrase or something.

She looked at me with the same expression of almost maternal pity that had come over her face when she was speaking about Brendan the night before.

"No."

Unintended Consequences of Being Temporally Challenged

Generally speaking, the American Crossword Puzzle Tournament is a well-run affair—it has to be, in a sense, because crossword puzzlers tend to be, well, a little anxious to find out where they've placed this year, and they are wont to gripe when that knowledge isn't made available to them at the time it has been promised them on the tournament schedule. Perfectionists just seem to be that way, and anyone who does a crossword regularly tends to be a fan of perfectionism. Throw in the fact that we're talking here about *competitive* perfectionists, and you can imagine how tense and nervous was the crowd at the Stamford Marriott waiting in the hotel lobby, many wallowing in their despair (though a remarkably large proportion of them were merrily doing puzzles), as the scheduled time for posting the final tournament results came and went with nary an indication as to when, if ever, those results would appear.

At this point in the tournament, there was a strong undercurrent of dissatisfaction about the organizers' decision to use those high school girls as proctors in the sixth round. Rumor had it that, hidden away in their basement tabulation room, Will Shortz, Fred Piscop, and the rest of the counting crew were tearing out their hair trying to figure out a way to recover from the disaster—and not making much progress at it. The crowd at Stamford is, again, unusually civil as crowds go, but as the clock struck eleven A.M., when the A, B, and C division winners were slated to face off in round eight, the championship round, and the Grand Ballroom had been partitioned off in preparation, and Will Shortz had yet to appear for even the preliminary bout of banter and last-minute word-quizzing—well, it felt like a Red Sox game in which the Yankees have just committed some especially grievous foul and the home-team fans are waiting to see what the umpires are going to do about it. (A side note: Now that the Sox have actually defeated the Yankees in the World Series, Boston fans are generally more mellow. I'm talking Boston fans in the years before the 2004 *annus mirabilis*.)

The very best solvers—those who place in the top 10 percent or so at the tournament—tend to be the least nerve-addled when something goes wrong with the standings. Now, as I've said, these people are freaks of nature; there's no denying the fact that someone who can get through a Saturday-level *New York Times* puzzle in ten minutes or less is somehow different from the rest of us. And they are—they're more disciplined, more confident in their abilities, and icier-blooded than their cocompetitors, which is what probably gives them their edge: Under pressure, they simply can think better than everyone else. Anyone who had paid attention at the tournament knew who the top-three Division A finalists would be, just from the standings after the first five puzzles: Jon Delfin, Al Sanders, and Trip Payne, all of whom had placed among the final three many times before. The sight of *those* guys nervously pacing around, the occasional cries of complaint from within the gathered crowd, and the fact that, by now, very few people were actually doing puzzles must have unnerved the tournament organizers. Under the circumstances, they figured they should do the logical thing: Set up an impromptu round of trivia and word games.

The extent to which the crowd eagerly accepted this new set of circumstances tells you two things. First, that the collective thirst for eggheaded intellectual games had not, as yet, been entirely slaked. Second, that everyone, in their general niceness, was hoping that someone in the group would shout out the funny thing at the right moment and would perfectly defuse the gathering tension. We were, you see, at the American Crossword Puzzle Tournament, which is meant to represent—it had always represented—the one weekend in the collective year devoid even of the possibility of nastiness. When the distractive trivia games began, it suddenly dawned on me what that bit of soothing whimsy would be.

On the previous night, remember, constructor Mel Rosen and his wife had hosted their trivia bar game, in which someone inevitably yelled out the word "Switzerland," to general hilarity, after a particularly impenetrable question had been posed. On this anxious Sunday morning, I was standing in the far back of the room, having a chat with a very easygoing fellow of about my age named John Old, a stay-at-home dad from Illinois. I couldn't hear the trivia questions being asked, since the room was too noisy. I knew, though, that somebody needed to yell "Switzerland!" I also knew that I had neither the inclination nor the sense of comic timing to do so myself. Peter Gordon was standing to the other side of me; from our late Friday and Saturday activities, I knew he was just the ticket this crowd needed, being the sort of quiet introvert who makes for the better kind of improvisational comedian. I mentioned the idea to him, he nodded, and I returned to my chat with John Old. Sure enough, a minute or two later the crowd fell silent, pondering some complicated question involving anagrams. Peter shouted out "Switzerland!" and the place fell apart—amid the laughter, good humor was reinstated as the reigning sentiment of the day, and I sat back and basked in the highly reflected glory that constituted the single most positive thing I'd ever or likely ever would contribute to a national crossword-puzzle tournament.

As if on cue, Will Shortz walked into the room. His opening words were a tonic to his audience—anyone who has heard him on his weekly National Public Radio "Puzzler" segment knows that he can speak, but you have to see him before a large, live audience to realize that he may have one of the best-developed sets of rhetorical armamentarium you're likely to encounter anywhere but on the floor of Parliament when a particularly poised British prime minister is defending his political policies. Will informed us that a drama other than the one having to do with the temporal skills of local high school girls had befallen the tournament that day. Cathy Millhauser, a gifted and prolific constructor whose work is very familiar to anyone who regularly tackles the *New York Times* puzzle, had, that morning, lost an envelope containing close to a thousand dollars in cash, the proceeds of what had obviously been a successful weekend flogging copies of her crossword books. And someone at the tournament had found it and turned it in to Will.

"And that"—I'm quoting Will from memory, since I didn't write down his exact words—"is one of the things this tournament is all about. I can't think of any other large group of people in the world you could rely on to hand over a very large chunk of lost cash if any one of them found it."

Will's words wowed the audience—not to mention that his appearance heralded the fact the tabulators had at last worked out the final tournament standings. He may have simply been using a lucky break and some fancy rhetorical footwork to win over a crowd, but I know Will truly believes that there is something inherently moral

about doing crossword puzzles and that that morality finds a reflection in the people who come to compete at Stamford every year.
And I agree with him; maybe it's because there's so much pleasure
in the game itself, maybe it's because the financial stakes are so low,
maybe it's a combination of both. All I can say is that I would have
turned in Cathy Millhauser's money had I found it, too, and it's my
absolute conviction that so would have anyone you'll meet in this
book—Will, Brendan, Michael Shteyman, Peter Gordon, Stan Newman, Katherine Bryant, Helene Hovanec, or indeed any person who
thinks doing crosswords is worthwhile and something to be proud
of. (The only individual I'd exclude from this blanket praise would
be the girl who asked for my completed Saturday *Times* puzzle on
the ferry—I bet she would have pocketed the pelf.) Consciously or
unconsciously, Will knows this, as well; and, consciously or unconsciously, he knew on this Sunday that his praise of his audience's
moral probity would strike the chord that transformed their mass
pique, in the wake of the high school girls, back into mass enthusiasm.

How to Make Difficult Crosswords

The first thing you notice when you look at the setup for the three
championship rounds at Stamford is that all three titles are fought
out on the exact same puzzle with the same grid and fill, even though
the Division A puzzle is tougher than the Division B one, and both
are of course harder than the Division C one. Since the fill is the
same in all three cases, the only difference—the only thing that
makes the puzzles progressively more problematic to solve—is the
cluing. Comparing the clues, therefore, gives us an ideal opportunity
to take a closer look at the arcane art of the crossword-puzzle editor.

One of the ways Will Shortz makes sure a Monday puzzle will be solvable by most of the people who attempt it most of the time, a Wednesday by a fair but not substantially fewer number much of the time, and the occasional Saturday by only the most determined and capable solvers around some of the time (barring people who use Internet search engines, dictionaries, and telephone calls to their sister-in-law to fill in grids, which is legitimate for a civilian but forbidden to a competitive solver) is by carefully calibrating the difficulty of the clues he uses to solicit answers.

For instance, say you have a fairly open puzzle—a puzzle in which the ratio of white squares to black is relatively high—in which one of the answers is SAGAN. (A very open puzzle will usually be very hard, simply because the likelihood is high that it will include one or more stacks of three fifteen-letter answers, which are challenging to even very experienced or talented solvers; a closed puzzle will be easier for everyone, since the words in it will be both shorter and less numerous. Let's say this grid can go either way in terms of potential difficulty.) In a Monday puzzle, regardless of what the constructor submitted originally, Will would choose something like "*Cosmos* host Carl _____"; most people know that the famous "BIL-lions and BIL-lions of stars" quote comes from the PBS TV science series. In a Wednesday puzzle, he might opt for "*Broca's Brain* author Carl _____"; fewer people are familiar with Carl Sagan's written works than they are with his televised ones. For a Saturday puzzle, he'd throw in a real doozy of a clue, for instance "French writer Françoise _____."

The reason for this is that very few people who want to publish a puzzle sit down and say, "Today I'm building me a Thursday-level puzzle—hope Will likes it." No, what they do is construct the sort of crossword they want according to whatever has taken their fancy: the aesthetics of the arrangement—the number and distribution—of the black squares in it, for instance, or a particular theme they've stumbled on that they think is suitable to build a crossword puzzle around. As long as their construction is symmetrical from corner to corner and reasonably akin in terms of content to the sort of stuff you see in the *New York Times* puzzle every day, Shortz will likely think it acceptable for publication—eventually. (The only constructor, it's said, whose work Shortz will use with almost no editing is Stanley Newman.) Once he has accepted your puzzle, it's Will's job to schedule it and edit its cluing to make it a reasonable candidate for the day of the week on which it's going to appear. He writes about 50 percent of the clues in the *Times* puzzle simply because he's the only person responsible for making it consistently easier on Tuesday than it is on Friday—and that work is both a science and an art.

An hour and a half late, that Sunday in Stamford, Will announced the three top finishers in Divisions A, B, and C; before the audience in the hall stood three whiteboards upon which this final contest would be decided. On each of the boards appeared the same rather open fifteen-by-fifteen grid (constructed by Bob Klahn, who is known for the elegance of his grids and the distinct whimsy of his fills). While Will was speaking, tournament officials handed out to us three sets of clues corresponding to each of the three divisional heats. There was something of a glitch after the announcement of the highest placers in Division C. Since those folks can't really know who their direct competition is (it would have to be a superlatively determined attendee who memorized the standings at all twenty-six previous American Crossword Puzzle Tournaments), they're more likely, as a group, to head home instead of waiting through a couple-hour-long tabulating delay. The first place in the Division C competition was won by Neil Singer, a retiree from Washington, D.C. who sauntered up to the stage. In second place came Joseph Kartheiser of Boca Raton, Florida, but he's a technical editor who had to be at work on Monday, so he'd left. Next in line was Arthur Schulman of Charlottesville, Virginia, a retired psychology professor, who had also left. His stand-in was Dan Katz of Providence, Rhode Island, an actor. After Schulman was my new friend John Old—housedads from Illinois apparently enjoy more free time than editors and academics emeritus. There was some grumbling from the audience about the unfairness to Kartheiser and then Schulman—but what else could be done?

The Division B winners were Scott Weiss, a computer science professor from Maryland; Joshua Kosman, a music critic from San Francisco, and Will Johnston, a textbook editor and host of the *New York Times* online crossword forum from Massachusetts. All were present and accounted for, as were the Division A winners: again, Al Sanders, the project manager from Colorado, Jon Delfin, the musician from New York, and Trip Payne, a crossword constructor from Florida.

The way the playoff works is that the winner in each division gets to start work on the puzzle first; his (or her, some years) runner-up starts one second later for each 10 points he trails the winner by in the standings; the second runner-up follows in turn according to the same rules. When the second runner-up starts, the clock begins counting down for all, in this case from fifteen minutes to zero. All finalists wear sound-damping ear sets to ensure sensory deprivation while they're working at their whiteboards; as an added guarantee, the earphones pipe random white noise into their skulls. I have never been in a finals round at the American Crossword Puzzle Tournament and probably never will, but the lucky ducks (actually, the extremely talented ducks) who have experienced that rare thrill tell me that the white noise is in fact an endless-loop recording of the conversational hum you can hear every day in the main lobby of the United Nations building in New

York City. I'm not sure if this bit of trivia contains an element of irony or not, given the cultural specificity of the kind of puzzle the finalists are working on.

Now, in terms of excitement, watching three people race to complete a grid is about what you'd expect it to be—which is no great thrill. In various venues Will Shortz has speculated that televising the tournament finals is something someone might want to do; I suppose people televise sheepdog contests, too, but unless you're a fanatic partisan of either crossword puzzles or sheepdogs, you're probably not going to watch more than three seconds of either.

What was really interesting, though, was the way Will Shortz had taken Bob Klahn's puzzle and fill and altered the cluing to make three separate puzzles, each tailored to the skills of the finalists in each division. For Old, Katz, and Singer, the result was about halfway between a Monday and Tuesday *Times* puzzle; for Johnston, Kosman, and Weiss, it was about a Thursday-level puzzle; for Sanders, Delfin, and Payne, it was a solid Saturday.

Take, for instance, 1-Down. In the fill, the answer was FIEDLER. In terms of the levels of difficulty for the A, B, and C finalists, the clues were these: "Boston leader for half a century," "Longtime Boston pops leader," and "Conductor Arthur." For the A finalists, the clue was vague and imprecise; only the phrase "for half a century" gives you an opening to crack it, while the B solvers got a more solid clue, and the C solvers almost had a gimme. For 19-Across, DESERTBLOOM, the clues in the same order were "Symbol of beauty in harsh conditions," "1986 coming-of-age movie set in Las Vegas," and "Cactus flower, e.g." For 30-Down, DANDELION, the clues were "Plant named for the teeth of a big cat," "Kind of wine," and "Yard nuisance." It's quite clear that many solvers would get the Division C clues without necessarily having to rely on hints from the cross clues; the overwhelming bulk of us, though, would spend our allotted fifteen minutes trying to figure out what letter ("d") could possibly represent a cross between the middle letter of "Boston leader for half a century" and the first of "Symbol of beauty in harsh conditions."

To give you an idea of how different top-flight solvers are from you and me, in Division A Al Sanders came in third at 10:38. Jon Delfin came in second at 10:24. The winner, Trip Payne, roared his way through this extremely difficult grid in an astounding 5:16. I placed in the top 40 percent of the contestants at the Twenty-seventh American Crossword Puzzle Tournament, which wasn't bad for a rookie. When I tried to complete the Division A version of the finalists' challenge at home many months later (it took supreme self-discipline to hold off on it so long) it took me fifteen minutes and twelve seconds.

This particular puzzle was represented as being themeless, which means that it contained no set of related words or phrases that would provide you a hook with which to pry it open. The only consolations I derived while watching Sanders, Delfin, and especially Payne utterly blow me and my pathetic time out of the water were the facts that at least I came near to making the time limit, that no matter that I'm one of the few people in the country who can do a difficult Saturday *Times* puzzle in less than twenty minutes, and that as I was doing it I'm fairly sure I detected a theme carefully hidden inside—with PINKLADY, TOPER, TEA, AMBROSIA, and PALEALE, there was a definite focus to it on drinks and drinking. If you counted the Division B clue for 30-Down (DANDELION) and imagined an apostrophe and "s" tacked on to the back of 1-Across (FOSTER), you'd be forgiven the suspicion that Bob Klahn knows perfectly well what goes on late at night in the hotel bar during a puzzle weekend at Stamford and was making a sly comment about it.

Water, Food, and Sleep, the Doctor
Recommended Afterward

With the finals over and Trip Payne now supplanting Stan Newman as the fastest solver of American-style crossword puzzles in the world, all that was left was the celebratory lunch (at which I sat beside a perfectly equanimous but singularly uncommunicative Al Sanders) and the final reckoning of our standings. Unfortunately, according to these the final puzzle had scuppered my hopes of beating Brendan Emmett Quigley, who placed 173rd with a total score of 9,805 versus my 204th with 9,530. That meant I'd in fact been trailing him by 105 points after the six puzzles of the day before—I wondered if that was right for about two seconds before realizing I was too tired to bother thinking about it.

What I did find interesting were the places the competing constructors occupied in the standings relative to me. Trip Payne placed first overall with 11,960 points. (Al Sanders scored 12,060, but, of course, lost in the final.) Sometime constructor Jon Delfin was second. Of the others whose names I recognized, I noted Tyler Hinman at 12, Will Johnston at 18, Peter Gordon at 22, Frank Longo at 35, Rich Norris at 49, Peter Abide at 90, and Brendan at 173 all bested me. I was surprised to come in before Cathy Millhauser (228; maybe she was distracted by selling all those books), Jim Jenista (286), and Nancy Erskine (402), all puzzle makers whose work I admire. (Of the nonconstructors, Katherine Bryant came in tenth, Laura Bauer, twenty-ninth; Stephanie Parsons, the star of Christina Kelly's video, ranked three hundred first.) One of the things you'll note is how tight the spread is in scores—Brendan beat me by 275 points, which represents a thirty-one-place difference. Had I not gotten a mere four squares wrong out of seven puzzles and paid attention to the bonus in the fourth round, I would have ended up, overall, around 55th; had I made no errors but missed the bonus, my place would have been around 127th. Competition is tough at the American Crossword Puzzle Tournament, and the margin between wholesale defeat and potential victory is slim; in Division C, the one I was competing in, John Old and Dan Katz at 60 and 56, respectively, both placed below the score I ideally could and should have chalked up.

It was now three in the afternoon and lunch not halfway over. (I was too busy speaking to people to eat.) I had arranged to stay with friends in Providence for a day or two after the tournament, so I said my various good-byes, checked out, and hoofed it to the Stamford train station, which accommodates both Amtrak and the New Haven commuter line to New York. When I got there, I was told Amtrak had no seats on a northbound train until ten that night—it was totally overbooked. I was ravenous, thirsty, woozy, weak, and strangely overheated, so instead of waiting caught the next commuter train back to the city. I thought about having something to eat, but the only possibilities at the station were doughnuts or vending-machine candy, and I had no appetite for either.

New York happened to be practicing a major counterterrorism operation that day, as it turned out, and it was a Sunday, a combination that guarantees a certain amount of disruption in the city's subway system. After an hour or so of delays, I finally reached the Canal Street station of the 6 line, where the train stopped and I, out of frustration, decided to take a taxi home to Brooklyn. There were none to be found, so I made my way on foot across the Brooklyn Bridge and then, at last, home. I ate some walnuts, which immediately insisted on coming back up again.

Just then my younger sister called, wanting to find out about the tournament. To make a long and very painful story short, she came over to my place and made a lovely pasta at the first bite of which I again was sick—I suppose my body was so hungry for fuel that it reacted violently when I tried to give it some. My sister went out for bananas and milk, which were the only foods I could imagine tolerating, and in the ten minutes she was away, something strange happened to me: I noticed my right arm involuntarily (or at least against my volition) rising in an arc over my head. I heard a snapping sound, as if a peal of thunder had broken out across the room, and I felt a sharp pain in my head, as if a ten-ton weight had fallen on it. The next thing I knew, I was on my bedroom floor, drenched in sweat, with, kneeling around me, my sobbing sister, my distraught good friend and downstairs neighbor, and three burly New York City EMTs, one of whom was inserting a saline drip into my arm.

Many hours later, returning from the hospital, feeling groggy and weak though somewhat restored by an intravenous feed of some description, I recalled the attending doctor's words: "You haven't eaten anything? For two days? You know, you're not fifteen anymore. If your body doesn't like what you're doing to it, it's going to tell you, and at thirty-eight it's old enough to know how."

So, tottering into bed at three in the morning, I thought of the weekend's lessons. Well, first of the words the doctor wrote on my release sheet: "Make sure to eat, sleep, and hydrate yourself." Then of my performance at the tournament: Don't rush yourself just because you want to do better than Brendan Emmett Quigley—but, at the same time, practice beforehand by doing crosswords on paper, not on a computer screen, because you weren't fast enough in actual competition. Finally, of the implicit threat made by my I guess aging body: "You pull a stunt like that again, and I'll take you down faster than you can say boo."

I pondered all this for a few seconds, then sank into the river Lethe and slept—for the next fifteen hours.

Chapter 8

THE PUZZLEMASTER
IN HIS LABYRINTH

"Brendan's way too hard on himself."

Will Shortz was sitting on one of the two overstuffed chairs in his upstairs library, surrounded by a couple thousand or so books, most of which were about games, puzzles, code-making and code-breaking, puns and anagrams, and like subjects. I had just asked him what he thought of Brendan Emmett Quigley's constructing style, and, as is often the case when you put that question to crossword people, inevitably the subject of his personality comes up, too.

"He's fascinated by grids and loves wide-open diagrams. He doesn't really care about the clues. But he's extremely talented—I don't know why he doesn't always seem to give himself enough credit for it."

I thought, as I sat there listening to Will talking about Brendan, that you'd be hard put to find a more contrasting pair of personalities. Both are very smart, of course; it wouldn't be a leap into sycophancy to say they're both brilliant. But while Brendan's psychic life seems to be an endlessly mutating obstacle course he has to navigate at great peril, Will's is, comparatively speaking, a broad, straight autobahn lined every couple of miles with pleasant country inns. Brendan feeds on self-doubt; Will positively glows with the energy of a man who knows that his life's work is an unmitigatedly good thing, both for himself and the thousands—if not millions—of people it touches.

The very environment Will has built for himself reflects the choices he has made about the way he will lead his life. His house, a smallish Tudor-style affair perched on the side of a steep hill in a perfectly conventional suburban town, is what an interior decorator might call spartan (Will calls the style "Arts & Crafts"—and the decor admittedly does include some very nice pieces). The kitchen was spotless, but that was because the cleaning lady had just been by; apart from a display case containing the cream of Will's collection of puzzle memorabilia, the living room is furnished with a couch, a coffee table, and, off in the corner, what looks to be a revolving credenza of some sort. (On later examination, it turns out to be a rack of vintage crossword-themed postcards.) The dining room contains a table, some chairs, a stereo cluttered with CDs, and a bunch of boxes. ("I haven't gotten around to putting that stuff away yet.")

If you're lucky, Will might treat you to a guided tour of the things in that living-room display case: puzzles and puzzle-themed toys dating from the early nineteenth century on, boxed games, artifacts produced during the Great American Crossword Puzzle Craze of 1924 and 1925. There's an issue of *The Massachusetts Magazine* dating from February 1789, that includes an essay by "Q.S." entitled "On the Antiquity and Dignity of Riddles." Will speaks ruefully of wanting to get his hands on a copy of the extremely rare *Samuel Danforth's Almanac* of 1647, only the seventeenth book as yet published in what was to become the United States, which features an "enigma," or riddle, for each day of that year.

"In American history," Will explains, "there have always been explosions of interest in puzzles that come in the wake of major cultural developments. There was a huge fascination with puzzles starting around 1789, when magazines first started getting published in earnest."

Shortz's undergraduate dissertation at Indiana University focused on the history of puzzles and games in America from the earliest settlements to 1850; it's difficult to think of anyone else, at least in my circle of acquaintances, who has single-mindedly and for so long continued amplifying on the theme that informed his senior essay in college. Will Shortz was, in 2004, fifty-two years old; he's thus been at it for more than thirty years, and shows no sign of flagging either in his interest or his energy for pursuing the minutia of puzzles.

"So what about the crossword craze in the twenties?" I asked. "I mean, apart from the onset of the Jazz Age and the Wall Street boom, you couldn't say there was a huge cultural leap forward in America—every American writer and painter had moved to Paris by then anyway."

"No, that's not true." Will appeared to bristle momentarily, a phenomenon I'd witnessed once or twice before with him, for instance when I asked him in 2003 if the partitions between puzzlers at the Stamford tournament were placed there to help discourage potential cheaters; but then as now he recovered quickly. "First, there was a rapid increase in newspaper circulation at the time, plus the development of better printing techniques that allowed them to publish crosswords. Everyone was past all the World War I silliness. The fact that it was the first big period for celebrities helped—if someone famous did crosswords, other people wanted to do them, too. But the biggest thing was that the nation reached a tipping point where all of a sudden everyone had more leisure time."

"I see."

"And the craze didn't last that long in any case. It started around November 1924 and had pretty much died down by March 1925."

"But a lot of people still do crosswords today."

"Yeah, but it's a lot mellower now. No one's writing hit songs about puzzles."

I asked if I could see Will's basement, which is where he stores the overflow of his gigantic puzzle collection (the bulk being scattered through the rest of his house), and he agreed to show it to me with all the alacrity of your young nephew when you ask to see his favorite video game in action.

Out of the living room, through the kitchen, down a flight of rickety stairs—and there was a version in miniature of that last scene in *Indiana Jones*, when the Ark of the Covenant is wheeled into a cavernous U.S. Government warehouse, where it will be lost again forever. Will's basement is literally packed, breathtakingly packed, with crossword stuff: books, magazines, tournament results for twenty-six years . . . in short, enough material to one day form the core collection of a Museum of Enigmatology, should anyone ever want to endow such a thing.

(Then again, maybe a crossword museum isn't so unlikely a possibility. Eugene T. Maleska, who had been superintendent of New York City's Board of Education District 10 before his career editing the *Times* puzzle, actually has a school named after him—the Eugene T. Maleska Middle School in the Bronx. I tried contacting its current principal, Anthony Orzo, to see if ETMMS has some sort of puzzle focus. Orzo was way too busy to talk to me himself—he's a rising young star in New York education circles who apparently spends twenty-four hours a day working—but he got a colleague, Mike Michaels, a retired official with the United Federation of Teachers and the font of institutional memory at Eugene T.

Maleska, to call me back. Eugene T. Maleska, it turns out, is a wonderful place for its 1,500 students, but no more crossword-oriented than any other middle school in the city. "We've never gotten any preferential treatment from the *Times*, either," Mike dryly put it. I didn't ask him what he thought of the fact that his principal's last name is one of the six hundred four-letter words most frequently used in the Shortz-era puzzle.)

"Here, let me show you this."

Will led me through the thickets in his basement toward an object that, though it was covered with boxes and framed posters, looked suspiciously like an arcade game. Will cleared it off and then stepped aside.

"Holy moly!" I exclaimed. "A crossword pinball machine!"

Which is what it was; I mean, it was a plain-vanilla pinball game, but the body of the thing was covered with crossword grids as opposed to half-naked girls. Will explained that he'd been walking down the street ten years before when he spotted the thing at an antiques mart. He'd been about to walk on by, thinking the dealer would want thousands of dollars for it, but then decided to ask about it anyway. The dealer said he could have it for $200, and Will reached for his wallet.

"I used to play a lot, but I haven't fired it up for a while." Will reached under the thing, grunted, and plugged it in. It blinked and ker-chinged for a few moments, then settled down and looked ready for business. "If I was tired and needed a break, I'd come down and play a few games to relax."

He fired off the first ball while I stood there, watching with the kind of amazement you'd reserve for, say, the race-car driver who wins the Indy 500 and then goes home to race electronic cars on his Nintendo game. It was practically unbelievable to me that Will's idea of a few moments' relief from crosswords, which he deals with 365 days a year, was to come downstairs and play a crossword-themed pinball game.

"Hey, look at that!" One of the little metal balls Will had launched into the machine had got caught between two of the little metal cushions at the top of the board, and the counter was ringing furiously and racking up an astronomical score. "That's never happened before!" When that game was over, Will started another—and again one of the balls got caught in a scoring loop that raised his score to even more vertiginous heights.

"Wow," Will said after that game was over and he'd unplugged the machine again. "Twice in a row. That was really, really neat."

Helene Explains Will

"You'll want to take along a tape recorder when you see him."

For the last twelve years, Helene Hovanec has been Will Shortz's right-hand person and chief of staff, at least insofar as his activities with the American Crossword Puzzle Tournament are concerned. Two months after the 2004 event, she told me what to expect from my first visit to Will's house, which was scheduled for the following week. I couldn't help shake the feeling that she was the Company agent briefing my Marlow for the trip up the Congo to confront Kurtz. My sentiment darkened when it struck me that there was a disturbing congruence of names operating here. "Marc"/"Marlow," "Shortz"/"Kurtz"—it just makes a fellow think.

Helene is a slight woman, filled with energy, who looks at you and the world with wide-eyed interest. There's something about those eyes that sets you instantly at ease; they make you think you

can say anything on your mind to their owner in the complete as-
surance that you'll be both listened to and understood. In medieval
Europe, ladies used to drink a decoction of belladonna before meeting a prospective suitor; being mildly psychotropic, the stuff dilates
the pupils, and since dilated pupils can be, among other things, a
sign of interest in one's interlocutor, it helps gull the poor guy in
question into believing he's making some real headway with this
gal—"belladonna" in Italian means "pretty woman," because any
man will think attractive any woman who thinks him irresistible
(even if that impression in fact is dependent on the woman's suffering from a case of low-grade alkaloid poisoning). Helene's eyes
make you understand why, given its history of fiascos with missing
clocks and all-too-present high school girls, the American Crossword Puzzle Tournament consistently produces fond memories in
its participants—it's hard to bear a grudge for long when the person
you bring any of your complaints to looks at you with eyes that even
Bambi would envy.

Like so many others who have made a career out of crosswords,
Helene was bitten by the puzzle bug young. In 1973, when she was
in her second year at college, she became a member of an organiza-
tion called the National Puzzlers' League (which is still going strong;
Katherine Bryant edits its monthly magazine). Among its literature
she ran across a piece about Will Shortz and the subject of enigmatology; she wrote to him, he wrote back, and in 1975 he came to visit
her.

"He's my oldest puzzle friend," Helene said. "Back then someone had asked him to write a book about crosswords, but he didn't
have the time, so he asked me if I'd want to do it. I did. Soon after
The Puzzler's Paradise came out in 1976, he decided to stage a National Puzzlers' League convention. I helped organize—I'm good at

chattering and Will isn't, or at least it's not something he's going to go out of his way to do. I mean, you know he can do it—you've seen him. It's just that if you're going to have a division of labor, you divide it the way everything is going to turn out for the best. That convention was just wonderful—twenty-six people each paying $50 for the weekend, and that included rooms and three meals a day. To spend a weekend with other people who share the same passion is fantastic—you get to feel a real connection, the thrill of recognition. It's what people still come to Stamford for today."

Will Shortz started the American Crossword Puzzle Tournament in 1978, choosing the Stamford Marriott as the venue. Helene acted as a proctor and judge at more than a half-dozen of the early meets and for various reasons missed as many again; by this time, she was producing a string of crossword books for kids. In 1993 she moved to New York City, and Will asked her to take over some of the administrative responsibilities for the event.

"It was unbelievable—there were literally hundreds of phone calls from people who wanted to take part. I stayed on with Will after 1993, and gradually I came to help him run the tournament itself, which allowed him to concentrate more on the puzzles themselves and on being the emcee." (He still, though, does a staggering amount of the grunt work itself.)

For Helene, the most memorable tournament—and the one that definitively transformed it from a two- or three-hundred-participant affair into the much larger event it has since become—was the twenty-fifth.

"We hired a publicist for it who was absolutely wonderful. We—"

A dim suspicion stirred in the back of my mind about who this publicist was. I'm not a terribly attentive friend, in terms of keeping track of what the people I know happen to be doing month in and month out, but when you have dinner with someone a couple of times a year for a decade or more . . .

"Was the publicist . . . Rose Marie Morse?" Rose Marie, a tall, beautiful, blond, and wickedly intelligent Croat, had been my first boss, at Grove Press, when I moved to New York. She left for William Morrow six months before I quit publishing in favor of full-time translating, and then a few years later she left Morrow to start her own company. Rose Marie is an exquisite cook, and I'm afraid I must have been concentrating more on her gnocchi than on her words when she told me, in early 2002, that her company had been hired by Will Shortz. In the instant before Helene answered, I pondered, as I had at least five times a year for the twelve years I'd lived in the city, the odd fact of how small New York actually is—it may officially have 8 million residents, but when you live there for a while you begin suspecting that there are really only a couple of hundred of you, with a supporting cast of maybe fifty thousand extras.

"Yes! Rose Marie! She had the magazines, the networks in to cover it. The tournament went up a couple of notches after that. But, you know, it was a story that told itself—for twenty-five years the tournament had been held in the same place. And all of that's because of Will. Nobody's as loyal as he is, even to a hotel."

"What about the people who go to Stamford year after year?" I asked. "I mean, it's fun, but at the same time it's sort of stress-inducing—Stamford's not the most relaxing weekend in the world."

Helene pondered for a while before replying.

"I suppose," she said, "it's like being deprived for a long time of something, like chocolate, and then all of a sudden having as much of it as you want. And it's a way to test yourself. To make sure you're actually becoming better at doing puzzles."

I was silent, thinking that what you're really doing at Stamford is finding out whether you're getting better not at crosswords per se, but at doing them under the pleasant-but-pressure-cooker conditions of the American Crossword Puzzle Tournament.

"Listen," Helene said, "why don't you call up my niece Bree? She was a judge in March and could tell you what it was like to be a first-time participant from that angle. Let me give you her cell-phone number."

My heart skipped a beat. Gosh, I thought to myself, and a picture of Brendan Quigley mouthing the words "Humbert Humbert" flashed across my mental screen.

"Ah, no—that's all right. I think I'm already talking to the people I need to."

I didn't have the heart to add that I wouldn't be bringing a tape recorder along when I saw Will, either; precious as any master's words are on the subject of his or her expertise, there's nothing so mind-numbing as transcribing conversations in which every third word is "er." And there's no better way to train yourself to listen to someone than forcing yourself to learn how to ask them a question and write down their answer while you're asking your next.

At the time, I was only just beginning to feel the first stirrings of the crosswords-as-ethical-force theme that pervades this book, so it was with no more than a slight catch in my throat that I said, "But I'm definitely running out now to get a tape recorder for the Will interview."

The Puzzlemaster in His Labyrinth, Revisited

"In about two minutes I can be out of bed and at work."

Will has led me back upstairs to the second story of his house, where there are four small rooms: his study, his office, a boudoir (not really; I just didn't want to say "room" again), and a bathroom. When I first asked if I could come up and see him, I mentioned that I would very much like to see all phases of the *New York Times* crossword operation firsthand, including editorial meetings and testing. "That cracks me up," Will had said at the time. "It's just me."

And it is, which is admirable enough. Will personally edits all the *Times* crosswords and handles all crossword correspondence himself, including some sixty to seventy unsolicited puzzles per week ("A lot of them are perfectly fine but just don't excite me") and, of course, the occasional irate letter from dissatisfied solvers. He works a heavy schedule of about sixty hours a week—it was more, he says, when he first started at the *Times,* but his stable of contributors is large and well trained enough that he no longer needs to spend quite so much time editing.

"Do you ever get tired of it?" I asked.

"No," he said without hesitation. "It involves so many diverse activities, like coming up with the NPR puzzles and organizing the tournament; even if all I did was the crosswords, I'd still be learning something every day and feeling challenged by it. Plus, I like the people who do crosswords."

"I've been wondering about that. Everyone I met at Stamford was great—why *are* people so nice there?"

Will laughed. "I really don't know. I'm not sure if puzzles attract nice people or if puzzles bring out the niceness in people. But they're a pretty pleasant bunch, overall."

Hanging on the wall in the corridor between his study and office was a framed letter that I was surprised to see is from President Bill Clinton. It's a birthday greeting Clinton had sent two years before. As Will tells it, Helene Hovanec had asked the by then expresident to come to Will's fiftieth birthday party; although Clinton begged off, he had sent this message instead. Given the *Times*'s relentless pursuit of the Clintons from the Whitewater episode on, the text is actually pretty funny: The crossword puzzle, the president wrote, was about the only section of the paper he consistently enjoyed.

"There's a story behind that letter," Will said.

And a fairly remarkable tale, too. When Will was still at *Games* magazine just before taking over the editorship of the *Times* puzzle, his publisher—a big Clinton supporter who eventually became finance chief of the then-governor's presidential campaign—had set up a meeting among the candidate, the puzzlemaster, and now–*Wall Street Journal* crossword editor Mike Shenk, from whom Will had commissioned a puzzle they hoped the candidate would attempt. This was just after Clinton had won his party's nomination at the Democratic National Convention. Clinton was a bit suspicious about the whole thing—it does seem odd for a polititian and a crossword maven to meet in the heat of a presidential run—and had made clear to Will and Mike Shenk that their time in his hotel room with him would likely be interrupted by all sorts of urgent phone calls, quick talks with campaign workers, and the like. The puzzle Shenk had brought along was a fifteen-by-fifteen clued to about the difficulty level of a Wednesday *Times* crossword.

Once Clinton saw that Will was in earnest, he agreed to doing the puzzle. He told an aide that only the most urgent calls were to be passed through, clicked the timer on his wristwatch, and set about solving Shenk's grid. Will fell silent, but Clinton said, "Go ahead; don't stop asking me questions," and he answered them as he filled in the puzzle. About three minutes into the proceedings, the phone rang; Clinton clicked the timer off and answered the call, which was long and involved. (Will later found out it was from the Reverend Jesse Jackson.) When he was done, he clicked on the timer again and finished the puzzle—in six minutes fifty-four seconds.

When the meeting was over, Will and Shenk looked at Clinton's answers. They were 100 percent correct; the ex-president would do well at the American Crossword Puzzle Tournament, if he can find the time for it given his busy schedule, and if the Secret Service don't take away everybody else's no. 2 pencils, just in case.

"When did you first start doing puzzles?" I asked Will when we were seated in his study.

Will thought for a moment.

"Well, I can't say I remember when I first solved them—I started making them when I was eight or nine. I remember sneaking into my older sister's room and taking a puzzle book she had on her shelf."

Will stood up and pulled something off his own shelf—a small book entitled *We Dare You to Solve This!*, which when opened revealed the spidery hand of a small child that had filled every page in. My God, I thought to myself as I handed the book back and he put it away again—it's Will Shortz's Rosebud!

"I don't know why it's so, but like a lot of people, I feel compelled to do puzzles. It's a way to refresh yourself mentally, and it distracts you from anything that's bothering you. I don't do a lot of solving myself anymore—but if I'm on vacation I'll take along a couple of puzzle books and go on a solving binge with them."

I asked him the question I'd put to Brendan, about what other endeavors in the field of human activities might be equivalent, in terms of time and energy, to creating a crossword puzzle.

"Well," Will said after a pause, "I don't really know. At a tournament Stanley Newman ran maybe fifteen years ago, they set a challenge for constructor William Lutwiniak. They set up a blank fifteen-by-fifteen grid on a display easel. William asked the audience for a couple of words to start with, then constructed a whole puzzle in fifteen minutes. I don't know if you could write a poem that fast. The only other constructor I know who could do what William did is Mike Shenk, but he's not a very public person." (That was a diplomatic understatement—Shenk is notoriously reclusive.)

"Speaking of speed, how can I do better at Stamford next year?"

"Well, how well did you do this year?"

"Came in two hundred and fourth."

"Hmm. That's actually not bad for your first time out. Of the squares you got wrong, how many were mistakes and how many were inadvertent errors?"

"Four, and three of them were errors. I didn't manage my time very well—I didn't go back and check the grids."

"Well, duh!"

"Um, thanks, Will. That's helpful."

"You should always run out the minute—and then use an extra minute after that. If you'd done that, you'd have lost a total of 175 points overall, but won 585 by catching those errors."

"Plus another 100 for the bonus on the fourth puzzle—I would have gotten that if I'd spent a few more seconds looking at it."

"And if you think you're going to make it to the playoffs, practice solving crosswords standing up. Take Al Sanders—he does very, very well on paper, and he often makes the finals, but he trips up at the board."

"What about handwriting? I did all my practicing online; when it came to the crunch in competition, I found that I was thinking a lot faster than I was writing."

"You should rethink the way you shape your letters. I mean, years and years ago I changed the way I wrote out my "e"s. By doing that, I've saved time both solving and in life."

"Now, the tournament itself—Helene says you have a great relationship with the Stamford Marriott and want to keep it there as long as possible. But more and more people seem to be coming, from a handful in the early days to a couple hundred in the nineties to more than five hundred now. What happens if the tournament gets too big for the Marriott?"

Will answered quickly—obviously, this is a topic he has thought about a lot. "Well, the first thing is, the Marriott has a second ball-room available if we ever need it. There aren't many places 25 percent larger that we could graduate to, so it's either that or a convention center somewhere, which would mean people would stay at different hotels. But I think the tournament is self-limiting in terms of size. It's always going to be somewhat difficult to get people to come. It's peculiar to spend a weekend doing something in a group you usually do alone."

Then the phone rang, and Will ran off to his office for fifteen minutes or so, and I took the opportunity to look more closely at the books on his shelves. In the fiction section, which isn't very large, there was nothing but crossword-themed mystery novels—I quoted Will's take on one, John Garland's *Crime of the Crossword*, in chapter 2. Among the other titles were Patricia Moyes's *A Six-Word Letter for Death* (Holt, Rinehart and Winston, 1983) and Barbara Delinsky's *Twelve Across* (New York: Harlequin Books, 1987); I had high hopes the latter would be a crossword bodice ripper, but it's the story of a beautiful crossword constructor from New York who moves to the woods of Maine and falls in love with a burly out-doorsman, and unfortunately there isn't any talk of puzzles any-where in it. Beside it was Nero Blanc's *Corpus de Crossword* (New York: Berkley Prime Crime, 2003); "Nero Blanc" is the pseudonym of Cordelia Frances Biddle and Steve Zettler, a couple who have a whole series of crossword mysteries in print.

My favorite of the lot (I later returned to Will's house to take a closer look at them) is E. R. Punshon's *The Crossword Murder* (New York: Alfred A. Knopf, 1934), whose opening paragraph reads:

> It was one of the loveliest days of a lovely summer, and Detective-Constable Bobby Owen, B.A. (Oxon. Pass degree only), as he jogged placidly along on a brand-new motor-cycle (Government property) at a quiet forty or fifty m.p.h., with an occasional burst up to seventy or eighty when he was quite sure there were no traffic police about, was almost able to persuade himself that after all there are on this earth, though rare, worse jobs than police jobs.

The mystery involves Nazi gold, a crossword-obsessed murder victim, and an abandoned lighthouse, and the puzzle the murdered man was working on before his untimely demise of course provides the clues that bring all the threads of the conundrum together. It's a neat read, well written and tightly plotted, and a lot of fun.

But the book got me thinking. Will Shortz seems to have built a cocoonlike world that apparently has little room in it for anything *not* having to do with puzzles. It's no doubt a pleasant world to inhabit, if you're the benign Darth Vader of the crossword business, but a little disconcerting to a civilian visitor. If Will went away for a fortnight and asked someone to house-sit for him, he'd better hope it was a polylingual puzzle fiend who took him up on the offer, since anyone else would go bonkers there by sundown of the second day. As a place to drop by, though, it's simply a treat to someone like me—for a while. (I'm being unfair. Will is obviously widely read in a lot of topics, and I'm here to talk only about crosswords—but still.)

"Yes," said Will when I asked him about the books. "Crosswords and mysteries share a huge thing in common—they both depend on a natural compulsion for solving things."

I suppose it was Will's use of the word "compulsion," but I couldn't, given what at this point I thought I knew about him, help but ask the question that had been stewing in the back of my mind for the last two years:

"Okay. Let's say there was some bizarre hiccup in the space-time continuum that resulted in all of us living in this exact same world, except for the fact that this time there were no puzzles in it. What would you do instead?"

It took a while for Will to answer—I suppose no one had asked him a question like it before, since to most it seems so natural that Will Shortz, puzzlemaster, should be doing exactly what he is doing and nothing else, and I guess he hadn't thought about it much, either.

"There was a period," he said at last, "between my time at the Penny Press and *Games* magazine when I was unemployed for about six months. If I wasn't going to do puzzles, I thought, maybe I should do something like copywriting for an advertising agency. I mean, fundamentally I think of myself as a creative person. But then I gave up the idea as soon as I was at *Games*." Will paused, and then his eyes brightened and he went on. "You know, over the years I've really gotten into table tennis. Sometimes I think that if I wasn't doing this, what I'd really like to do is move to Europe and do it professionally."

I thought he was joking, but then he proceeded to rattle off the names of the reigning Greek, Dutch, and French stars of the game today, and I said to myself, "Holy mother of God—he's actually *serious* about playing table tennis professionally."

Months later, Brendan Quigley stopped by Will's house for the evening on his way down to New York from Boston in his aged

Hyundai. They had dinner and hung around Will's place until eleven or so (it was the first time Brendan had visited Will at home), and the next day he and I spoke. Brendan knew that I thought of Will as something of an obsessive type as far as crosswords were concerned; like any rational person, Brendan knows that it's somewhat unusual for a person to be as wholly absorbed by one subject as Will is, but he was afraid I was going to paint the puzzlemaster as a freak freaky beyond the freakiness of most of the people in the crossword world. I wasn't going to, since I frankly think of Shortz as one of the more grounded people I've met, but I could understand Brendan's worry—because the fact is, most people who spend a good part of their waking hours doing crosswords or thinking about them probably have a screw or two loose.

"Because he's not *only* into crosswords, man," Brendan said. "He's really into sixties-era garage bands and knows a shitload about them." (Brendan, a rocker himself, had occasionally given Will tapes of his own bands before.) "And we had a *really* great time talking about all sorts of stuff. But you're right about one thing—I was looking through his photo albums and saw one from about 1978 where he was playing Ping-Pong. The guy looked good at it. I think he's a bit too into the game—yeah, okay, he's obsessed with it."

When it was time for me to go, after that first visit to Will's, he offered to drive me down to the train station half a mile away. Since it was a nice day, I said I'd walk, so he came along, too; he wanted to mail a couple of letters, and in an oddly European way for a midwesterner transplanted to a New York suburb who possesses a car, he didn't feel the need to drive to the local post office to do so. As we ambled down his street, a neighbor across the way who was planting her spring flowers waved at Will, who smiled broadly and waved back. I wondered if that person knew her pleasant, unassuming, kindly neighbor was just that, or simultaneously the most gifted puzzle editor the planet has ever seen. On that lovely, sunny day in late April, I'm not sure she did, or that Will would care one way or the other. He was just enjoying the prospect of a pleasant stroll, in much the same way, I guess, that he enjoys getting up every morning to the prospect of another eight hours vexing and delighting the inhabitants of his otherworld—the millions of folks who consider a day without doing the *New York Times* crossword a day misspent.

The Lord of "the Puzzler"

National Public Radio's New York bureau is an unexpectedly small and cluttered office located in the grim and colorless commercial zone between the United Nations building and Grand Central Station. At a couple of minutes before one in the afternoon on a Friday the week after I first visited Will at his house, I was sitting in the reception area, waiting for him to appear. He was running late, but no one seemed to care; given that Will's weekly "Puzzler" installment won't air until Sunday morning, there's no real pressure to keep rigidly close to schedule.

I'm not much of a radio listener, although I enjoy, when I hear them, both Will's program and *Car Talk,* the WGBH/Boston radio show featuring two wisecracking brothers/mechanics who answer call-in automotive problems. The only time I remember even hearing about Will's "Puzzler" show came several years earlier, when a woman I'd been set up with was deeply impressed solely because I'd answered in less than thirty seconds one of Will's verbal enigmas she'd been unable to figure out since the Sunday before our date. The question then had been "What work of international literature has five words in its title, each of which is four letters long?" I thought first, irrationally, of *The Old Man and the Sea*, which was wrong, of course, but it immediately set a train of thought rolling. When that train reached its station a few seconds later, I had my answer, *All's Well That Ends Well* by William Shakespeare (the trick is that punctuation marks like possessive apostrophes don't count as letters) and, consequently, a new bedmate. I told this story to Will at the 2003 American Crossword Puzzle Tournament; he had been smiling, as people do when someone's telling them what appears to be an amusing anecdote, but by the time I ended it his smile had become a frozen rictus of the sort your Aunt Edna would display if she suddenly realized the songs you were belting out at her afternoon tea party were ribald sea shanties. (Alas, the woman in question and I didn't work out; a few weeks afterward, she left town for law school.)

When Will strode into the bureau office a few minutes after one, he had a copy of that day's *Times* under his arm that, it turned out, he'd picked up on the train. With a wan half-smile, he showed me the crossword: a fifteen-by-fifteen by Manny Nosowsky in which the only two filled-in words were ILOVEYOU—the answer to the question "Lyric sung three times in a row in the Beatles' 'Michelle'— and ERR for "Go wrong." At Stamford, that puzzle would have earned its owner a mere 20 points. Whoever did it can rest easy in the knowledge that it also produced a degree of amusement for Will Shortz and his interlocutor there amid the NPR clutter.

It's a brisk and efficient business, taping the "Puzzler" episode—after all, most of the work has been done by Will Shortz long before it happens. On this Friday, Will was recording the show that would air on Mother's Day; it was his seventeenth Mother's Day–themed broadcast, so you can imagine what a chore it must have been to come up with something fresh and different (and you can be sure that at this moment he's at least subconsciously thinking about his eighteenth one).

The trick with this Mother's Day puzzler was that Will gave the caller a word that, when anagrammed and saddled with the suffix "ma," produced a legitimate word two letters longer than the original. My favorite was "earldom"—if you shuffle its letters around and add "ma" to the end, you get "melodrama." I was in the sound booth with the engineer and rattled off the answer to each question as it was posed. At the end, the engineer turned around and said, "You know, I've been doing this for ten years and not once have I gotten a single question right. How the hell do you come up with answers for this stuff?"

The really funny thing about it, as far as I was concerned, was the fact that, in the banter between Will and Liane Hansen, the NPR host, it emerged that Shortz's mother's first name is Wilma—if you're a Freudian analyst, you can make of that all you care to.

Will's challenge to NPR listeners for the next week was to take a word, reverse its phonetic halves, and stick them together to make a completely different word. As an example, he cited the word "welfare," which if reversed produces "farewell." The actual question was "A nineties fad that becomes an item of apparel." As soon as Will said the words, I cranked through nineties fads—Furbies, Tickle Me Elmo, and so on—until I settled on Tae-Bo. (That karate-cum-aerobics routine you'd see pirate vendors peddling VCR tapes of on the streets of New York from about 1992 on; being extremely vowel-friendly, it rapidly became the new darling of crossword constructors nationwide.) If you reverse its syllables, you get "bowtie."

When Will emerged from his isolation booth, I said to him, "Gee, Will. The late Senator Paul Simon would really have loved that one."

"Gosh, you're fast," Will replied, with a leery look in his eye that made me think what he really wanted to say was "If you're so good, how come you only placed two hundred and fourth at Stamford this year?"

My only answer can be that yes, I can be fast at this stuff—unless I've stayed up until two in the morning the previous night, swilling beer with a score of overexcited word-and-grid fiends. I don't say this to Will Shortz, though. Because, chances are, I'll probably do the very same thing again at Stamford next year.

Chapter 9

■ THE NICE AND
■ THE NASTY

By now it should be fairly clear that, if you want to experience collective geniality in its purest and most unadulterated form, you should probably think about attending the American Crossword Puzzle Tournament someday. It's hard to determine precisely where the font of all this pleasantness lies: They say the fish rots from the head downward, so I suppose you could take the inverse of that statement and apply it to Will Shortz himself—perhaps it's because he is so genuinely open and friendly that the people who come to his tournament are that way, too, either because it's inborn in them or because braggarts, liars, and cheats find the hyperhonest and hyperethical world of crosswords a complete turnoff and don't show up in Stamford more than once.

There are at Stamford, of course, varying degrees of niceness. Most repeat customers attend the tournament largely because of the puzzle friends they've made there over the years, so there's a vague soupçon of cliquishness that attaches to some of the clots of people you'll see hanging together there. The Cru wine-and-cheese get-togethers sort of fall into this category. ("Sort of" because the Cru is actually pretty democratic; if you post on the *New York Times* crossword electronic bulletin board once or twice, you're in.) For a couple of years, the "Bizarro Brew" Sunday-night homemade beer party hosted by a young woman from Somerville, Massachusetts, named Jenny Gutbezahl was pretty popular among the under-thirty crowd, but she was a no-show in 2004, so maybe that's all over. (In crossword terms, "Bizarro" means any puzzle by a syndicated service such as the *Times*'s that appears in print elsewhere three to six weeks after the original publication date; the term—which derives from Superman comic books and not, as many believe, from the *Seinfeld* TV comedy show—refers to bulletin board posters from Florida or California or what-have-you who ask for pointers about how to solve 32-Across and who are in fact referring not to today's crossword but one that appeared a month or more ago, which everyone else has entirely forgotten.)

Being what they are, crossword puzzles also tend to attract a disproportionate number of people who are deeply introspective and less adept at normal social interactions than someone grabbed at random from the greater population; a lot of the folks you'll meet at Stamford, for instance, will be perfectly happy to let you assume the whole burden of any conversation you wish to maintain with them, which can be a pretty unsettling experience—these are the kind of people who, if they ever went to a shrink, would bitterly frustrate their therapist by lying on their couch for the whole hour, staring at the ceiling and feeling perfectly comfortable not saying a word except for "Hello" and "Good-bye." On the other hand, as we've seen, when a bunch of introverts come together, they tend to act, collectively, like extroverts, which explains the stentorian levels of conversational volume that greet you when you walk into the Stamford Marriott on a tournament weekend.

The other thing about Stamford is that it can be a pretty intimidating experience to the first-timer, who may find himself or herself a little daunted by both the enthusiasm and the patent skill at
doing crosswords of the other attendees. Let's remember that it
takes most people the better part of a week to finish a given Sunday
New York Times puzzle, if they finish it at all, and that here you're
given no more than forty-five minutes to turn in the very same
grid—and keep in mind that at least 50 percent of the people solving the same puzzle in that great big room look on such a generous
time limit as an outright gift. If you're not ready for it, walking into
the Grand Ballroom of the Stamford Marriott on tournament
weekend is sort of like pulling off Exit 23, your usual route home,
and suddenly finding yourself in the final three laps of a Formula 1
auto race—the speed and skill of the people using the same road as
you can be intimidating.

However, if you aren't already acquainted with one or more
people on the constructing side of the crossword equation, at Stamford you're likely to spend most of your time rubbing elbows with
fellow solvers. You'll want to stride up and give your greetings to
Will Shortz, but chances are he'll look too busy, or he'll be too surrounded by crossword-biz folks who've been waiting a year for a
chance at a face-to-face, and you'll be too daunted to walk up and
say hello. Unless you've been to Stamford once or twice before, or
unless you're there with someone who has been there in the past,
you'll find that it requires significant effort to get beyond the pleasantries and establish real personal ties, over the course of one brief
weekend, with anybody else there. If you're an alumnus returning
for the second or third time, though, you'll have no problem—in-
troverted people can recognize their own, and they'll open up to
you readily enough if this is the second or third year in a row they've
seen your face among all those other familiar ones. (Of course, you

could be inordinately charismatic or even slightly famous and have a different experience altogether—being neither charismatic nor famous, I couldn't tell you one way or the other, though I can say that being a reporter helps.)

With respect to constructors, though, the same social dynamic among solvers at the American Crossword Puzzle Tournament doesn't apply. Brendan gets mobbed by the young and the not-so-young alike. Cathy Millhauser, Manny Nosowsky, Merl Reagle, and a score or so like them (including the decidedly charismatic couple of Henry Rathvon and Emily Cox, who create the *Boston Globe* Sunday puzzle every other week and publish a highly popular acrostic puzzle in the *New York Times* twice a month) get asked for autographs and, occasionally, for free tutoring about how to get the puzzle a fan has worked on for months into publishable condition. These people are Stamford's superstars, and it doesn't matter if they're personable or cold and off-putting—without them, you see, you wouldn't be here at all.

What all puzzle constructors are supposed to display is a sort of collaborative goodwill toward the solver—a crossword that is too hard, that uses too many obscurities in its fill and too many overly ambiguous phrasings in its cluing, is, simply put, not a very good one. For instance, in my opinion the most difficult puzzle published in the *Times* in 2004 was Brendan Emmett Quigley's unthemed one of Friday, September 10, which it took me a humiliating thirty-nine minutes and forty-two seconds to fill in correctly, or about twice as long, for me, as your average Friday crossword. The reason it required so much of my time to do it was that I'm simply not as conversant with contemporary sports and pop culture as Brendan is, and in this I case I wasn't on his mental wavelength, either—but every single word in that very open puzzle was legitimate and fair, so I didn't begrudge him the time or the effort it took me to crack it. (I do hope, though, that he signs up for the American Crossword Puzzle Tournament next year, since participants are of course barred from having their grids used in competition.)

So it might be a beneficial thing, in terms of contributing to the sociology of the crossword world, to take a constructor many consider to be an ornery character and one many think particularly nice and see what makes them tick respectively. If you've read this far, you'll know exactly whom I intend to look at more closely: Stanley Newman, the constructor of the Passchendaele of all puzzles, the fifth of the 2004 tournament, and Michael Shteyman, the precocious and extremely gifted author of the same tournament's first one. The hope here is to limn from a comparison of the two constructors a sense of what fairness is, in crossword terms, and the beginnings, based on that information, of what a crossword ethics might look like—though, to fall back on a retort both Brendan Emmett Quigley and Cold War scholars might appreciate, I won't postulate that being mean is unethical or that being nice is its moral antithesis, at least when we're talking about puzzles. I will say that if you're interested in solving crosswords better, or in solving them faster than you currently do, both Newman and Shteyman are well worth hearing out.

A Crossword Mephistopheles

Back in the days when he was actively competing, Stanley Newman was known as the fastest crossword solver around—only Trip Payne's five-minutes-and-change polishing off of the final puzzle at Stamford in 2004 comes close to emulating Newman's feats. (He has since concentrated mainly on making puzzles, editing the *New York*

Newsday puzzle and hosting yearly cruise-ship junkets that double as constructing seminars.) Newman's speed is the subject of a tale sometimes heard at Stamford (though it's untrue; the real story involves another quick solver and turns out quite differently, with the constructor winning). It goes like this:

"At one point, a constructor decided he'd set up a challenge for Stanley. He designed a puzzle especially for him, then challenged him to a head-to-head public solving contest; the constructor figured there was no way he could be outsolved in a puzzle he himself had made. Stanley agreed and they got down to it—and, sure enough, Stan won handily.

Deeply shaken, the constructor vowed to do the same thing again the next year—only this time he not only created the crossword, but spent a couple of hours the night before the rematch memorizing the fill. Again they set to it. After just over two minutes of furiously filling in the words he had memorized, the constructor glanced up to see how Stan was faring. To his utter dismay, Stan was sitting there with his arms folded across his chest and a Cheshire-cat smile on his face. On the table before him was the constructor's puzzle, all done and all correct. He had done it in two minutes."

Like many people who are at the top of the field in terms of what they do, Newman has a reputation for cockiness; at Random House, whose crossword-publishing operation he ran for some years (he now writes crossword books for them), a few individuals basically told me to avoid him if at all possible. I don't know if Stanley rubs some people the wrong way, or if he's intolerant of those he considers less than competent, but all I can say is, in my conversations with him, he came off as entirely charming and very happy to be of help. The only hint of a real mean streak in him I've encountered was that dread puzzle five at the 2004 tournament. The first time I spoke with him, someone was mowing his lawn, his dog was obviously hoping to attract his attention, and a stream of calls came in that he put off for the forty-five minutes we talked—not quite the behavior you'd expect of an irascible self-involved sadist, in other words.

Stanley Newman's background is a pretty classic one, for a crossword maven, since it's heavily math-oriented. He started out as a kid from Long Island (as you'd guess if you ever hear him talk) with an internship at Goldman Sachs during the summer of 1971, where his boss was future Clinton-era Treasury secretary Robert Rubin, and, after college, worked for the next fifteen years as a quantitative analyst at various Wall Street firms. When he was young, he did the *TV Guide* puzzle ("I don't know if they still think it's okay to run two-letter solves"), but doesn't remember exactly when or how he graduated to the big leagues.

"A couple people wrote something about crosswords in my high school yearbook; I wish I could say I have vivid memories of that time, but I don't. Later on, there was this trader I ran with on Wall Street in my early years there who wanted me to solve puzzles in bars and have people bet on my performance, so I guess I was already into crosswords then. But my life changed dramatically after I first started attending the U.S. Open Puzzle Championship. I won twice, and that got me started in the business—very gingerly. I published my first crossword in *Games* magazine in 1983, with Will Shortz as editor. Constructing puzzles is a skill that has to be learned."

I interrupted at this point, suggesting that being in a position to make a successful puzzle is sort of like being a glassblower, in the sense that you need to have a whole range of skills at your disposal before you can even hope to produce anything that looks like blown glass.

"Well, yes, and for a while I couldn't be sure I could finish every one—when you make a puzzle you know is hard, you need to make up the clues as you go, and you can find yourself worked into impossible spots. All that's gone now, of course, because of the constructing software that's available. That said, though, it's still me selecting the words, the theme, and the cluing elements—not the computer. Instead of being impossibly hard, constructing is now just really hard."

"So how did you come up with the theme for 'Compound Fractures'?"

"Ah. I was driving from Amsterdam to Arnhem, in Holland, for the World Puzzle Championship. Holland, especially northern Holland, is particularly flat and dreary, in terms of landscape. The phrase 'tedium car-ride' just popped into my head. I needed to have a puzzle for the 2004 Stamford tournament, so I started scribbling down all these bogus compound names to see which ones would work. I wanted the grid to look impressive, but it was going to be the fifth puzzle, so I wanted to make it very difficult. It was mean, and I meant to clue it hard."

"Hard"? I didn't tell Stanley that, had the Stamford Marriott's amenities for its guests included pitchforks and burning torches, he would have been in for quite a run that Saturday afternoon—he had already told me it was a much-anticipated thrill for him actually to see the competitors fill in his crossword, so I suppose he must have seen and felt the level of collective animus grow as the clock ticked down to zero. And made good his escape through a side door, I suppose; at least, I tried to spot him when I came back to watch after having finished that monster, and Stanley was nowhere to be seen.

"Why," I asked, "do you think people with mathematics or music backgrounds do so well at Stamford?"

"Well, back in the old days, constructors were usually coming from the humanities—teaching, writing, things like that. I don't know what to make of the fact that these days they're not so high-profile in terms of constructing. I used to think that math people brought precision to a grid, but I just don't know."

"What about the ability to recognize and pick up on patterns?"

"I'd say it's key—absolutely *key*—for a solver to be able to visualize what a long word or phrase might be from just two letters. I don't know what sort of mind it takes to do that; I mean, I don't know if you can define that sort of mind or not. As far as I can tell, you either have it or you don't."

"Have crosswords changed your life?"

There was a long pause before Newman replied. "There's no question about it. I started constructing and then editing full time after the market crash in 1987. The life expectancy of crossword editors is actually quite high, and there aren't many slots that need to be filled—so, instead of hanging around and waiting for someone to die, I started my own puzzle publication. By the time people started to pay attention to what I was doing, I was a crossword professional. And I will say that it has enriched my life far beyond measure. It's not just that I don't have to commute to Wall Street anymore and sit there in an office doing the same thing day after day. Crosswords have brought me psychic success in ways I never would have imagined."

Hmm—I rang off at that point, thinking that the picture of a monster I had developed about Stanley Newman was all wrong. And mean? If this guy's behavior is mean, I remember a couple of schoolyard bullies who could take a few lessons from him.

A week or so later we spoke again; this time I was more interested in hearing what tips Stan might have for me after I described my performance at the 2004 tournament to him.

"First, I have to say that making a mistake in four puzzles isn't so good. You overthought it. You should train yourself to automatically look the other way, to make sure that the crosses add up. That doesn't take thinking, it takes looking. Accuracy is king. I never say do puzzles faster—solve them smarter. And when you're training for Stamford, stop doing puzzles online. Print them out and do them on paper insanely slowly, so you train your eye to look both ways. I swept Stamford in 1982, but only after I'd done well over fifteen hundred puzzles by way of practice. They didn't have electronic versions back then."

"What about changing my handwriting?"

"Well, I didn't want to do it myself. But that's just me—you have to play your own game, and changing the way I write my vowels isn't mine. Just remember that most of the people at Stamford aren't there to compete. People have their rituals with crosswords as with anything else, and it would never be my goal as an editor to have people solve them more quickly if they don't want to. If you plan on competing better, just make sure you're not overthinking your fills—train your eyes by practicing, then let them do the checking while the clock's running down."

Misha the Nice

Six years ago, the youngest regular contributor to the *New York Times* crossword was Brendan Emmett Quigley—he was twenty-four then. Although Brendan has what your Gypsy grandmother would call an "old soul," he's no old man now, at thirty. But his mantle as boy wonder has passed on to Michael Shteyman, the slight, elfin, black-haired Johns Hopkins junior who authored the 2004 tournament's first puzzle.

Again, the amazing thing about Michael—"Misha" to those who speak to him in Russian—is that he's only been in the United States since 1997, when he was thirteen. By the time he was nineteen, he had gone from functionally speaking no English at all to being one of the more frequent names appearing in the credit line of the *Times* puzzle; it's a remarkable feat that only underscores how bright and how intensely hardworking this college premed actually is. (His appearance at Stamford in March was a sort of two-day holiday for him; the epic games of phone tag we played a month later, when he was gearing up for his year-end exams, took place largely because he was off at the library six or seven nights a week, an orgy of concentrated study that was exhausting merely to hear about, let alone experience. When I think that he was producing a half-dozen *Times* grids over the same period, as well, I'm deeply tempted to take a sympathetic nap on my couch.)

"What was the transition to English-language puzzles like for you—I mean, did you do crosswords in Russia before you came?"

"Yes. By the time I was ten, I was helping my mother with the *St. Petersburg Times* puzzle. I published my first crossword in a local weekly when I was eleven. So, when we came here, all I had was the English we'd learned in school, which was nothing—if I speak English now, it's mainly because of immersion. I got a book of English grammar and decided to try putting English words into a Russian grid, crossing every second letter, to make puzzles that would help some friends learn English, too. The word 'begin' would only be crossed at the 'b,' 'g,' and 'n,' and so on."

"What did you make of American puzzles when you first saw them?"

"Oh—I immediately picked up a *Baltimore Sun* puzzle. I thought it was horrible and didn't make sense. There was too much wordplay, and the fact that every letter was keyed made it very confusing. But in high school, one of my classmates was Ethan Cooper, who'd just sent his first puzzle to Will. He showed it to me; I didn't even know what the word 'layup' meant. He explained that to me, as well as how a wholly keyed puzzle works—the grid, the fill, the cluing. I began to get interested, and I used Ethan as a guide to perfect in English the constructing skills I'd learned in Russian."

"What was it like for you to be at Stamford—what, seven years after you came to America?"

"To see five hundred or more people doing the puzzle you constructed—that was incredible."

"And why did you leave Russia in the first place?"

Misha laughed. "We're Jewish. But, yes, I know it sounds corny, but in my family America was always perceived as this great country where you can fulfill your dreams. I know it sounds bad, but it's true."

(In the summer of 2004, Misha became a U.S. citizen, a fact that was wildly celebrated on the Cru bulletin boards; he's well liked in the crossword community, of course, so the event of his naturalization was much celebrated by his fellow puzzlers, who understandably don't get all that many chances to welcome another crossword fiend into citizenship. That a first-generation American with seven years' experience speaking English is *publishing* crosswords in the nation's highest-profile venue for them is nothing short of astounding.)

I'd just been looking at the Wednesday, April 21, 2004, *Times* puzzle that Misha had done—a grid whose theme reflected, I'd supposed, the fact that the constructor was neck-deep in the academic whirl. The themed entries are PASSFAIL, FINALEXAM, MIDTERM, POPQUIZ, RESEARCHPAPER, and ESSAYTEST; KAPPA and

DAWNS aren't meant to be part of the theme, but, when you think about it, most students want to make Phi Beta Kappa, and certainly many of them see their share of dawns, either because they're pulling all-nighters or staying out too late of a Saturday night.

"So, does this puzzle reflect a certain preoccupation on your part with matters academic?"

Misha laughed. "Yes, basically, although I wrote it two years ago. I walk around and whatever I see or think about can become a theme. For example, I was on a bus the other day and saw a sign that said 'Private Property'—that's fifteen letters. Then I noticed that 'No Trespassing' has a 'p' in the middle. The two phrases can cross and still fit into a weekday grid. A puzzle is a reflection of something I'm doing or interested in at the time. For instance, I like to play pool, so I've been thinking of a way to make a puzzle out of that—with a pocket on the corners and both sides, perhaps. You can never tell what will or what won't work out until you try it. The great thing about puzzles is that they encourage you to try. Except for cryptics, which are devious when you make them and even more devious when you try to solve them."

Learning from the Nice and the Mean

It's one thing to do a puzzle in the quiet of your own space, where you can put the thing down and come back to it later if you wish and no one will much care. It's quite another to do it at Stamford, with the clock practically booming and the motion of the proctors and the other participants a faint, distracting irritant out of the corner of your eye. But, in between the lines of what Newman and Shteyman are saying, you can begin to glean solving tricks that should stand you in good stead no matter where you are when you're doing a crossword.

The first thing to remember is that, themed or not, a puzzle is built by one person at one specific point in time. The constructor has been driven by something to construct the puzzle in this specific way. In the case of the *New York Times* puzzles especially, there's also the editor's contribution to take into account, although from the solver's point of view this latter isn't necessarily all that important— Will Shortz can accept and work on a puzzle but not run it for several years or (as in the case of the Brendan Quigley puzzle I mentioned before) turn it around in a matter of days, so you can't reasonably expect to see a recurrent leitmotif introduced by him in a given week's puzzles. As you're doing a specific puzzle, however, you can keep it in the back of your mind that there may be some overarching connection among at least some of the clues, because constructors are human, too, and like the rest of us they have unconscious minds that can throw a pattern into an otherwise perfectly random-looking selection of words. It takes effort to keep an eye out for themes, conscious or unconscious, but it's a skill that can be acquired and honed. After all, it can't be sheer luck that the same names keep appearing in the finals year after year at the American Crossword Puzzle Tournament; the people who win have developed their ability to pick up on and exploit subtle recurrences in the grids. There's no reason you or I can't do the same; it just takes practice—a lot of it, granted, but plain practice nonetheless.

Another thing to keep in mind is that constructors have personal styles; after you do a couple of Brendan Quigley's puzzles, you learn that when you do the next one, you're going to have to set your mind to the topics of sports and popular culture—in his words, again, you have to steel yourself to play *Jeopardy!* on acid. With a

Michael Shteyman puzzle, you can expect a very creative, very open grid whose fill isn't going to be, on average, all that recondite or recherché; at least for the next few years, while his English-language skills improve and as he becomes exposed to reading (and listening, and watching) matter less limited than medical textbooks. Each of the major constructors has his or her specific talents, interests, and limitations—it's no easy task to identify them and then keep them all straight, but if you do the work, if you go back and examine each filled-in grid with an eye to how it differs from grids by other constructors, you'll find, after a while, that you'll get a sort of second sense about what a given constructor might be trying to do with the grid on the table in front of you. In this sense, solvers of British-style cryptics have an edge over their American cousins—the puzzle they're doing today was made by the same person who made yesterday's and the day before's, so the chances are greater, over time, that the solver will internalize the individual quirks and idiosyncrasies that make up the functional rules governing the creation of that puzzle.

What the cognoscenti call "crosswordese"—that bizarre patois of nouns and phrases you see nowhere else but in crosswords—has seen its star fall somewhat since Will Shortz became editor of the *Times* puzzle, but in a vestigial form it still is and always will be there. ANOA ("Celebes ox") and ADIT ("Mine entrance") may be gone; SST, ESNE, and many others still remain. In his essay "How to Solve the *New York Times* Crossword Puzzles," which appears on the premium games page of the newspaper's Web site, Will Shortz cautions readers to look out for question-marked clues (these represent puns or stretched definitions) and common abbreviations such as RANDR for "rest and recreation"; more important, he makes the point that each and every answer must be interchangeable, if you were to use it in a sentence, with the clue that produces it: A clue that's a noun cannot produce a fill that's an adjective, for instance. If you're not familiar with this fundamental rule, make sure to memorize it; doing so will save you from going on a lot of wild-goose chases, since the more dastardly constructors will arrange matters to exploit your tendency toward choosing the simple and straightforward answer that can be made to look like a different part of speech from the original clue.

The second most important skill to master in order to consistently solve the *Times* puzzle is intraword pattern recognition. If you see a seven-letter space with a "d" in the second position and an "l" in the last, with a little prompting from the clue (say, "Floating general?"), you should be able to get ADMIRAL pretty quickly. One way to get better at doing this is, again, to practice. When you're showering or mowing the lawn or shaving (but not driving, please), think of words of random length with two letters placed somewhere within them and try to come up with real words or phrases by filling in the blank spaces. Take an eight-letter word or phrase beginning with an "o" and ending in a "y," for instance. That could yield OVEREASY; it could also yield any of a couple of score of adverbs beginning with the letter "o." The point isn't to memorize all the possible combinations that will fit the conditions you set; it's to train your mind to recognize as many combinations as it can in the least amount of time, because that enables you to concentrate on producing an additional cross, which in turn radically increases your chances of getting the answer right. Part of training yourself to do this hinges on your innate ability to identify which letter combinations are statistically the most common and to make inspired guesses based on that information. This last factor may be why quantitatively oriented people do better at crossword competitions than do the nonquantitatively oriented; on the other hand, constructors are aware of frequency analysis, too, and will do their best to come up with unexpected word forms to trip up the smarty-pants statistics-oriented folks among us.

The most important thing you can do to make yourself a better solver, though, is the most difficult. You need to be able to rearrange your brain into an information storage and retrieval system of the highest order; you need to cram it with facts neatly relative to one another, each living in its own assigned place, with the things nearest it being the things most like it. You need, in other words, to become a highly organized collector of data about the world around you.

This is a tall order for many, since our memory system evolved to handle tasks quite different from the storage of abstract data. (And, unless you live there and travel a lot, your knowing the names of every capital city around the Pacific rim counts as your having possession of some pretty abstract data.) It was built to deal with fairly concrete information, such as where that stand of nut trees is in relation to home, where that trail leads to, and why this smell or that represents something good or something bad; we think we're pretty sophisticated, in terms of memory, but we're actually using the same hardware designed hundreds of millennia ago—there is no equivalent of Moore's law for the human brain. It's only our software that differentiates us from our early ancestors, and for all of us the publisher of that software is the same entity—the problematic firm of Genetics, Environment & Co.

You obviously can't change genetics; I'd love to be able to carry a tune, for instance, but the best I can do of a morning in the shower is a fairly convincing imitation of late-career Bob Dylan (or, if I'm hung over, the late Jim Morrison). Given that the American Crossword Puzzle Tournament is so overwhelmingly dominated by people with math and music on the brain, it's a pretty good bet that, short of overwhelming luck, I'll never do better there than place between the top fifty and the top hundred. But I go— and I do crosswords—not because I want to prove to anyone that I'm highly skilled at solving puzzles, but because I find that the effort I put into developing a crossword solver's way of thinking has repercussions that redound positively in all the other aspects of my life.

If you're not quantitatively oriented by virtue of your genetic payload, you can at least train your brain—or rewrite your software—by making conscious decisions to remember abstract data in an associative way. Since the time I was a small child, making a forced conversion from being a French-language thinker to being an English-language one, I've approached the problem of information acquisition sort of like the way a librarian decides how to shelve the new book that has just come in. Take the word "kapok," which, you'll recall, provided me with the key that allowed me to solve Stan Newman's fifth puzzle at the 2004 tournament. Several years before I'd read Dan Kurzman's *Fatal Voyage*, an account of the sinking of the heavy cruiser USS *Indianapolis* late in World War II. For reasons of national security, the ship was operating under conditions of radio silence, so no one realized it had been sunk until about five days after the event; most of the ship's complement perished by drowning, of thirst, or of being eaten by sharks. I learned, reading the book, that kapok, the filler of most U.S. Navy life vests during that time, was admirably buoyant for about twenty-four hours; after that, it became waterlogged, and the fellow wearing it might as well have been wrapped up in a length of anchor cable for all the good it would do him after that. When I first encountered that new word, I filed it away under the general umbrella of (I'll try to do this Library of Congress–style) "Flotation devices—Not so effective over the long haul—World War II—Sharks." And it was there at my fingertips when I needed it; all I had to do was concentrate, and it was suddenly being written out, almost automatically, by my hand holding that no. 2 pencil in that crowded but deathly silent room.

Chapter 10

HOW TO SOLVE
a crossword

Up to now, the focus of this book has been mainly on the constructor side of the equation, and there's a reason for that. In constructing, the difference between the creations of a seasoned pro such as Brendan Emmett Quigley and those of a novice are a matter of degree; Brendan makes beautiful grids and knows how to get himself out of the constructing jams they sometimes create, but fundamentally he uses the same rules and techniques a neophyte does, only to better effect. Every solver, however, approaches a puzzle in his own unique way.

My method of filling in a grid is to look for definite patterns in the cluing and concentrate on breaking into the puzzle through them. In Christina Kelly's video of the 2004 American Crossword Puzzle Tournament, Tyler Hinman speaks just after I do and says something quite different:

> I don't really think about what I'm doing. I do sections at a
> time. . . . You know, I don't read down all the acrosses; I fill
> the grid, basically.

Hinman is saying that he starts in one of the corners and works his way through the puzzle from there; since all the answers in that section are interconnected, they provide mutually reinforcing hooks, and exploiting these is probably what makes Hinman a faster solver than I. The thing is, Hinman's not necessarily a *better* solver than I—at Stamford, anyone placing in the top half in the standings is likely to be as good as everyone else within that subgroup, if only because all will likely have solved most of the puzzles correctly. The trick in competition is to achieve 100 percent accuracy while writing words down as fast as you can, which means you need to be able to simultaneously write down one correct answer while reading the next clue, and so on until the puzzle is done.

It's sort of embarrassing to report that, even after scores of conversations with puzzlers in which I put the question to each, none could say precisely what advice to give to someone who has never touched a puzzle in his life. The only thing the crossword mavens can offer is advice about how to better your scores in competition: cross-checking your answers, making the clock your friend instead of your enemy, remaining calm, and practicing—lots and lots of practice is, indeed, apparently the one thing all top solvers have in common.

Months after the 2004 event, I got in touch with Al Sanders, who scored highest at the tournament although he placed third in the finals, and asked him what he would tell a complete novice. (Sanders was far from incommunicative; he was funny, animated, and very willing to take forty minutes out of a busy dad's weekend schedule to talk to me. I realized he'd been so reserved at the awards lunch for the wholly understandable reason that he just, for the third straight year, won the rankings race yet lost top place in the final heat.)

"Do a lot of puzzles. Don't worry about memorizing obscure

words or anything, because that really won't help you. If you practice a lot, you start to see the same words over and over; the better puzzles use common words and phrases, but use good cluing to make them work. Pretty soon you'll be amazed by how much you'll be able to fill in. The reason I'm good at puzzles, I guess, is that I've been doing them since I was seven and am extraordinarily comfortable with them."

"You need flexibility of mind—the ability to rapidly figure out where the twists are, what's a pun, what's a rebus," said Katherine Bryant when I asked her the same question. "You need an ear for the quirks of language, and you need to be good at pattern recognition. I don't know what I'd tell someone about to do their first puzzle. I don't try to make a point of learning—it's something that just happens. My brain needs the stimulation of a puzzle; it's like an itch you want to scratch."

Contrary to the way it may seem, Hinman, Sanders, Bryant, and I aren't trying to throw a wet blanket over anyone's hopes of becoming an accomplished puzzle solver overnight; it's just that it's as impossible to tell someone how to do puzzles as it is to tell them how to be a great basketball or chess or tennis player. Partly it's innate—I will say that the better solvers tend to be introverts who are most comfortable when they're alone with themselves and who have polymathic minds. If you don't answer to that description, the chances don't seem good that you'll be accepting a trophy and a check from Will Shortz at Stamford. (On the other hand, if you're not six feet six or taller, it's also unlikely that you'll ever be a star forward for the L.A. Lakers). If you're the sort of person who likes puzzles in the first place, you may have a chance, although I can tell you that it's a devilishly hard and close race, a crossword tournament, and, as with any sport, to do well at it you need to think strategically (about the clock, about making sure you get enough rest, about keeping hydrated) and to practice lots and make sure you do so using pencil and paper, not a computer and a keyboard.

"I think the hardest thing to get good at," Sanders also suggested, "is the concept of the look-ahead; while you're writing down one answer, you're reading the next two or three clues. It's difficult and it takes practice. Take Monday and Tuesday puzzles and really push yourself to complete them in half the time you're doing now. That, and being good at getting the cluing, plus a small amount of luck, is all it really takes. I hope I'm not jinxing myself, but one reason I've done well is that I haven't made a mistake in six tournaments."

In case you're getting goose-pimply with anticipatory excitement, I'll add that when Al says "all it really takes," he's talking about himself and not about you or me. To me, that's a bitter pill to swallow; but I comfort myself thinking that no amount of coaching and practice will transform me into any semblance of a star athlete. I may shave off a microsecond or two from my speed in the hundred-meter dash, but not even Carl Lewis could teach me to make that distance faster than a reasonably fit dog—which is why, I guess, I don't make a habit of sneaking into top-secret military installations all that often.

The Cru

A good place to start learning more about crossword puzzles, both if you're new to them or have been doing them for years, is the crossword bulletin board—the Cru—on the *New York Times* Web site. (You don't have to be a member of the paper's premium puzzle service to post.) Both in person—at its periodic dinners and lunches held in New York, and of course the wine-and-cheese orgies at the Stamford Marriott—and in its virtual form, the Cru is as warm and welcoming as the American Crossword Puzzle Tournament can be. More important for our purposes, though, it's an incredibly valuable crossword resource.

Once you learn to obey the no-spoiler rule (do not discuss a puzzle from 10 P.M., when it's posted, to noon of the day of its publication), you can ask the board why a particular clue yields a particular answer, what a word's etymology is, how to go about solving other types of puzzles, even trivia questions. Since it's populated almost exclusively by introverts, the Cru tends to be a lively place—an introvert whose social inhibitions are obviated by electronic quasi-anonymousness tends toward outright giddiness. What this means for you, who's posting for the first time and just introducing yourself, is a torrent of welcomes and question. Six months after the tournament, for instance, a person named Gary came on with a question, and in the process of asking it let slip that he was a sometime writer for the *New York Times*. I don't know why this struck the collective nerve, but it took forty-eight hours for the chorus of responses to him to begin quieting down. If you're a person who can bandy about the crossword terms introduced in the preface of this book, and you want virtual company, there's no better place to be.

When you're posting at the Cru, though, you'll need to watch your language. Under the vigilant eye of its moderator, Will Johnston (the constructor and math-textbook editor from Boston who, you'll recall, placed third at the Division C American Crossword Puzzle Tournament in 2004), swear words and the like are uniformly removed from messages, so that the whole thing sounds not only as if you'd entered an animate version of the *Times* puzzle but, indeed, as if you were at Stamford in person—Brendan Quigley is the only person there I've ever heard utter an oath, but he does that enough to make up for everyone else.

The Cru is like being at Stamford for another reason, too: It's the only place on the planet where you get to interact personally with a very large proportion of the best solvers and constructors alive. Over the summer, for instance, a couple of posters were discussing Puns & Anagrams, a type of puzzle that appears with the *Times* Sunday crossword every couple of months or so. When I logged on to the Cru the morning after this particular exchange, I read the following informative post:

History of Puns & Anagrams

Puns & Anagrams were invented by Albert Morehead, the bridge and games expert, and first appeared in *Games Digest* magazine in 1937. They were meant to be an American version of the English cryptic crosswords, which at that time were still in their formative stage. Soon P&A were also appearing regularly in *Redbook*, the women's magazine, and various puzzle magazines and books.

The main difference between P&A and cryptics was that the former had fully-checked grids (like regular American crosswords) while the latter didn't. Also, P&A clues contained lots more anagrams (generally unsignaled) than cryptics, as well as more straight puns. And over the years P&A developed various uniquely American idiosyncrasies, like the name "Elsie" representing the letters L-C, and clues like "Kind of ear" for END (where the parts and the whole have no etymological connection).

When the *Times* inaugurated its Sunday crossword in 1942, editor Margaret Farrar made P&A a recurring feature on the bottom of the page, where it has been ever since.

Mel Taub became one of several P&A makers beginning in the 1950s. Today, since he's reliable and popular, he's the only P&A contributor I'll accept (not that anyone else is trying).

Eugene T. Maleska tried to eliminate P&A in the late 1970s and replace them with cryptics, but the outcry was too great. He compromised and reinstated them, printing one P&A every eight weeks, with cryptics appearing in the intervening months.

When I became the editor in 1993, I planned to phase out P&A gradually in favor of cryptics, which I think are more interesting puzzles. But, like ETM, I discovered that P&A have many diehard fans. So I put them back into the schedule—but just once every 18 weeks. Cryptics appear twice every 18 weeks.

As far as I know, the *Times* is the only publication today that still publishes P&A.

The message, of course, was signed by Will Shortz; it's a typical example of the sort of thing he weighs in with every month or so, and a representative sample (complete with a hyphenated adverbial compound with the adverb ending in -ly, which appears to be the only grammatical mistake Shortz ever makes). When you post on the Cru board, you can be sure what you write will be read not only by the two Wills, but by Al Sanders (a frequent lurker), Jon Delfin, Trip Payne—almost all the experts you've encountered in this book. Your post on a basketball board won't be read by Shaquille O'Neal; your post on a comedy board won't be read by Al Franken or Jon

Stewart. But your Cru post will be read by everyone who's anyone in the crossword world.

Crossword Fun

When you spend the better part of a year thinking about and doing crossword puzzles, certain leitmotifs begin to crop up. One of the most common of these, which I heard from two dozen or so constructors, is that puzzles are no more and no less than entertainment.

I suppose that, in a tautological sense, crosswords are entertaining—a statement that's a tautology because you need to be the kind of person who likes them in order to see them as objects of pleasant diversion. Whenever anyone expressed such an opinion to me, I always thought of the people who don't find puzzles entertaining; these individuals consider them, if they ever think of crosswords at all, a frustrating waste of time. The image that kept coming to me is of the nonathletic poor fellow gulled into participating in one of those ten-kilometer Fun Runs you see advertised on the bulletin boards of schools, libraries, and churches—if you're not a runner, six miles and change of slow, sweaty progress with the prospect of shin splints and acute respiratory distress ever looming sound like no "fun" at all.

Determining precisely what percentage of the general population regularly does crosswords is very hard to do. In the business, it's generally assumed that around 60 million Americans fill them in at least occasionally, though I don't know—and no one has been able to tell me—how that figure was calculated or even what "occasionally" means (once a day? once a month?). The best estimate I can come up with is based on the marginally valid extrapolation of the fact that the *Boston Globe* once forgot to run its daily puzzle and received forty thousand letters of complaint about it; given that the *Globe*'s circulation is just under five hundred thousand, that means that just under 9 percent of its readership felt strongly enough about the matter to bring it to the editors' attention. If the same readership-to-puzzlers ratio holds true for the *New York Times*, then up to a hundred thousand people buy it or subscribe to it largely because of the crossword. If this is multiplied across all the other crossword-publishing papers in the nation, and if you add to that figure the puzzles that appear in *TV Guide*, airline magazines, and those cheap little books you see people filling in on the subway, then maybe the total approaches the tens of millions—and that's a very big maybe.

Of the five people in my immediate family, I'm the only one who does puzzles. Of the eight to ten people who spent a given weekend at my summer time-share, on average usually only one other would be motivated to go out and buy another copy of the *Times* of a Sunday morning. So let's say that, based on very rough calculations and extremely flimsy anecdotal information, 5 to 10 percent of the folks you see on the street every day are likely to be cruciverbalists. I think that's a reasonable hypothesis, even though it was pulled out of thin air, so let's say that on a given day about 20 or 30 million Americans are going to do a crossword puzzle, or at least try to.

There are probably as many reasons for filling in grids as there are people who do so, but there are certain overarching ones that I'm fairly sure everybody shares. As I mentioned in the first chapter, they're a great way to occupy your mind for fifteen or twenty minutes, of course. For the hard-core puzzler, they're also things of beauty in and of themselves—a really good-looking grid combined with an interesting fill and challenging clues has both esthetic and intellectual appeal. But I suspect that, deep down, people who do lots of crosswords are attempting to create order by proxy. Certainly I dived headfirst into compulsive solving (as opposed to the ordinary, once-a-day-while-commuting-to-work kind); Brendan Emmett Quigley is by his own admission a little ridden by angst; Stanley Newman made crosswords his career only after his first one on Wall Street imploded; during his term in office, of course, Bill Clinton desperately needed to think about things other than the responsibilities of high office and those legal woes circling him like so many condors. Will Shortz is a different creature entirely—he seems simply to have been born to puzzle. For many solvers, especially those who do more than seven a week, crosswords are something of an emotional crutch. Certainly you'd begin to think so if you saw those people at the Stamford Marriott, feverishly getting through a score or more grids over the weekend above and beyond the competition puzzles; something, you know, has to be feeding that manic energy.

Without making too broad a psychological statement or belaboring this point over much, I'd say that, by and large, crossword solvers tend to be of an introspective ilk; some people may think it fun to do them in tandem with others, but mostly crosswords are filled in alone (as they were meant to be, the traditionalist in me screams). In this respect, casually asking whether the other person in the room knows a seven-letter word for "banner" that starts with "c" (the answer would be CRESSET) isn't really asking for help on the grid; like chocolate mousse eaten off someone else's plate, it's a lapse that doesn't count. This introspection also, as we've seen, explains why the American Crossword Puzzle Tournament is so unexpectedly a raucous event—all these introverts get together at the same time, a collective swing of the psychic pendulum (ENANTIO-

DROMIA, if you need a fancy thirteen-letter word for your next grid) takes place, and suddenly you're in *Animal House*.

The hedge fund I used to work for made a point of hiring just about anybody as long as they had IQs thirty or forty percentage points or more above the norm. While that policy didn't work out too well in the long run for the company (if you ever start an investment bank, remember that more than anything else you'll want brash salesmen and sober, conscientious accountants, not poets and punk rockers however brainy), it did make it possible for you to attend Friday-evening happy hours where the conversation of topics ran from physics to medieval political theology; apart from the beer and food, you might well have been sitting in on a graduate seminar. Stamford is a bit like that, too—it has to be, when you get so many seriously smart people together in the same hotel for a weekend.

In addition to being just plain fun for some, then, crosswords are also something of a didactic tool. If you perform a Web search for the term "crossword," a huge proportion of the results you get will be sites that provide or let you create grids to be used in a classroom setting. This is because, just as you're more likely to get your daily dose of exercise playing squash or tennis or something other than running, you're more likely to learn about a topic if you make a game of it. Of course, a *New York Times* puzzle is going to cover a whole lot more history, science, and culture than a grammar-school state-capitals crossword. You don't have to consciously realize, as you solve it over the course of many years, that you're not just playing a game but also constantly broadening your intellectual horizons—it's no coincidence that another recurring motif of my year in crosswords was the oft-repeated contention, on the part of both constructors and solvers, that one of the great rewards of puzzling is the constant injunction it places before you to learn and incorporate ever-greater masses of information. Granted, so does reading; but if you dislike classical music or sports, if you're frightened of math, if you detest science, you're not going to pick up a book on any of those subjects, whereas if you do crossword puzzles, you'll have to cope with them every day.

Now, there's a net positive good to this, and it strikes you the moment you walk into the American Crossword Puzzle Tournament; in fact, it was another leitmotif of my year. Everybody—as I've said quite a few times before, but the point bears repetition—is really, really *nice* there. It wouldn't be such a stretch, I believe, to say that this general atmosphere of pleasantness is in very large part due to the fact that everyone at the tournament spends a lot of time looking at and learning about the world around them: You pretty much have to if you want to develop the accumulated store of factual information you'll need to get through a crossword puzzle. It's sort of like the person we all know who hated people who were gay just because they're gay until his own brother or good friend came out; after that, "all gays" became just plain folks to him, each to be judged according to his individual attributes. I think puzzle people are nice because they have to be—the more you know about the world, the more you tend to give all things in it the benefit of the doubt before deciding if you like them or not. The more your mind is filled with real facts about the real world, in other words, the less room there will be in your heart for hatred.

The Seamy Side of Puzzles

On May 4, 2004, the puzzle editor of the British *Daily Telegraph*, Val Gilbert, published a short article within its pages about the first time the paper made puzzle history—that was when, just before the

Normandy D-Day invasion, then-editor Leonard Dawe was hauled before the authorities because his cryptic puzzle included, in rapid succession, the highly secret code names for various aspects of the impending military operation, but all of which were rapidly identified not as the work of a master spy, but as a series of innocent if astonishing coincidences.

In her article, Gilbert wrote that a man named Ronald French had just come forward with a startling story. In addition to being a puzzle constructor, Dawe was also the headmaster of the Strand School; French said that it was Dawe's habit to have his pupils into his study and, as an exercise in "mental discipline," would have them fill words and phrases into a blank grid, which Dawe would then later clue. When he was fourteen, French claimed, he was one of these pupils. The school had been evacuated to the countryside of Surrey in the wake of the London Blitz, and, since this was 1944, the area was dotted with the encampments of Allied troops who would be opening up the western front against the forces of Nazi Germany. French claims that he had picked up mention of the code words in question while he and his chums were hanging around the American camps and promptly used them when Dawe asked him to fill his grids.

Now, the story is implausible for a world of reasons. First, I've yet to hear of a constructor going through such an elaborate routine to build a puzzle or of one who builds a grid before worrying about the nature of the fill—not to mention that one tends to think of a cryptic clue and its answer as a gestalt rather than as two discrete entities, nor that it would be damnably ("deucedly," I guess Dawe would have said) harder to come up with a cryptic clue for a randomly selected word. Second, it's a huge source of complaint in memoirs and reminiscences of those days that the Allied soldiers were effectively quarantined from the general British population in the months leading up to the assault, and not too many fourteen-year-old boys would have had the resources to get in and out of what were in essence well-guarded fortified camps during a hot war. Most important, "Omaha," "Neptune," "Mulberry," "Utah," and "Overlord" weren't terms the grunts would have been bandying about—as code words, they were probably known to no more than fifty people in the world at that time, if that, and most if not all those being fellows with three stars or more on their shoulders. I'd be willing to grant at the very outside that, being the code names of the beaches the American infantrymen were slated to assault, "Omaha" and "Utah" might possibly have percolated down to the ranks, though I very much doubt it. Under no circumstances would foot soldiers know the code name for the naval covering operation ("Neptune"), the artificial harbors the British were going to tow to the Norman coast after the initial landings ("Mulberry"), or the whole complicated operation itself ("Overlord"). The guys who were going to set their boots on the ground would in any case have been much more interested in the name of the operational sectors they were assigned to—"Dog Green 2," for instance—and no such terms appeared in Dawe's puzzles.

No—instead of being the cause of a fundamental reformulating of puzzle history, the *Daily Telegraph* story of May 2004 was most likely the result of a cranky old man's desire to pull the leg of an overly credulous newspaperman too young to be able to confirm or deny the thrust of his tale. Gilbert ends her piece with the request that any reader who knows more about the story write in to her about it at the *Telegraph*. I suspect she'll be waiting beside her mailbox for a very long time to come.

What lengths you're willing to go to in order to have a filled-in grid before you at the end of the day is wholly your concern; your puzzle belongs to you, and you can complete it in Tagalog or Romansh for all that anyone cares. The *New York Times* offers solvers a telephone cheat line that costs $1.20 per minute; this is fair enough, and I hope the paper makes enough off the operation to give Will Shortz a nice raise every year. Paying for answers is no different, except for the cost of the transaction, from asking your spouse, plumber, or librarian the same thing—or from using the Google search engine. I don't do any of these things, and nor does, I'd guess, anybody who practices for the American Crossword Puzzle Tournament, where the only thing you can bring into the room with you is a no. 2 pencil and a sharpener.

But some people out there do like to cheat at crosswords, and for the life of me I can't figure out why this is so. In the first chapter I mentioned the young woman who wanted, I can only conjecture, my completed Saturday puzzle in order to impress her friends with it; since then I've twice noticed people picking up and pocketing a *Times* puzzle I had just completed. (I don't know what the motivation is—except when in competition, I always solve with a pen rather than a pencil, and maybe an inked-in grid is sexier than a penciled-in one.) And of course there are all those people who like to post absurd solving speeds on the *Times* puzzle Web site, for what form of satisfaction I have no way to tell; I'd just like to see some of those people try their luck at Stamford one day. Any potential payoff you might get from cheating on a crossword seems far too small to make it worth the risk—though I do sometimes wonder if at dinner that night the friends of the girl on the ferry, to her intense shame, said, "Amy, this isn't your handwriting, is it?"

As I mentioned in chapter 7 about the 2004 tournament, someone found and returned to Cathy Millhauser an unmarked envelope containing a very fair amount of untraceable cash. I'll let that fact speak for itself, but in the meantime will ask you: If the same thing were to happen at, say, a fairground or a gun collectors' convention, do you think that money would have been returned? I don't, either. I'm not saying that all crossword lovers are honest folk dripping with goodness. I would say, though, that if I had to toss my keys and wallet to someone before leaping off the pier to save the little drowning girl, I'd look for the fellow in the crowd with the daily crossword in his hand.

Chapter 11

THE ESCHATOLOGY
OF PUZZLES

At this point, I'm ready to admit it: I believe—I strongly believe—that doing crosswords is more than just amusing oneself for
a little while with a bit of intellectual game-playing. I think solving
puzzles is an active step you can take to make yourself a better, more
informed, fairer, and more tolerant person. At the same time,
though, I realize that most of the people you see around you are
averse to crosswords for whatever reason. Some may just plain consider them boring; others might not have the verbal and symbolic
skills necessary to getting through them, and when you're bad at
something you tend to avoid it.

Sitting and solving crossword puzzles under the timed and
competitive conditions of the Stamford tournament is a nerve-
racking experience I wouldn't recommend to everybody. I plan to
do better in 2005 than I did in 2004, though, but that's going to be
an exercise in keeping my cool under stressful conditions, which I'm
not, I realize, terribly good at doing. But I would recommend that
as many people as possible try to do at least the Monday and Tuesday *Times* puzzles for a while in the hopes that the puzzle bug bites,
because if it does, you'll never have to be bored again. A long trip by

train, bus, or plane is made immeasurably better if you have a collection of Brendan Emmett Quigley crosswords to battle your way through while you're in tedious transit; the hours literally pass like minutes. There's also nothing quite like the feeling of a job well done that comes from finishing a truly tough puzzle; granted, you crinkle the thing up or flip to the next page when you're done, depending on whether you're working with a newspaper page or a book, but you will remember many of those facts and words you spent so much energy wresting from the clues, and when you come across them again in future puzzles you'll have the delightful experience of meeting old friends after a long separation.

In the chapter on crossword history, I wrote about the mysterious Phaistos Disk, whose enigmatic, whorled pattern of words or letters has been confounding linguists, anthropologists, and historians for roughly a century now. I thought about it again as I was lying for several hours, with nothing to do and too weak to move, on an emergency-room bed a few hours after the 2004 American Crossword Puzzle Tournament concluded. As I tried not to listen to the ghastly rattle of the old woman across the ward or to watch the cocky detectives guard the gunshot victim in the bed catty-corner to mine or to talk to my neighbor, who was my age and had come in because he, too, had suddenly fainted that evening, I concentrated instead on the anonymous artisan who had fired that weird and singular artifact. It dawned on me that, unable as modern linguists are to decipher what the symbols impressed on it mean, we tend to project onto them the product of our wildest imaginings. For me, all of a sudden, it was this: Some ancient genius, way back in the days of King Minos, discovered the secret of the crossword. The priests in the temple, seeing it, realized at once what damage this magical thing would wreak—absorbed in their solving, the peasants in the field, the huntsmen in the woods, and the fishermen by the sea would neglect their work, and who then would till or bring back the wild boar or shake the fish from their nets? In secret, the priests wrested the thing from its maker and hid it in the deepest corner of their temple, where only the gods could see it.

Three thousand years later, knowing the moment was propitious, the gods caused the disk to be uncovered; five years after it was found, they breathed its secret into the ear of Arthur Wynne. "Take this wonder of the word-cross and heal yourself," they said. "And you should probably copyright it, by the way."

So, nearly a century after the crossword was born or breathed into the fertile mind of Arthur Wynne, you may find yourself in an airport or on a train or in the subway, watching the man or woman beside you assiduously fill in a puzzle. Whatever you do, don't disturb that person—he or she is solving a mystery and at the same time putting back together, word by word, the pieces of our broken world.

On the following pages are the seven grids that competitors were faced with at the 2004 American Crossword Puzzle Tournament. For a full re-creation of that event (minus the bar tab), try to complete them within the times listed on pages 109 and 110. If you ace all seven, try either the A-, B-, or C-level version of the championship puzzle, which appears after them. Good luck!

Puzzle #1

CONTRADICTION by Michael Shteyman

A warm-up puzzle with a simple—and elegant—interlocking theme.

WORDS	MINUTES	LETTERS	SCORE

Copyright © 2004 American Crossword Puzzle Tournament

ACROSS

1 Penny pincher
6 Change for a five
10 Opposite of dele, to a typesetter
14 Refrigerator brand
15 Pepsi or Coke
16 _____ Alto, Calif.
17 2002 DiCaprio/Hanks movie
20 Former partners
21 Butterfingers
22 Alternative to 15-Across
23 Garden bloom
25 "Come in!"
26 Some figures in *The X-Files*
30 Many millennia
32 Draw a bead on
33 "_____ out of it!"
34 Soybean curd
38 Old Glory
41 Private eyes, slangily
43 Ship's pole
43 J.F.K. often used his: Abbr.
44 Out of one's ever-lovin' mind
45 Corner fold
46 Thick
50 Cabbage, on a wiener
52 Shows disapproval
54 Hit up for, as a cigarette
55 Island of Napoleon's exile
59 "Row, Row, Row Your Boat" line
62 The "A" of U.S.N.A.: Abbr.
63 Attend
64 TV news source
65 London's _____ Gallery
66 Itar-_____ (Russian news agency)
67 Greek Z's

DOWN

1 Nutmeg spice
2 Giant-screen theater
3 Fill
4 Envelope extras: Abbr.
5 "Go, team!"
6 70% of the Earth's surface
7 Familiar phrase that contradicts 17-, 38-, and 59-Across
8 Assistant for Santa
9 Utters
10 Reject
11 Unspoken
12 Make very happy
13 Laser printer need
18 Pitiful cry
19 Dentist's request
23 Cats and dogs
24 Breadmaking need
26 Speedy
27 Dentist's request
28 Apple computer
29 Home now for NASA's Spirit and Opportunity
31 Choose, with "for"
33 Nosh
34 Triangle's sound
35 *The Andy Griffith Show* boy
36 Greek cheese
37 Brezhnev's land
39 Te _____ cigars
40 Hilarious thing
44 Late filmmaker Riefenstahl
45 Russian parliament
46 Half a tone above C
47 Author Jong
48 Jack Sprat's diet
49 Stockholm native
51 Detroit products
53 Army N.C.O.
55 Scottish Gaelic
56 Gave temporarily
57 "Ali _____ and the Forty Thieves"
58 Old Gremlins and Pacers
60 Feathery scarf
61 Neutral area, for short

Puzzle #2

A COMEDY OF ERRORS by Fred Piscop

We hope the only "blunders" in your solution are the intended ones.

WORDS	MINUTES	LETTERS	SCORE

20 MINUTES / 98 WORDS

ACROSS

1 Eur. carrier
4 Pain in the neck
8 Bring down
12 Prefix with sphere
15 *Lou Dobbs Tonight* airer
16 Black-and-white beast
17 Word with pigeon or square
18 Pointillist's mark
19 In vitro items
20 The dieter _____
23 Instrument that goes tootle-te-tootle
25 It's good to break
26 Slots spot
27 The maid _____
34 German wife
35 Road postings
38 Reply implying everyone's doing it
41 Poor people
43 Richard III's request
44 Bell-ringing company
46 Live
47 The Web surfer _____
52 Cabin sleeper
53 Baseball family name
54 Country singer Tubb
55 Side in the Peloponnesian War
59 Oscar Wilde works
61 Directs
62 Battle of behemoths
63 The overhead lighting technician _____
70 Need ibuprofen
73 In the past
74 Devil-like
75 The jazzman _____
82 Model T contemporary
83 It must be tended
84 Cuddly movie alien
85 MacLachlan of *Twin Peaks*
86 Titled Turk
87 Yeoman's assent
88 Classic theater name
89 Cry out loud
90 To this point

DOWN

1 Show disdain
2 Sight at a smithy
3 Super blooper
4 Down for the count
5 Like some verbs: Abbr.
6 Cpl., e.g.
7 Key letter
8 Places of prenatal development
9 Sign of approval
10 It glistens
11 Lofty lyric
12 Nose out
13 Joseph McCarthy aide
14 Comics bulldog
21 Mushy fare
22 Golfer Hale
24 Elbow grease
28 Curly, in Paris
29 Moved carefully
30 Horse color
31 Grassy expanse
32 Actress Tyler
33 Cockney's abode
36 Perfectly
37 Cause of burnout
38 Worrisome cry in a china shop
39 Loudly deride
40 Pre-kickoff call
41 Incantation start
42 Painter José Maria
43 Simple stuff
45 Brandy letters
48 Medieval guild
49 Gathered, informally
50 Like a certain ballerina
51 Shed one's clothes
56 Mend over
57 Gumshoe
58 Flight board abbr.
60 Sun Devils' sch.
64 Nutso
65 It may be bruised
66 Nerdish
67 A sunblock blocks it
68 Feudal subject
69 Get too big
70 "Mamma Mia" group
71 1844 loser to Polk
72 "Take this!"
76 Part of H.R.H.
77 World War II battle site, for short
78 Beantown nine
79 Carrie or Louis
80 Bracket shape
81 Rolodex no.

Puzzle #3

RE-FILLS by Merl Reagle

A puzzle jam-packed with gags that probably only a crossword fan would appreciate.

WORDS	MINUTES	LETTERS	SCORE

30 MINUTES / 128 WORDS   Copyright © 2004 American Crossword Puzzle Tournament

ACROSS

1 Holey order?
6 Lucknow dress
10 Less-than-cute-fruit
14 *The Beverly Hillbillies* airer
17 Bona _____
19 Word after air or knuckle
20 Easy place to get stuck
21 The Zuider _____
22 Jai_____
24 Film director Craven
25 Fictional newspaper magnate
26 Mind expander?
27 Secret target?
28 Colony that's now part of Yemen
30 _____ B'rith
35 Sleepers and diners
39 Fizzler
40 "Go figure"
41 Pork Place?
42 Agnus _____
45 *The Lion King* critter
47 See 102-Down
48 Father with a #1 son
49 Verizon, once
51 _____ cotta
54 Neighbor of Can.
55 Diamondlike
56 Get with sweat
58 Le Carré characters
60 Recess ender
62 _____ de Cologne
64 Raison d'_____
66 Picnic dish
67 Child of renown
69 Average guy?
71 Don Juan's mother
73 Apt name for a C.P.A.?
74 _____ l'oeil
76 Org. for shooters
77 *Quo Vadis?* role
78 Like Bacon or Byron: Abbr.
79 Part of 18-Down
81 I. M. _____
84 Letters on a Cardinal's cap
87 Eastern ideal
88 TV's Arthur
89 Affront
90 _____ Saud
94 Imbroglio
98 Flying-related
99 Kind of symbol
100 Both: Prefix
104 Big name in Indian literature
105 _____ Amin
108 Mai _____
111 Old French coin
112 One of the Corleones
113 Fleur-de-_____
114 Kind of symbol
115 Part of Nasdaq: Abbr.
116 Word after air or knuckle
117 Ones who may be engaged

DOWN

1 The "a" sound in "tournament"
2 Tried to win
3 Operating
4 S.F.'s are famous
5 Try to locate
6 Phaser setting
7 Wasn't well
8 Future perch
9 Officeholders
10 "I'm still listening" comment
11 It includes tectonics
12 Firm concern
13 Gilbert & Sullivan princess
14 Statements of principle
15 Wholesale purchase?
16 Like van Gogh's "Night"
18 Org. for shooters
23 _____-cone
26 Busy co. around Feb. 14
29 Two-striper, e.g.: Abbr.
31 Sultan's haven
32 Polite push
33 Actor Cobb
34 Comedian Leary
36 Duke's introduction?
37 Ford Clinic's forte
38 Barak's successor
42 Tourist's spot
43 By word of mouth
44 Place for a victory dance
45 Jane Eyre, e.g.
46 Road-tour load
47 Predicate's partner: Abbr.
50 Black goo
52 Setting
53 Pines
57 "Haven't heard anything yet"
59 Stolen simoleons, e.g.
61 Train line to N.Y.C.
63 Sphere
65 Wild
68 Singer Baker
70 Pub pals
72 *Germinal* author
75 Many miles away
80 Plumlike fruits of Japan
82 Conned
83 Spin stat
84 They may get high in Vegas
85 From that place
86 *The Phantom of the Opera* author Gaston
88 Ballpoint brand
91 _____ de grâce
92 Author Sinclair
93 Stand for something?
95 Undercut
96 Site of 1692 trials
97 Like washer water
101 European bird of the genus *Turdus*
102 With 47-Across, part of California
103 *Cast Away* setting
106 The Mountain State: Abbr.
107 Towel stitching
108 Bird's beak
109 Some sac contents
110 Curbside container

Puzzle #4

WHAT IS THE ANSWER? by Patrick Merrell

The puzzle will tell you.

WORDS	MINUTES	LETTERS	SCORE

SEMIS
LDA
ROY
NODULE
REZONED
SANEST
AS
NOTE
NOD

20 MINUTES / 76 WORDS

Copyright © 2004 American Crossword Puzzle Tournament

ACROSS

1 Prosperity
5 Matrix
9 Loot hideaway
14 Chronometer
16 First step at many ATMs
17 Figure made by waving the arms and legs
18 Prefinal round
19 Dire
21 Captures
22 *The _____ Club* (1970s–'80s TV show)
25 "_____ Beso" (Paul Anka hit)
26 Bonsai, e.g.
27 Sailing hazard
29 Mauna _____ Observatory
31 Dale's Western partner
33 Pro golfer from South Africa
35 Knobby growth
39 Boot camp figure
40 Like some city property, after a commissioners' meeting
41 Most clearheaded
42 Turning heads?
43 Assent at sea
44 Western hemis. group
45 Do, re, or mi
46 Soft mineral
49 50 Cent piece
51 Nap, with "off"
52 Sizzling server
53 Copyists
58 Marketing aids
60 Followers
64 Hibernian
65 How dogs are walked
66 Fidgety
67 With 29-Down, where hints #1 and #2 will lead you
68 Scads

DOWN

1 Lb. and oz.
2 A for Hans
3 _____, amas, amat...
4 In questionable taste
5 Actress Lollobrigida
6 Rules, for short
7 Summer refreshers
8 They may have lox stocked and barrels
9 Draft no. designator
10 Hint #2 to solving this puzzle's title
11 One about to shoot
12 Vengeful behavior
13 *Steppenwolf* author
15 Tee posting
20 Meeting points
22 Gets ready, quickly
23 _____ incognita
24 Revolutionary leader
28 Hint #1 to solving this puzzle's title
29 See 67-Across
30 Señor's chant
32 Seep
34 "Calm down"
36 Factory organizer
37 Slow tempo
38 Fringed
40 HDTV maker
42 Micaëla in *Carmen*, e.g.
46 Shire of *Rocky*
47 Fall burial item
48 Not bogus
50 _____ God
54 Northern home: Var.
55 Boxer Max
56 She, in Brazil
57 Slamming Sammy
59 Retiring
61 Org. for Orr
62 Old Metro or Prizm
63 Atl. crosser, once

Puzzle #5

COMPOUND FRACTURES by Stanley Newman

This puzzle's theme may look elementary, but it isn't.

WORDS	MINUTES	LETTERS	SCORE

Copyright © 2004 American Crossword Puzzle Tournament

ACROSS

1 Base
7 Rhyme scheme
11 Clearing
16 *The Princess Bride* director
17 Encouraging words
18 Hard to explain
19 Prison riot participant
22 Plant pest
23 "_____ luck!"
25 Elusive one
26 Primed
27 Kwik-E-Mart clerk on *The Simpsons*
28 "J to _____ Lo" (2002 CD)
30 Metal holder
32 Start of some addresses
34 *King Lear* duke
37 Nominal
42 Robert Caro biographical subj.
44 Net org.
45 1928 Winter Olympics star
46 A goldfish would be a likely one
51 Objet d'art
52 Scanning-software function
53 Uncouth one
54 Big name in beans
55 Quidnunc's quest
57 Jesse Jackson once wore one
61 Travel guide
62 Designate
64 "OK"
65 Black-nosed breed
69 "_____ out!"
71 Less often seen
73 Thirst for knowledge
77 Shoplifter
80 *Zodiaco* beast
81 Bob Hoskins film role
82 Editor's need
83 Shavers
84 Dispose of
85 Term of endearment

DOWN

1 Artist who let his sculpture "create itself"
2 Wildflower locale
3 Discovery of 1922
4 Where Chimborazo is
5 Ogle
6 "Garfield" waitress
7 P.G.A. nickname
8 1994 Winter Olympics star
9 Very busy
10 Real estate ad abbr.
11 Art class
12 Preliminary proposition, in math
13 "This is _____!" (buster's shout)
14 Short number
15 Very wide
20 Tower in Los Angeles?
21 French suffix
23 ___-di-dah
24 Withdraw, with "out"
29 Mecca visitor
30 Recorded
31 Clancy character
33 Elementary
35 Frame-up
36 Where part of *My Fair Lady* takes place
37 Send off
38 Niece of Circe
39 Narita Airport client
40 English _____
41 Quarter toward which the wind blows
43 Tito's real name
46 Leipzig lament
47 N.H. neighbor
48 William Tell setting
49 *The Daily Bruin* publisher
50 Raw material
56 Throat culture finding
58 China setting
59 One that's seeded, maybe
60 Finish'd
61 The Valley Isle
63 A follower
65 Former House majority leader from Texas
66 Life-jacket stuffing
67 Melded
68 Flags
69 World War I battle area
70 Foil cousins
72 Up
73 Sixer rival
74 Requirement
75 Shot
76 Tough trip
78 Simple top
79 Directional suffix

Puzzle #6

CLOTHES CALL by Maura Jacobson

More smile inducers from the queen of crossword puns.

WORDS	MINUTES	LETTERS	SCORE

30 MINUTES / 120 WORDS

ACROSS

1 Posse leader, perhaps
8 Chews the fat
12 "Fernando" pop group
16 Russia is in it
17 Out on _____ (vulnerable)
19 Once more
20 May birthstone
21 Hat for a woman having her hair set?
23 Immigrant's course: Abbr.
24 High-hat
25 Bout segments
26 Lummoxes
29 Hawaii county
31 Tom or Benedict
33 Politician's footwear?
36 Part of a mechanic's bill
40 Order after "Ready?"
41 Cheap
42 Train stop: Abbr.
44 Identical
45 Half CXII
46 Matching pieces
47 Ordained one
50 Pig _____ poke
51 Egotist's concern
53 Analyst's lingerie?
56 Thumbs up
58 ___ Paulo, Brazil
59 Biddy
60 ___ Mahal
61 Metropolis rainwear?
65 Salad fish
68 Uganda's ___ Amin
69 Most ill-mannered
70 Beauty preceder?
73 Small business co-owner
74 High-schooler
76 Crosses out
77 Wall Street type
80 Harper Valley org.
81 Relieves tension
83 G-men's underwear?
86 First name on *Hollywood Squares*
88 Big butte
89 Greek war god
90 Sandy Africa
92 No mere talker
94 Neither's partner
96 Shorts worn in court?
98 Pilot's postal load
102 Toughen gradually
103 Fictional Lorna
104 One or two
105 Put back in
106 Spanish digits
107 Huron or Erie

DOWN

1 "Get it?"
2 Good engine sound
3 Palindromic preposition
4 Least cooked
5 "Beauty _____ beauty does"
6 13th President
7 Craze
8 Food embellishment
9 Baseball's Felipe
10 Spanish museum city
11 Size options: Abbr.
12 To-do lists
13 Shakespeare, with "the"
14 Drool catchers
15 Whichever
18 *West Side Story* composer
19 Never _____ moment
22 Kanga's baby
24 Arithmetic homework
26 Milky gems
27 Partner of kicking
28 Mafia neckwear?
30 What the suspicious smell
32 Dwells
34 Garrisons: Abbr.
35 Ballyhoo
37 Dress for one saving a sinking boat?
38 Discontinued Dodge
39 Opposite of sow
43 Middle of a simile
48 Germany's _____ Valley
49 Explosive
52 Elfin
53 Confronts unpleasantness, with "to"
54 Korean G.I.s
55 Got lucky on the subway
57 State under Stalin: Abbr.
58 Dining room furnishing
61 Quote
62 Mental flash
63 Camay competitor
64 Feminine ending
66 Our, in Orne
67 Stockpile
70 Says further
71 Garden plant also called a cranesbill
72 Cenozoic, for one
75 1980s sitcom named for its star
78 Name of several pharaohs
79 Mischa of old films
82 Sedimentary rock
84 Use, as a buggy
85 Not as cool
87 Sphere
90 Faxed, e.g.
91 Malaria symptom
93 _____ concern (unimportant)
95 *Coffee, Tea _____?* (1967 bestseller)
96 Article in *Paris Match*
97 Debtor's chit
98 "Gimme _____" (Auburn cheer)
99 *Exodus* protagonist
100 Scottish John
101 Legal deg. abroad

Puzzle #7

AND THE LAST SHALL BE FIRST by Mike Shenk

Containing eight ingeniously related phrases, compactly presented.

WORDS	MINUTES	LETTERS	SCORE

45 MINUTES / 140 WORDS   Copyright © 2004 American Crossword Puzzle Tournament

ACROSS

1 Listing type
7 Like Indian summer days
14 Easy out
19 Religious doctrines
20 Colombian airline
21 Pepperidge Farm cookie
22 The U.S.S. *Maine* was built there
24 Brief sketch
25 Editorial page features
26 Monk
27 Brahma, to Hindus
28 Possess
29 Bittersweet Italian apéritif
31 River called Aigyptos in the *Odyssey*
32 Public prosecutors, in brief
35 "I mean now!"
39 Steamed
40 Matures
42 Pitcher
43 Groom one's brows
45 Monopoly token choice
46 Cole ____
47 6 on a telephone
49 Practices parsimony
52 *Don Carlos* composer
54 Stock holder
55 Serengeti carnivore
57 Socially dominant
58 Summer setting in D.C.
59 Scout activity
63 Rate of speed
64 "Let me repeat"
66 Dude
67 "Tiny Bubbles" singer
69 Häagen-Dazs buy
71 Procrastinate
76 Thanksgiving side dish
79 Consul coverings
81 Targets of water cannons
82 Salon offering
83 Disney elephant
85 Designate officially
87 N.B.A. stat
88 Salt holder?
89 Gerber's first baby food
90 Get situated
92 Homicidal farmer
93 Informal recipe amount
95 Diploma-awarding exam: Abbr.
97 Visit the widow, e.g.
101 Ring around the collar?
102 Showing temerity
104 Explore Carlsbad
105 In the style of
106 Clothed
108 Grounded flier
109 Best Picture of 1933
115 Tulsa native
116 As late as possible
118 Political ousters
119 Wolfish activity
120 MTV viewer, often
121 Mill output
122 Car radio buttons
123 *Gunsmoke* star

DOWN

1 Atlas, e.g., for short
2 Where Mammy and Prissy worked
3 *Década* divisions
4 Sack
5 Item to dip a quill into
6 *The Screwtape Letters* author
7 Prop for Harry Potter
8 Gardner and others
9 Bob Randall play *6 Rms ___ Vu*
10 Fashionable part of London
11 Ready for war
12 Pickle
13 Suckered
14 Holmes trademark
15 Wow! chips ingredient
16 Source of some student funds
17 7-Up nickname
18 Rained cats and dogs
21 "The few" and "the proud" group
23 Masculine force
27 Field flapper
29 Enjoy some caramels
30 Overture follower
32 Get-up-and-go
33 Showed on TV
34 Ball carrier, of a sort
36 Paris obsession
37 Nashville sound
38 Ten: Prefix
41 Purpose
44 A big goose egg
46 Arachnophobe's fear
47 He has fleas
48 Genealogy chart word
50 Upsilon follower
51 Easy mark
53 Mrs. McKinley
55 Devil features
56 Accountant's work
60 It may be well-raised
61 Parting words?
62 Stadium surface
65 Flight segment
68 Aussie outlaw Kelly
69 Sch. monitor
70 Saturn model
72 Proceed cautiously
73 On a roll
74 Funnies unit
75 Grammy winner Cleo
77 Eastern summers?
78 Dayan of Israel
80 Barbershop sound
84 AP alternative
86 "Coming up next" ads
88 Enjoy the limelight
91 Det. Sipowicz's org.
92 Alonzo Mourning and Shaquille O'Neal
93 Hawks' home
94 Devotional book
95 Comprehends
96 Patronize a restaurant
98 Site of "the Troubles"
99 Future brother, maybe
100 Stop resisting, slangily
103 Gate feature
107 Stagger
109 100th of a rand
110 Dow numbers: Abbr.
111 Joan of *Twin Peaks*
112 Super-duper
113 Union jack?
114 Screws up
116 Yodeler's perch
117 Creative story

Puzzle #8 (Set A)

CORNER TO CORNER by Bob Klahn

A final, themeless challenge with just 68 finely interlocked entries.

WORDS	MINUTES	LETTERS	SCORE

15 MINUTES / 68 WORDS   Copyright © 2004 American Crossword Puzzle Tournament

ACROSS

1 Rear
7 Hard look
15 Gaga, possibly
16 Fable
17 Absconds
18 Trail
19 Symbol of beauty in harsh conditions
21 Better
22 "If I Only Had the Nerve" singer
23 Delays
24 Pinpoints
25 Threshold
26 Put on
27 Some spirals
28 Alerts
30 Setting of many Thomas Hardy novels
31 Abundant
32 Guarded
33 Far from deferential
36 Cocktail with gin and grenadine
40 Nick name?
41 Teen idol Moore
42 Place to start a drive
43 They always turn up at the end
44 Swell
45 Nation's foes
46 Social
47 No-vacancy situation
49 Divine dessert
51 Under control
52 Titanic
53 Secrecy sworn to by oath
54 Opening for a secretary
55 Home maker

DOWN

1 Boston leader for half a century
2 Ashore
3 Spilled over
4 Member of high society?
5 By any chance
6 Isn't worrying
7 Faux fireplace items
8 Stylish
9 Plaza de _____
10 Smacker
11 Keep to oneself
12 Game in which the players would rather not catch any breaks
13 Knee-length trouser
14 Doesn't stop
20 *Men Against the Sea* captain
24 Hall of Hall & Oates
26 High wind
27 Member of *Our Gang*
29 Darts
30 Plant named for the teeth of a big cat
32 Flappers
33 Separate, as tables
34 1990s fad
35 Supple
36 Rhyming beverage
37 Was humiliated
38 Thaw
39 Marital accord
41 Seven-time N.L. batting champ of the 1940s–'50s
44 Don Pasquale, for one
45 Cambria, today
47 Claptrap
48 "Down _____" (Janis Joplin song)
50 Certain buck

Puzzle #8 (Set B)

CORNER TO CORNER by Bob Klahn

A final, themeless challenge with just 68 finely interlocked entries.

WORDS	MINUTES	LETTERS	SCORE

15 MINUTES / 68 WORDS

ACROSS

1 Nurture
7 Test of courage
15 Smitten
16 Didactic narrative
17 Runs off (with)
18 Wander
19 1986 coming-of-age movie set in Las Vegas
21 Crown
22 MGM lion
23 Impedes
24 Stipples
25 First offender?
26 Fake
27 Salad ingredient, maybe
28 500 signals?
30 County on the English Channel
31 Tosspot
32 Circumspect
33 On one's high horse
36 Cocktail with gin and grenadine
40 *Jefferson in Paris* star
41 Barry Manilow's first #1 hit
42 Souvenir shirt
43 Cross-country runners
44 Dieter's battle
45 Antiprohibitionists
46 Afternoon affair
47 With no place left to put anyone
49 Nectar go-with
51 Queued up
52 Stupendous
53 Mario Puzo's last novel
54 It may be between your drawers
55 Bird, at times

DOWN

1 Longtime Boston Pops leader
2 Away for a while
3 Pie-eyed
4 Pub crawler
5 Always
6 Remains carefree
7 Faux fireplace items
8 Posh
9 Ring opponents
10 Shut (up)
11 _____ wild
12 Messy party game
13 Woman's trouser
14 Doesn't stop doing
20 Captain in literature
24 Singer Hall of Hall & Oates
26 Champagne glass
27 Rather fat
29 Flutters
30 Kind of wine
32 First Oscar-winning film
33 Separate, as chairs
34 Big name in kids' collectibles
35 Flexible
36 It's lighter than a porter
37 Had to swallow one's pride
38 Tension reducer
39 Words from the resigned
41 Longtime Cardinal
44 Operatic voice
45 Prince of _____
47 Hokum
48 "Take _____" (a-ha chart-topper)
50 Old World deer

Puzzle #8 (Set C)

CORNER TO CORNER by Bob Klahn

A final, themeless challenge with just 68 finely interlocked entries.

WORDS	MINUTES	LETTERS	SCORE

15 MINUTES / 68 WORDS

ACROSS

1 Songwriter Stephen
7 Realistic assessment
15 Like Shakespeare, according to a 1998 film
16 Allegorical narrative with a moral
17 Leaves the bedroom via a ladder, say
18 Wander off the direct course
19 Cactus flower, e.g.
21 Spinner
22 Bert of *The Wizard of Oz*
23 Brakes
24 "i" completers
25 Garden of Eden resident
26 Pretend
27 Trattoria staple
28 Warning signals
30 Breed of white-faced sheep
31 Luxurious, as foliage
32 Hardly trusting
33 Too big for one's britches
36 Cocktail with gin and grenadine
40 Actor Nick
41 In a 1975 #1 hit, she "kissed me and stopped me from shaking"
42 Golf peg
43 Enjoys Vail, perhaps
44 Battle of the _____
45 Dampens
46 Twinings product
47 With runners everywhere
49 Food of the gods
51 Kind of skates
52 Gigantic
53 Sicilian code of silence
54 Desk opening
55 Empty _____ (many an older parent)

DOWN

1 Conductor Arthur
2 Taking extended time off from work
3 Three sheets to the wind
4 Big drinker
5 At any time
6 Has a load off one's mind
7 Nonnatural fireplace burners
8 Like streets in the '60s and '70s, in Manhattan
9 Bullfight bulls
10 Sea creature with a shell
11 Swine
12 Party game with a breakable item
13 Woman's skirtlike trouser
14 Continues doing
20 *Mutiny on the Bounty* captain
24 Actress Hannah
26 Instrument with finger holes
27 _____ Pig
29 Flies like a hummingbird
30 Yard nuisance
32 Angel features
33 Distribute, as plates
34 1990s fad from Japan
35 Easily bent
36 Amber libation
37 Suffered humiliation
38 Thaw in relations
39 Reply to a spouse's request
41 Longtime Cardinal Stan
44 Low voice
45 Part of the United Kingdom
47 "Nonsense!"
48 "This one's _____"
50 Caviar

■ ACKNOWLEDGMENTS

I want to thank the score or more people who generously shared their time and expertise with me as I wrote *Crossworld*; all those who are mentioned by name, but especially Brendan Emmett Quigley, Will Shortz, Helene Hovanec, Stanley Newman, and Michael Shteyman. I'm grateful to Doubleday's David Phethean for his early comments on the manuscript, to Debby Manette for her sharp copyediting eye, as well as to David Micklethwait for his pointers about British cryptic puzzles. My particular thanks go to Jin Auh of the Wylie Agency and to Sarah Rainone of Doubleday— as formidable a combination of agent and editor as any writer could hope to have on his side. None of these individuals bears any responsibility for errors of fact or infelicities of style that appear in the book—blame for those lies almost entirely with Mrs. Gladys B. Ambacher of Fond du Lac, Wisconsin, and to a lesser extent with me.

Marc Romano is a Yale graduate and a former staffer at the *New York Review of Books*. His work has been published in the *Village Voice* and the *Boston Globe*. He lives in Brooklyn, New York, where he averages four to ten minutes on the *New York Times* daily puzzle (sixteen on Sunday).

ANSWERS

1 — CONTRADICTION

2 — A COMEDY OF ERRORS

3 — RE-FILLS

4 — WHAT IS THE ANSWER?

Bonus answer: WHAT

5 — COMPOUND FRACTURES

6 — CLOTHES CALL

7 — AND THE LAST SHALL BE FIRST

8 — CORNER TO CORNER